Crispin de Passe, *Hortus Floridus,* 1614. This view of spring planting illustrates the style of *parterre de pièces coupées*: flower beds cut into various figures on a base of gravel, sand or stone and edged with a herb or an inorganic material. These 'cut-work' gardens flourished in different forms in Germany and the Low Countries during the seventeenth century. Crispin de Passe depicts the central bed as planted sparsely with exotics such as the crown imperial; this sparse style was still apparent in the Low Countries at the time of Het Loo (1680s–90s). The flanking beds of tulip are more typical of close planting.

MARK LAIRD

The Formal Garden

TRADITIONS OF ART AND NATURE

Photographs by Hugh Palmer

*With 306 illustrations,
151 in color*

THAMES AND HUDSON

To my mother
and in memory of my father

On the half-title and title pages: design from André Mollet,
Le Jardin de plaisir, 1651.

Endpapers: engraving of the Grosser Garten, Herrenhausen,
by J. van Sasse after J. J. Müller, *c*. 1720.

© 1992 Thames and Hudson Ltd, London

First published in the United States in 1992 by
Thames and Hudson Inc., 500 Fifth Avenue,
New York, New York 10110

Library of Congress Catalog Card Number 92-70867

Printed and bound in Singapore by Toppan

Contents

INTRODUCTION
Nature and Formality

THE IDEA of a 'formal garden' evokes in all of us a clear and vivid impression: from the immense vistas of Versailles to the intimate knots and mazes of Hampton Court or Hatfield House. We recall the terraces and fountains of Villa Lante, the box parterres and hornbeam hedges of Herrenhausen. We remember the quaint topiary of Levens Hall, the boxwork of Williamsburg and the pebblework of Dumbarton Oaks. As through a madrigal by Monteverdi or through a motet by Bach, we seem to be transported by such gardens to a world of unsullied order and harmony.

At the heart of these varied images are traditional notions of what makes the formal garden formal. First, there is the idea of architectural rules as extended to the outdoor spaces around the house or palace; this results in vast terraces as at Vaux-le-Vicomte or hedged rooms as at Hidcote. The mansion is either at the centre of the design, or, if off to one side, still exerts an influence on the spatial character of the regular layout; straight lines predominate. Inseparable from this view of extension are the principles of geometry, proportion and symmetry which have helped shape architecture and thereby garden architecture from the time of Alberti (1404–72).

Second, there is the idea of man's dominance over nature: water constrained in rectilinear canals or in fountains, shrubs clipped into dwarf hedges or giant curtains, identical trees planted in avenues and allées. And third, there is the sense of stiffness or artificiality; as represented in trelliswork and topiary, and as mirrored in the etiquette of formal ceremony – those rules that have always helped determine hierarchical spaces. Kenneth Woodbridge wrote, for example, that 'formal' was the apposite term for the French style of the sixteenth or seventeenth centuries; it described the axial approach to 'a hierarchy of courtyards with the garden as the climax; a scheme calculated to demonstrate the status of the owner'.

Is a formal garden, however, such a clear-cut thing? Is it the opposite of the landscape garden, by virtue of its architectural structure, its geometry and symmetry? Is it artificial where the landscape garden is natural? Is it the work of 'art' rather than of 'nature' as the theorists often claimed? Moreover, is the formal garden we see today the same as it was fifty or two hundred or four hundred years ago, in form, content and function – as a symbol of the arts and of power, as a museum, as a setting for theatre, entertainment and sport? Above all, does it remain true to the original as conceived and perceived by its makers?

These questions are prompted as soon as one delves into the background of any one formal garden. Consider Villa Lante for example. The restful composition of *palazzine*, terraces, fountains and fishponds displays an order based on the square. Yet Vignola's architectural design was once perceived as part of a more irregular, natural park, now neglected and overlooked. The beautifully crisp boxwork of the main terrace looks as immutable as the Renaissance stonework. Yet it was made by later generations, who abandoned the original design of twelve squares of flowers enclosed by laurustinus hedge, latticework and fruit trees. It was this lush planting that once softened the architectural lines and that lent to art the balance of nature.

6

Versailles, view of palace and gardens from the Bassin d'Apollon, after 1775. Traditional notions of the 'formal garden' come readily to mind in André Le Nôtre's layout at Versailles – the immense vistas, the geometry and regularity, and above all, the dominance of man over nature. This engraving by F. D. Née, after a drawing by the Chevalier de Lespinasse, shows, however, an unfamiliar aspect of Versailles – the replanted grounds one hundred years after Le Nôtre's initial design. It illustrates how a garden's appearance changes over time, especially through planting; Jules Hardouin-Mansart's Colonnade of 1685–89, for example, towers over the new bosquets. It also suggests how the royal garden, which had been open to the public since the time of Louis XIV, was alive with the movement of people and dogs.

A formal garden then is not always a clear-cut entity. Equally, historical periods or art-historical labels, however useful in describing the past, are often only partially applicable to gardens as they survive today. When we visit Herrenhausen, we are in the presence of the restoration of the 1930s as much as in the world of the Baroque, and when we gaze on the knot gardens of Hampton Court we are glimpsing the 1920s more than the Renaissance. To state this is not to imply a purist attitude to conservation, for in many instances the additions and accretions are part of what gives a garden its charm and repose; later interpretations of the past may be valuable and beautiful in themselves. It is merely to acknowledge that a garden, more than most other works of art, is subject to change and that compositions of trees, shrubs and flowers are particularly susceptible to alteration, decay and renewal.

If the nature of a formal garden is hard to define, so too the relationship of the formal to informal is sometimes ambiguous. It has always been customary to talk of formal gardens being destroyed by the landscape gardens of 'Capability' Brown; of the Baroque being banished on the Continent of Europe by the mode for *le jardin anglais, der englische Garten* or *il giardino inglese*. While this is undoubtedly true, a simple explanation conceals a more interesting complexity. Many of the great formal gardens we shall visit in this book, such as Chantilly and Schwetzingen, are composed of a sympathetic union of formal structure (Baroque or Rococo) and landscape additions; at Wilhelmshöhe a mighty axial cascade was integrated into a Picturesque or romantic park. Even the great landscape gardener 'Capability' Brown was not immune to compromise, albeit against the grain. During a final phase of work at Wrest Park in 1778 he left the axis of canal and pavilion intact and contented himself with a few clumps; 'to do more, he thought, would be to unravel the mystery of the garden . . . unless the whole style of the place was changed', recalled his client, Jemima Marchioness Grey.

Fusion of the formal and informal is particularly apparent in planting design. Consider, for example, a photograph of Claude Monet in his garden at Giverny. The setting is not the familiar water-lily pond of his paintings, but rather the flower garden close to the house. With sun hat and white beard, he stands rather stiffly on a gravel path. In front of him there is a long straight border, edged with a ruff of grey-green leaves and filled with scarlet and pink pelargoniums. Three ten-foot-tall tripods of bamboo and string support red morning glories and give architectural accent to the ends and middle of the bed. Behind the painter is another long straight border of formal standard roses. We might imagine that

Monet is about to set off on one of his daily rounds, scrutinizing every flower with the eye of a strict horticultural disciplinarian. As Claire Joyes recounts: 'No detail escaped him; he would correct a vista, recompose a clump of flowers, alter a pattern, and he insisted on the removal of fading blooms'.

Claude Monet is not a name we associate with 'formal gardening'. He detested French formal gardens like Versailles, preferring instead the naturalness of weeping willows and water-lilies. Yet when he came to plan his first garden at Giverny around 1890, he chose a rectilinear framework in which to display a rampant blaze of flowers; his borders were laid out in rectangles like the order beds of a botanic garden. He is said to have been influenced by a visit to the tulip fields of Holland. But the regular grid of gravel paths and the strong central axis of Monet's flower garden seem to draw inspiration directly from what we might call a 'formal tradition' of garden design that extends back to the Renaissance and beyond.

It was on a brilliant September day in 1990, gazing from Monet's front door down the central walk of nasturtiums, dahlias and sunflowers, that I first wondered about this strange 'formality'. I had come across it before in an equally unexpected place – the landscape garden in England. In my research into Georgian planting plans I had found, contrary to expectation, that certain designers in the naturalistic style of 'Capability' Brown continued to pay respect to principles of geometry and symmetry. Late into the eighteenth century, shrubberies and flower beds continued to be, in Batty Langley's phrase, remarkably 'stiff and stuffed up' despite the naturalness of the landscape style. If they were no longer formal, they were still influenced by a formal tradition.

In the light of these thoughts, it seemed reasonable to ask: what is 'formal' and what is 'informal'? This book is not an attempt to resolve such a large and complex question, although aspects of the theme will inevitably recur. It is more an opportunity to open up a fresh discussion of how, over five centuries, architecture and horticulture, art and nature were wedded and not divorced – often against the odds. The discussion will lead us to visit on the way some of the world's most captivating gardens.

The intention is to explore afresh the remarkable diversity and adaptability of that formal tradition. While many of the surviving gardens discussed will correspond to the conventional image of the 'formal garden', others like Chiswick House are chosen to defy the usual categorization (e.g. 'early landscape'). The scope is deliberately selective rather than comprehensive. The delimitation of period from the Renaissance to the present is determined in part by thematic constraints but also in part by the wish to illustrate a range of gardens in good upkeep (those, for example, of the ancient world are known to us more as archaeological sites, whilst those of the medieval world are either partially or entirely lost or exist only as theoretical restorations).

Choosing to concentrate on the mainstream traditions of Western Europe – from Italy and France to Germany, Holland and Great Britain – and on formal gardening in the eastern United States, implies a conscious bias but not an ignorance of the magnificent formal traditions of eastern Europe and Scandinavia, of the Iberian peninsula, of the Islamic world from Mogul India to Moorish Spain and of formal traditions exported to other lands through empire. That Schönbrunn in Vienna or Hellbrunn near Salzburg are omitted here should not obscure the fact that they fall within the wider German sphere or *Sprachraum*; and that such great formal gardens of California as Filoli are ignored should not be taken as indicative of their worth or of their isolation from the traditions of eastern North America. These are omissions more of necessity than of choice. The apparent quirks of selection are sometimes explained by chance: the Villa d'Este, at the moment of writing and photography, was waterless.

Claude Monet's flower garden at Giverny: view of Monet in his garden in about 1920 published in *L'Illustration*, 1927; and the garden as restored today. Fusion of the formal and informal is particularly apparent in planting design. Monet's flower garden combined a rectilinear structure with rampant planting – reminiscent of a cottage garden. It is noteworthy that even under very careful restoration, planting effects are not always replicated; here, for example, an alternative climber to the original morning glories has been chosen for the tripods.

Such is the present state of historical research and the present care of historic gardens that, even within these delimitations, a study of formal planting traditions remains especially challenging. Victorian carpet bedding, for instance, has only recently drawn the attention of scholars; yet it forms an important phase in the history of formal planting. Examples of this art of 'mosaiculture' can still be found at Versailles or in some municipal parks in Europe but not *in situ* in one Victorian layout alongside Italianate parterres or ribbon borders. Thus, guided in part by a fortuitous element in both scholarship and conservation, and above all by the chance factor of site survival, the emphasis of this study varies from chapter to chapter; while Italy features rather larger than other countries in the sixteenth century, and France and Holland likewise in the seventeenth, German gardens receive more attention in the eighteenth century. British gardens are well represented throughout but gain rather more attention in the nineteenth. American gardens come into their own both in the Colonial (or post-Colonial) period and in the twentieth century. It might also be stressed that the selection is made to please the eye as well as the mind.

As much as anything, this book should illustrate that gardens are subject to propaganda. While Monet made his garden at Giverny, there raged in England a battle between those who believed a garden should be architectural like the house and those who looked to nature as the guide. In 1892 Reginald Blomfield's *The Formal Garden in England* was published. He argued that the architectural tradition, which produced houses and gardens of 'well-ordered harmony', had been undermined from the middle of the eighteenth century. His opponents, notably William Robinson and H. E. Milner, contested that the garden 'should express by its breadth of treatment most unmistakably that nature has triumphed over art'.

Our sense of incompatibility between 'formal' and 'informal' has been shaped by this debate. But it can be traced back into the eighteenth century when the Earl of Shaftesbury celebrated 'Things of a *natural* kind . . . beyond the formal Mockery of Princely Gardens'; or further still to the seventeenth century when John Evelyn wrote to Sir Thomas Browne of his 'abhorrency of those painted and formal projections of our Cockney Gardens and plotts, which appeare like Gardens of past board and March pane, and smell more of paynt then of flowers and verdure'. It is to be hoped that this book will restore the scent of flowers and verdure to gardens in the formal tradition.

The parterre on the first terrace at Villa Lante, Bagnaia. Here
we are looking between the two pavilions towards the terrace
on the hillside; see the bird's-eye-view on p.27.

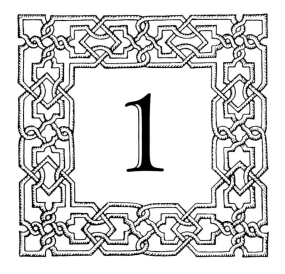

Gardens of the Renaissance
The Union of Architecture and Horticulture

I N EUROPE during the sixteenth century, laying out gardens according to architectural principles developed into a sophisticated art. What we think of as 'formal gardening', however, did not begin with the architects of the Renaissance. Thousands of years before, in Egypt and Babylon, there were planted architectural structures. The roots of Renaissance garden design extend back directly to the traditions of antiquity, especially those of ancient Rome. To the self-conscious revival of the ideas of Vitruvius and Pliny, there was added the influence of the Islamic world and of medieval theory and practice. The use of water and fountains and the organization of gardens into geometric quarters were part of that wider inheritance.

By 1452 Leon Battista Alberti had established a theoretical base for Renaissance garden design through his treatise on architecture; this was later published as *De re aedificatoria*. Drawing on the writings of Pliny and other classical texts, Alberti stressed anew the unity of house and garden. If the architect's province was thereby extended, this was not to the neglect of the countryside; siting and views of the wider, irregular landscape were important. Visual evocation of the past was provided by an equally influential text: Francesco Colonna's *Hypnerotomachia Poliphili*. Published in Venice in 1499, it was translated into French from 1546 and into English by 1592. Colonna's book illustrated garden structures, shrubs cut into figures (topiary) and intricate patterns for flower beds (knots). The resonance of these images and the symbolism they suggest, can be detected in garden design for centuries thereafter.

From 1504 the architect Bramante created a series of terraces and steps linking the Vatican to Pope Julius II's Villa Belvedere. This drew inspiration from the archaeology of classical sites, confirmed the practice of architects in designing gardens and established a prototype, on which terraced gardens of the Renaissance and Baroque were modelled. The lower level was designed as a setting for rituals and entertainments. The upper Statue Court was an outdoor museum of antiquities. In its union of antique statuary with garden structures and water, a symbolic vocabulary was established which reverberates well beyond Italy and the Renaissance.

The gardens of Villa d'Este, Villa Lante and Villa Farnese, laid out around Rome in the mid to late sixteenth century, suggest the range of effects that were realized on the basis of the terraced model. Pirro Ligorio's design for Cardinal d'Este at Tivoli (from 1560) was a complex achievement: the fountains expressed the ingenuity of the hydraulic engineer; the iconography of statues and sculpture reflected the inventiveness of poet and artist; and the flowers, pergolas, labyrinths and groves testified to the skill of the gardener. Vignola's treatment of water and stone in Cardinal Gambara's terraced garden at Bagnaia (from 1568) was just as inventive and lovely as at Villa d'Este. Moreover, in the integration of the formal terraces into a more informal park, Villa Lante anticipated future developments in garden design. As with the casino garden of Villa Farnese at Caprarola (from 1584), the park was inseparable from the garden.

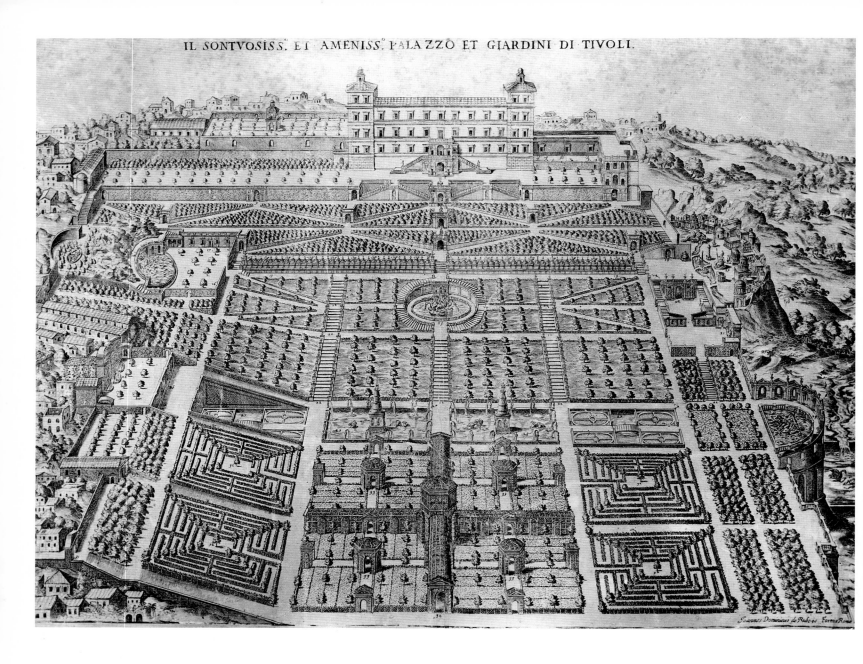

IL SONTVOSISS. ET AMENISS. PALAZZO ET GIARDINI DI TIVOLI.

Étienne du Pérac's bird's-eye perspective of Villa d'Este, Tivoli, 1573. In this view of Cardinal d'Este's terraced garden, a number of original features of planting are depicted that are now lost, replaced or overgrown. In the centre foreground were arbours and the flower garden or garden of *semplici*. To either side were labyrinths (only two of which were implemented but later removed). In the centre were orchards, including an area devoted to grapes. And on the steeply terraced ground below the villa, there was the *bosco* – planted with chestnut, fir, elm and laurel.

Elisabeth MacDougall, David Coffin and Claudia Lazzaro have all shown how such informal areas of woodland – the *boschetti* – were essential to the understanding of the formal garden.

The original design for the Villa Medici at Castello on more gently sloping terrain near Florence typifies aspects of Italian Renaissance planting and the interplay of art and nature. Niccolò Tribolo's layout for Cosimo de' Medici (1540s; continued by Giorgio Vasari after 1554) was illustrated in 1599 as one garden in the series of lunettes by Giusto Utens. The foreground, although idealized (like many images of gardens, which need to be treated with caution), conveys some sense of the animation in the life of the original household. There is a jousting match taking place in the forecourt. There are figures in motion in blues and reds and yellows. Faces peep out from every window. Fountains spout and swans glide across the twin pools.

On either side of the villa were small enclosures. These were the private flower gardens where the owner displayed his best loved exotics. To the traditional medieval palette of flowers – violets, columbines, roses, lilies and irises – there had been added by 1600 hyacinths, grape hyacinths, crown imperials and tulips from the east, African marigolds from the west. What we think of today as 'spring bulbs' were just then becoming the rage.

12

At the centre of the main terrace was a grove or labyrinth of cypress trees, planted in concentric circles and underplanted with strawberry tree, laurel and myrtle. This dark green crown must have cast welcome shade around the circular pool and fountain, where the figure of Florence wrung out her hair; for it was approached from the house across a sun-baked expanse of lawn. The visitor ascended a shallow set of steps on which evergreens in terracotta pots were cut into topiary. They were backed by an elaborate hedge, patterned and castellated like a palazzo; behind the hedge lay exotics in pots and the white fountain of Hercules and Antaeus in a setting of evergreens. On either side of this dramatic ensemble were square compartments of herbs and grasses. They were surrounded by small trees, hedges and topiary. These were miniature meadows framed as art. In spring it must have seemed as though little compartments of the countryside were blooming at Castello.

If flower gardens and meadows (or orchards) were two important elements of planting in any Italian Renaissance garden, the grove or wood was the third. At Castello, the *bosco* is apparent around the main garden, set out like the flowers and fruit trees in regular configurations. Such groves were sometimes all evergreen. Sometimes, however, they contained flowering trees and shrubs: the strawberry tree, the tamarisk and the cornel. As Claudia Lazzaro writes: 'The

Detail from a fresco showing the Villa Medici, Castello, by Giusto Utens, 1599. To either side of the villa are the flower gardens in the style later known as *parterre de pièces coupées*. In the centre is the evergreen grove or labyrinth, flanked by square compartments of herbs and grasses. The space in front of the villa has been arranged for a joust.

whole of a garden was therefore enclosed with greenery, and the basic subdivisions were also defined by vegetation'. This variety of textures and colours has been lost at Castello and at other surviving gardens of the Italian Renaissance. Elsewhere, the plantings that once softened the divisions of the garden – the hedges, trelliswork, arbours, climbers and espaliers – have vanished with time.

Today's visitor to the Villa Medici finds a vast expanse of boxwork in a later style replacing the cypress labyrinth and meadow squares. Refuge from the heat is found in the interior of the grotto. Here the original retains its integrity. The grotto is patterned architecturally in natural materials such as shells and pebbles. It is also embellished with sculptures of real and occasionally mythical animals: an elephant, a lion and a unicorn; a bear, a giraffe and a rhinoceros. Such exotic animals were given as tributes to the Medicis from foreign rulers like the Sultan of Egypt. But the grotto was not merely a record of nature's marvels; it also expressed the preoccupation with an interplay of art and nature: natural materials combined in art, art counterfeiting nature. Above all, water, as a life-giving substance, animated the grotto; it oozed out of the walls and it flowed out of the animals. Sometimes, however, it was there simply for amusement. Hidden trick fountains could be turned on to the delight and dismay of visitors caught admiring the art.

The visitor to the Villa Medici or the Villa d'Este at the end of the sixteenth century experienced the garden not just as something beautiful or curious, but as a setting for activities, whether in the sun or beneath the stars. The garden was at once a theatre, a museum or *Wunderkammer* of rare plants, rare minerals and rare animals, and a place in which to enjoy splendid festivities or to dine in intimate circles. The garden, profuse with plants, was animated by people, by water and by mythology.

The influence of Italian Renaissance theory and practice spread northwards gradually. The gardens of Ancy-le-Franc (c. 1546) and Anet (c. 1546–52) developed on flat terrain the axial formality of Italian prototypes first emulated in France at Bury around 1515–20. Canals began to unify designs on the flat as at Charleval (c. 1560–74). The terraces of Saint-Germain-en-Laye (1590s) suggested parallels with Villa d'Este.

Philibert de l'Orme, as architect to Henri II, was responsible for the château of Anet; the king had granted it to his mistress Diane de Poitiers in 1547. An elaborate gallery, a traditional feature of French Renaissance gardens, enclosed the layout. The iconography of the garden centred on Diana the huntress and her stags. At Anet, moreover, the French decorative style was already apparent in the emblematic knots; after 1582 these knots were turned into the first *comparti-ments en broderie* – that is, one large pattern entirely in box rather than the traditional small patterns in different herbs.

Philibert de l'Orme was also associated with Diane de Poitiers' garden at Chenonceaux (1550s). There, the festivities organized for Catherine de Médicis after Diane's demise involved elaborate fireworks, water spectacles and masques. As in Italy, the garden was a setting for diverse social functions both public and private. Those festive traditions were to pass on through France to England. Likewise, pastimes and recreations crossed the Channel. The game of pall mall, for example, involving mallets, boxwood balls and an iron hoop suspended at the end of a half-mile allée, became popular in England by the second quarter of the seventeenth century. It was to compete with bowls, which flourished on fine English turf.

Translations of Colonna's work had already begun in France by 1546, but England had to wait until 1592. This is indicative of the delayed spread of Italian Renaissance ideas northwards to English gardens; after 1540 contact with Italy was severed by Henry VIII's break with Rome. According to Roy Strong, Alberti's

The Grotto of the Animals at Villa Medici, Castello. The animals represented here include the exotic giraffe and rhinoceros.

Giovanni Guerra, Mount Parnassus and Theatre in the Villa Medici at Pratolino, 1604. From the shaded arc of benches, visitors could watch the concert of the Muses on Mount Parnassus; a water organ was hidden inside. The association of the garden with theatre and the imagery of Parnassus and Pegasus were to reverberate well beyond the Renaissance – for example, at Veitshöchheim in mid-eighteenth-century Germany.

The knot of the Tudor House Museum, Southampton, re-created in the early 1980s. This feature demonstrates the traditional use of different herbs to form a knot: lavender cotton, wall germander, box and winter savory. Such planting was gradually superseded by the box parterre, which developed in France after 1582. The 'open knot' was filled with inorganic materials, the 'closed knot' with flowers.

concept of the house and garden as unified by the architect only became widely accepted in England in the 1620s. Under Henry VIII, the gardens of Hampton Court and Whitehall emulated those of François I. At Fontainebleau, gardens had been located beneath the windows of state apartments, and at Hampton Court the same device followed; the knots could be looked at from above. The use of carved heraldic beasts to accompany the heraldic patterns of knots was a distinctly English characteristic.

The accession of James I to the throne of England in 1603 opened the way to Italy. Yet, as John Dixon Hunt has rightly pointed out, Italian influences are discernible before this, not least through the impact of individual visitors to Italy – for example, in Lord Lumley's alterations to Nonsuch after 1579. Salomon de Caus (1576–1626) and Isaac de Caus (1590–1648) were important figures in bringing knowledge of Italian and French gardens and of hydraulics to England in the early seventeenth century. The latter is associated with the Countess of Bedford's garden at Woburn and the 4th Earl of Pembroke's garden at Wilton (from 1632). Wilton continued the marvels of grotto-making, elaborated on Italian models and combined these with the new art of French broderie.

In the German-speaking world, princely gardens such as the Residenzgarten in Stuttgart (1550–1628) gradually absorbed influences from Italy and France. Salomon de Caus's incomplete Hortus Palatinus in Heidelberg (1614–19) represented one of the most distinguished manifestations of this process: Italian terracing but without axial dominance and a whole array of different parterres reflecting both the past and the future. The smaller gardens of the sixteenth-century elite in prosperous towns such as Augsburg, Frankfurt or Breslau remained, however, by Italian standards essentially small-scale and compartmentalized. There developed in these enclosed spaces a style of flower garden, whose patterns (later called *parterres de pièces coupées*) resembled the flower gardens of the Villa Medici at Castello. These are represented in paintings and engravings of the early seventeenth century, notably in the work of Joseph Furttenbach and in an anonymous painting of a garden near Hamburg.

The publication of Johan Vredeman de Vries's *Hortorum Formae* (from 1583), which had an important impact on European garden design, records somewhat similar traditions within the Flemish sphere. His perspectives illustrate enclosed layouts of arbours and fountains with flower beds of the same type – the *parterre de pièces coupées*. His Mannerist style extended to the Elizabethan garden world and remained detectable as an influence on features such as the arbour of Het Loo in Holland over one hundred years later. What has been called the Dutch classical garden of the early seventeenth century (represented first by the Buitenhof in the Hague c. 1620) reflected Vredeman de Vries's work. Yet by absorbing Italian Renaissance theory, as Florence Hopper argues, it was developed at Honselaarsdijk (c. 1621) into a new prototype for the Dutch canal garden of the seventeenth century. In turn, André Mollet's work at Honselaarsdijk in the 1630s helped shape the French formal garden as first systematized in Mollet's *Le Jardin de Plaisir* of 1651, and it was Mollet's work that looked forward to the Baroque planning of André Le Nôtre.

If Francesco Colonna's designs in *Hypnerotomachia Poliphili* (1499) are to be trusted, a flower compartment of the early Renaissance in Italy might well have resembled the knots that are more often associated with Tudor and Stuart England; this style seems to have come from the Islamic world, perhaps through the influence of the Crusades. The intertwining loops, rather like strips of pastry, make sense of Francis Bacon's and John Evelyn's later criticisms of flower gardens, as no better than 'Tarts' or 'Gardens of past board [pastry] and March pane [marzipan]'.

It would seem, however, by the later sixteenth century, in the days of Cardinal Gambara or Cosimo de' Medici, that an alternative arrangement to knots was more common in Italy: small individual beds of various geometric shapes, whose overall pattern was unified by narrow paths rather than by the lines of herbs (the type known as *parterre de pièces coupées*). These were often squares or rectangles, sometimes with circular or diagonal elements as in the Duke of Sermoneta's garden of the 1620s near Cisterna. Designs by Bartolomeus Menkins of 1584 range from configurations of stars and triangles to beds in the shape of a heart. The star seems to shine on beyond the Renaissance; it occurs in a plan in a manuscript for an unknown Italian villa of the late seventeenth century, and it recurs in the garden of Buonaccorsi near Ancona as it survived into the eighteenth century.

Despite the popularity of these 'cut-work flower beds' in the gardens of Germany and the Low Countries, other traditions continued to hold sway in Northern Europe during the sixteenth century. In England an indigenous tradition of knot-making seems to have existed from the fifteenth century. The knot, in its diverse configurations, no doubt absorbed influences from the Continent. It dominated English gardens until the early seventeenth century. At Hampton Court, for example, the German visitor Thomas Platter described the Privy Garden in 1599 as full of 'square cavities . . . some . . . filled with red brick-dust, some with white sand, and with green lawn, very much resembling a chessboard'. This was evidently what Gervase Markham would later define as an 'open knot': a pattern set out in lines of herbs – hyssop or thyme, for example, – and filled with inorganic materials such as sand or coal dust. It thus anticipates the Baroque parterres with patterns of coloured materials between flowing lines of box. The 'open knot' contrasted with the 'closed knot'; the latter was infilled with flowers instead of inorganic materials.

Variants on these two types included patterns of herbs in the form of arms or initials. Although occurring in France and Germany, such emblems were especially popular in England where the heraldic imagery was reinforced by a taste for heraldic beasts set on columns as at Hampton Court and Whitehall. The raised flower beds were surrounded by low wooden rails painted in Tudor colours – green and white stripes or chevrons. Topiary, which we have encountered before in the Medici gardens, also seems to have complemented the fanciful imagery at Hampton Court: not just in shapes of flowers and crenellations but also of men and women (perhaps after Colonna), and even figures of 'half men and half horse' – that is, centaurs.

The garden of Villa Lante, begun by Cardinal Gambara in 1568, was celebrated by contemporaries as 'exceedingly beautiful and delightful'; to this day Vignola's design is praised as the 'flower' of Italian Renaissance garden art. Over the centuries, alterations to the original concept and above all to the planting have changed the nature of the garden: the formal layout is no longer perceived as part of the informal park and the parterre has been redesigned and replanted; Cardinal Montalto's Fountain of the Moors (*right*) replaced Cardinal Gambara's 'sweating spire', probably in the late sixteenth century. In the composition of stone and water, however, Villa Lante still excels.

Villa Lante

Aᴠɪᴇᴡ of the parterre (*below*) illustrates further subtle alterations to the design: from the eighteenth century onwards boxwork was substituted for the original flower compartments. It is through the sensuous interplay of stone and water that Villa Lante remains closest to its original meaning. The Fountain of the Lights (*right*) was designed to resemble ancient oil lamps.

The Water Chain (*above*) recalled both the eddies of a
mountain stream and the crayfish or *gambero* of the
Cardinal's coat of arms. At the Fountain of the Table
(*right*), inspired by Pliny's description of floating
dinner-plates, a guest might be sprinkled by trick jets
while dining beneath the stars.

Villa Farnese, Caprarola

The casino garden or 'Barchetto', created by Cardinal Farnese as an outdoor dining area, was separated from the palace and main gardens by woods. First laid out from 1584, probably to designs by Giacomo del Duca, the garden was completed by Girolamo Rainaldi after 1620. Rainaldi's additions established a stronger architectonic character; the dominant central axis was made to extend beyond the garden, thus anticipating later Baroque layouts. Subsequent alterations to the planting have changed the nature of the design but without destroying its charm and beauty.

20

FRAMED by Rainaldi's stone herms, the terrace in front of the casino (*opposite and above*) was originally devoted to evergreens and to fruit trees in terracotta vases; the box parterre is more recent. The terrace to the rear of the casino (*right*) was developed as a meadow and flower garden in the 1620s. Of the earlier design, only the octagonal fountain was preserved; this now stands in pebble mosaic paving of a later date. A profusion of flowers once adorned the interiors of the stone compartments in the background.

In the approach to the casino, the Water Chain and River Gods (*left and above*) date from the late sixteenth century and are reminiscent of those at Villa Lante; Rainaldi provided the enclosing architectural setting in the 1620s.

21

Chenonceaux

Dating from the 1550s, the archival records of Diane de Poitiers' garden provide the 'most complete picture we have of gardening practice in mid-sixteenth-century France'. The garden consisted in a rectangle of around 2½ acres and was once filled with fruit and vegetables, bordered by violets, lilies and musk roses; there were also knots and a labyrinth. Today, the architecture of the rampart or *levée* survives, but the planting has been radically altered. The rectangular quarters have been replaced by one unified composition of diagonal and orthogonal walks and fanciful broderie and topiary.

Against the backdrop of an enchanting palace (*above*), cotton lavender broderie, standard hibiscus, clipped yews and bright annuals offer an attractive planting scheme, far from the original quarters of fruit and vegetables. From the château the view of the elevated garden in its woodland setting (*right*) conveys the splendour of Renaissance engineering.

Roy Strong has commented on the Elizabethan aesthetic as dominated by a love of pattern: from clothing to furnishing and from decorations to gardens. It would appear that the designer of knots was often conversant with designing embroidery in fabrics and marquetry in furniture. Such knot patterns were, however, by no means confined to England, and as late as 1620 they can be found in Salomon de Caus's *Hortus Palatinus* and even in Claude Mollet's *Théâtre des Plans* (1652); by which time the ascendant box parterre was firmly established.

It could be said that the Renaissance knot was the direct antecedent of the Baroque broderie, in so far as what were lines of herbs became lines of box. Equally, the tradition of 'cut-work' flower compartments (as in the Italian examples or the garden near Hamburg) was to flourish subsequently in the form of *parterre de pièces coupées pour des fleurs* – the Baroque flower compartments we shall encounter at Vaux-le-Vicomte in the following chapter. An important distinction in the planting of such discrete flower compartments was between the use of one species (or colour) and a mixture of species (or colours) in a single bed. This distinction assumed, however, a common purpose – a bright bold display of plants as pattern rather than as individuals.

In the Low Countries a variant in the flower garden was planting sparsely to show off the individual specimen. This is apparent in Crispin de Passe's illustrations of gardens in the four seasons (1614). As late as 1694 the same phenomenon can be observed in a quaint frontispiece to Johan Walther the Elder's volume celebrating the botanical collection of his patron, Johan of Nassau. The garden at Idstein is shown as containing flower beds in the shape of fruits. The crown imperials and tulips are spaced widely apart. That this was not merely artistic whim is indicated by the fact that the tradition of 'isolated planting' reappeared in the Baroque gardens of Het Loo.

In France, most of these diverse traditions are represented in the sixteenth century. At Anet, for example, there were heraldic designs, and Du Cerceau illustrates a wide range of geometric patterns in gardens of the mid-sixteenth century. In Charles Etienne and Jean Liébault's *L'Agriculture et Maison Rustique* (1564; later editions 1570, 1572 and 1582), knots are featured. The terminology is interesting for the future. *Parterre* was already used to describe the flower garden as a whole, *compartiment* being confined to the square knot; the older term *parquet* was gradually disappearing. According to Claude Mollet, it was Etienne du Pérac who showed him at Anet how to lay out a large *compartiment en broderie* in box. This was after 1582 when Du Pérac returned from Italy. From then on Mollet worked on a 'large scale' and the *compartiment en broderie* became the *parterre de broderie*.

As in Italy so in France box had been avoided until then on account of its smell. But Mollet explains that the fashion changed with the change from small knots to large parterres: 'At the time I began to make the first *compartiments en broderie*, box was still rarely used . . . so that I planted my *compartiments en broderie* with several kinds of garden plant which gave a variety of green. But such plants cannot last long in this French climate, because of the extremes of heat and cold that we have. It was the great labour and expense of remaking and replanting the compartments every three years which led me to experiment with the box plant, so as not to have the trouble of remaking so often'. After Anet, Saint-Germain-en-Laye and Fontainebleau both received box broderie in the 1590s; thereafter, box conquered France, the rest of Europe and, in due course, Colonial North America. But the traditions of the Old World only spread gradually across the Atlantic during the course of the seventeenth century; it was later in the eighteenth century that grand gardening first began in the New World.

In Italy as elsewhere, the flower gardens of the Renaissance have disappeared. Only in a few sites such as **Giardino Buonaccorsi**, near Ancona, do those planting traditions live on. The history of Buonaccorsi is obscure; the design may date back to the seventeenth century. Certainly it remains true to its likeness in a painting of the mid-eighteenth century – in the arrangement of statues, in the miniature obelisks and above all in the disposition of stone-edged beds. These configurations of stars and diamonds resemble the planting plans of Bartolomeus Menkins (1584). Although no longer the original anemones and tulips, the flowers spilling over the geometric beds evoke the Renaissance ideal.

Villa Lante

17–19 My first visit to Villa Lante was in the early spring, now more than a dozen years ago. The countryside around Rome was full of dainty anemones and exuberant spurge. The meadows and olive groves seemed lush after the cold days of March under northern skies. Entering the great terrace at Villa Lante from the little town of Bagnaia, we left the countryside behind; the hills and pine trees seemed far away beyond the walls. Within the garden everything felt ordered, timeless and almost seasonless: the massive clipped hedges, the stonework covered in lichens and behind the twin *palazzine* just the hint of yellow-green buds in the lofty plane trees. The visit was private, it was quiet and we could enjoy the sound of fountains and trickling water from the age of Vignola.

A visitor to Cardinal Gambara's garden in the 1570s would have had a rather different experience. First of all, there were private visitors and public visitors. A private visit was not always a quiet event. When the Pope came to stay, for example, an entourage accompanied him: 80 light horsemen and 180 Swiss guards. Pope Gregory XIII's visit in 1578 cost the Cardinal 4,000 *scudi*. Twenty years later on the visit of Clement VIII, the terrace was turned into a mock military spectacle: carved animals shot fire, there was the crack of artillery, and torches flared. On the second evening came fireworks and music. Other receptions were no doubt more intimate, but scarcely less exotic. The Cardinal's ordinary guests might have got sprinkled by a trick fountain while dining beneath the stars on the water table inspired by Pliny's description of floating dinner-plates.

When the Cardinal was in residence with his guests, the formal garden was closed to the outside world; the dignitaries entered the garden through the central portal, which was private. This is evident in Giacomo Lauro's engraving, 1612–28, which shows the entire layout. A tour was, therefore, from the bottom to the top. On the way up, the visitor moved through the sequence of terraces and into the park. In order to appreciate the significance of the garden's sculptural programme, however, a return down the terraces was required. And this is what Gregory XIII did in 1578.

On other days, when the Cardinal was back at work in Rome, the public were allowed to enter; they came in through the gateway to the park, on the right in Lauro's view. They followed, therefore, a circuit from the informal park with its sculptural allusions to the unfettered Golden Age through into the formal garden whose iconography was encoded to refer to the accomplishments of civilization. If some of this was lost on the average visitor, the overwhelming sense of splendour was certainly not.

It may come as a surprise to find that these noble gardens were open to the public. Access was guaranteed by the so-called *Lex Hortorum*, the 'law of gardens' inscribed on a plaque at the entrance. At the Villa Borghese, for example, one line of the inscription reads: 'As in the Golden Age when freedom from the cares of time made everything golden, the owner refuses to impose iron laws on the well behaved guest'. Such openness was not unique to Rome, but elsewhere in Europe access was scarcely guaranteed. Thus the Frenchman Michel de Montaigne remarked on the accessibility to all, 'even to sleep there'. This was not true, of course, of the outcasts of Renaissance Roman society, beggars or Jews. In 1581 the following event was recorded at the Villa Medici: 'This week some Jews having gone to see the Garden of the Cardinal de' Medici under the Trinità, the day being last Saturday, were against their will put to work with a wheelbarrow moving earth and then given a good meal as recompense'.

Fountain of the River Gods, Villa Lante, Bagnaia.

One of the miniature boats on the fishponds at Villa Lante, Bagnaia.

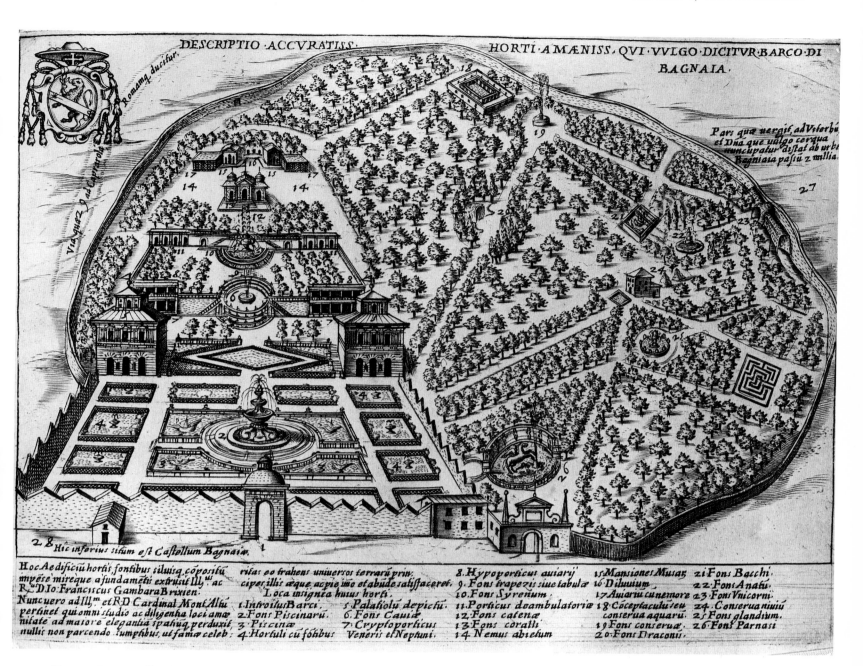

DESCRIPTIO·ACCVRATISS.   *Romamq ducitur.*   HORTI·AMÆNISS·QVI·VVLGO·DICITVR·BARCO·DI
BAGNAIA.

*Pars quæ uergit ad Viterbū
et Dña quæ uulgo cerqua
nuncupatur distat ab urbe
Bagnaia pasiu 2 millia.*

28 Hic inferius situm est Castellum Bagnaia.

Hoc Ædificiū hortis, fontibus, siluisq. cōpositū   risas eo trahens uniuersos terrarū prin-   8. Hypoporticus auiarij   15 Mansiones Musaꝝ   21 Fons Bacchi.
impese mireque a fundametī extruxit Illꝰ ac   cipes; illis æque, ac pie, imo et abūde satisfaceret.   9. Fons trapezis siue tabulæ   16 Diluuium   22 Fons Anatū.
Rꝰ D.Io: Franciscus Gambara Brixien.   *Loca insignia huius horti.*   10. Fons Syrenum.   17 Auiariū cū nemore   23 Fons Vnicorni.
Nuncuero ad IllꝮm et RD Cardinal Mont Altū   1. Introitus Barci.   5 Palatiolū depictū   11 Porticus deambulatoriæ   18 Cōceptaculū seu   24 Conserua niuiū
pertinet qui omni studio ac diligentia loci amœ-   2. Fons Piscinarū.   6. Fons Cauiæ   12 Fons catenæ   conserua aquarū   25 Fons glandium.
nitate ad maiore elegantia spatiuq perduxit,   3. Piscinæ   7. Cryptoporticus   13 Fons coralli.   19 Fons conseruæ   26 Fons Parnasi
nullis non parcendo sumptibus, ut fama celeb: 4. Hortuli cū fōtibus,   Veneris et Neptuni.   14 Nemus abietum   20 Fons Draconis.

Giacomo Lauro, Villa Lante, Bagnaia, from *Antiquae urbis splendor*, Rome, 1612–28. Many architectural features of the formal garden as shown here survive today. Photographs on p.10 show the view from the lower garden looking up; on p.17 the view in the opposite direction (the Fountain of the Moors now stands at the point numbered 2); on pp. 18–19 the Fountain of the Lights (No. 6), the Water Chain (No. 12) and the Fountain of the Table (No. 9); and here (opposite) the Fountain of the River Gods (No. 10) and the figure of a man in a boat on the fishpond (No. 3).

Modern visitors to Villa Lante, or indeed any historic site, will often try to photograph the garden as though there were no other people present; a work of art should be appreciated without visual distractions. In the days of Cardinal Gambara, however, the garden was a setting for activities and those activities brought animation. Against a backdrop of green we should visualize the colours of costumes; in the dark indigo sky we should imagine the colours of fireworks.

Villa Lante and the so-called 'Barchetto' or casino garden at Villa Farnese, Caprarola, remain two of the best preserved gardens of the environs of Renaissance Rome. They offer contrasting images of Renaissance garden design; and in the case of Caprarola, a turning-point in the direction of the Baroque. They are not, however, as I imagined on that first visit, works of art that have by some magic defied the march of time. Just as the Cardinal's guests, enjoying loud festivities and quiet intimacies, have been replaced by the tourist and the garden historian, so too the gardens and plants have changed with changing times. Renaissance stonework and fountains may remain but flowers vanish, arbours and trelliswork perish and trees grow old.

27

A tour of Villa Lante and the Villa Farnese, therefore, is a tour of the imagination as much as of the senses. Standing in the parterre at Villa Lante in May, overwhelmed by the musty scent of box and the sound of trickling fountains, we must imagine a walk through the gardens at the time of Cardinal Gambara. We shall take the guests' circuit.

To begin with, our impression of the parterre would be quite different. The scent of flowers and herbs – the *semplici* or 'simples' – would replace the scent of box. For this main terrace was devoted to flowers. They were planted in the same twelve squares that exist today but enclosed within compartments of laurustinus. The laurustinus (*Viburnum tinus*) was grown against low trelliswork, like a hedge. At regular intervals along the hedge were fruit trees, offering seasonal colours of blossom and fruit and a soft vertical accent to the terrace, where today all is remarkably architectonic and flat, box-green and brick-red.

In the fishponds at the centre of the terrace, the sound of water would be more intense. For in addition to the main fountain, each of the four pools contained small jets: three little men on a boat, whose harquebus and trumpet spurted forth water rather than the sound of shot and brass. Montaigne described the central fountain as 'a high pyramid which spouts water in many different ways: one jet rises, another falls'. This ornament, known as a 'sweating spire', was based on the *meta sudans* of the ancients. Indeed, the whole composition and the miniature military boats were intended to recall the ancient Roman *naumachia*, where naval battles took place. Today, the water parterre's beauty comes more from the glassy stillness of the pools and from the dark silhouette of the Fountain of the Moors, erected by Cardinal Montalto after the death of Cardinal Gambara.

The view across the parterre would have looked lopsided. For although Giacomo Lauro shows the terrace backed by two *palazzine*, only one was completed during Gambara's lifetime; the completion of the second had to wait for Cardinal Montalto and his architect, Carlo Maderno. The ascent to the second terrace was by steps to either side of the central axis. Today, the architectonic character of the main terrace is sustained up the grass slope by box hedges and box ornamentation. Originally, however, the openness of this area would have contrasted with the flowery terrace below. The Fountain of the Lights, evoking the flickering oil lamps of the ancients, would have dominated the central axis, where today magnificent twisted plane trees cast deep shade and soften the hillside behind the twin *palazzine*.

A visitor in 1578, Fabio Arditio, the papal secretary, remarked how, 'at first sight one does not imagine a single fountain but a thousand, indeed a whole hill'. From this second terrace it must have seemed as though the whole garden were animated by water. Beyond the Fountain of the Lights was the third terrace, laid out like a garden dining room. A stone table, with a central trough for cooling wine, was alive with water: bubbling in the centre, spouting out the end through a grotesque carving and sprinkling guests who approached from the side. Behind, lay the Fountain of the River Gods, fed by the Water Chain from the terrace above. This miniature cascade was designed to imitate both the eddies of a mountain stream and the crayfish, or *gambero*, of Cardinal Gambara's arms. Today, in this sensuous interplay of stone and water, Villa Lante remains faithfully preserved.

To imagine the setting of these fountains, however, we must visualize a wide, open meadow instead of the box hedges and shady groves. The meadow extended across the full width of the site; the square dimension of the parterre was repeated up the hillside. In that meadow were rows of planes and groves of trees in regular ranks.

The top of the formal garden was dominated by the Fountain of the Dolphins

Detail of the Fountain of the Dolphins, Villa Lante, Bagnaia.

and the Grotto of the Deluge, from where the garden's water first issued. This area was once animated by the sound of bird-song as well as splashing water. There were aviaries either side of the grotto and loggias; juniper, arbutus and myrtle provided berries for the song birds. Of the whole ensemble, only the Loggias of the Muses remain alongside the grotto. These may have offered a more intimate dining area than the monumental table below. Now all is tranquil.

For the educated visitor, returning to this formal climax after a prolonged walk in the informal park, the garden was not merely beautiful and spectacular; it intimated things historical and mythological. The fountains of the park – dedicated to Pegasus, acorns, ducks and Bacchus – recalled the Golden Age when society fed on 'acorns which had fallen from the broad tree of Jupiter', and when 'wine ran everywhere in streams'. Descending the formal terraces, the visitor gradually appreciated the meaning of the garden.

Just as Ovid relates the story of the Deluge after that of the Golden Age, so the Grotto of the Deluge forms the immediate feature adjacent to the park. The Fountain of the Dolphins takes up Ovid's account of how in the Deluge dolphins invaded the woods. The Houses of the Muses suggests how nature was then controlled by the inspiration of art; in the Water Chain, rivers and springs were appropriated as Cardinal Gambara had done. With sources of water – symbolized by the river gods Tiber and Arno – the land bore produce for the Cardinal's table. On the lowest level of the flower terrace, the material endowments of nature were transcended by the aesthetic. Art and nature were made one. As David Coffin concluded: 'The juxtaposition of rustic nature and man's formal design – nature and art – achieves a magnificent unification of meaning and form'.

Fountain of Pegasus, Villa Lante, Bagnaia, (No. 26 in the bird's-eye-view). One of the pavilions appears in the background.

Caprarola

20–21 In 1578, Gregory XIII made a stop immediately before Villa Lante; this was at Cardinal Farnese's villa at Caprarola. The summer to autumn exodus from Rome – or *villeggiatura* as it was known – was part of the church calendar. Cardinal Gambara was often a guest at the Villa Farnese. Sometimes, if the Pope requested a favoured villa, the owner would transfer himself to another resort, setting off what David Coffin has called 'a confusing game of "musical chairs" in which the only control was one's position in the social hierarchy'. September 1578 was merely a passing visit. Gregory found time, however, to have a quiet chat with the gardener, after which he dined informally in his apartment.

The fresco in the casino at Caprarola, dating from around 1586, gives some idea of what Cardinal Farnese planned in the years after the Pope's visit. Here was a private pleasure garden, sequestered from the palace and approached through woods of chestnut and firs; the fresco suggests a deer park. In the foreground there is a ramped architectural approach, in the background a series of terraces. The terrace in front of the casino looks very plain, while the one to the rear contains some beds and an enclosing arbour.

From a sketch by Giovanni Guerra of 1604, it is clear that a water chain, reminiscent of Villa Lante, was also part of Cardinal Farnese's scheme of approach. What we see today, however, is considerably embellished by subsequent alterations. These include the pavilions to either side of the Water Chain, added by Girolamo Rainaldi in the 1620s, and the later figures – quaintly called Prudence and Silence – that act as sentinels to the complex. As in Guerra's sketch, we should imagine the whole approach as a delightful interplay of stone and water transfigured in movement. If the Water Chain and River Gods recall Villa Lante, the later additions make this a more architectonic design, in which the central axis is emphasized by the embracing pavilions.

By the 1620s, the terrace in front of the casino had also undergone changes from the representation in the fresco. Unicorns, dolphins and sea-horses were added to the steps and fountains, giant male and female herms were incorporated into the perimeter balustrade. The planting, according to the inventory of 1626, was of greenery, but certainly not of box. There were fifty-five large plants of fruit trees in terracotta vases. Topiary was also listed and may have been intended for this area – peacocks and the heraldic Farnese lilies, for example, both cut out in myrtle. By the early eighteenth century, this terrace had become an intricate box parterre as indicated in a plan of 1748. Full of lilies as emblems, it was by then

The approach to the Casino Garden between rusticated pavilions added by Girolamo Rainaldi in the 1620s. In the plan on the right, we are standing at the bottom (*Primo ripiano*) looking up past the fountain, the Water Chain and the river gods to the casino.

Fresco in the Casino, Villa Farnese, Caprarola, dating from around 1586 and showing the original sequence of terraces and ramps.

Giuseppe Vasi, Casino Garden, Villa Farnese, Caprarola, from G.C. von Prenner, *Illustri fatti farnesiani coloriti nel real Palazzo di Caprarola*, Rome, 1748. The plan is dated 1746.

30

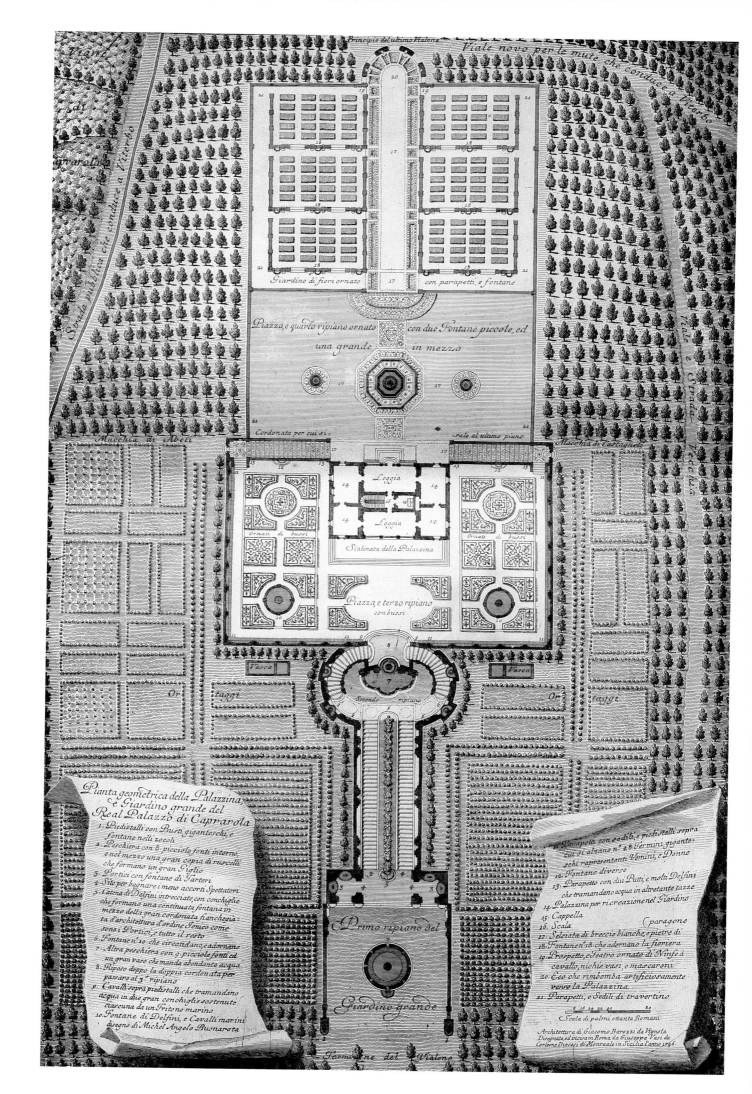

rather old-fashioned. Thus today, as we look out over the more recent box beds, we are in fact seeing the original design mediated by the vision of later interpreters, whether in the 1620s, the eighteenth century or the present day.

What was described as the 'flower garden' in 1626 was located on the third terrace behind the casino. This was no doubt the resting place for eighty-two vases with flowers itemized in the inventory. The area had been enlarged from the arbour enclosure shown in the fresco. Of the earlier design, only the fountain was kept in place. It was later surrounded by a pebble mosaic which picks up the Farnese lily emblem and which may have been used as the dining area. Both this mosaic and the series of flower beds are depicted on the 1748 plan. As Claudia Lazzaro has pointed out, this new design contrasts with the geometry based on the square at Villa Lante, producing an effect that 'appears neither measurable nor finite'. It anticipates the more expansive style of the Baroque.

Lacking the profusion of flowers, this terrace possesses today a rather different charm: a certain faded repose. At Caprarola, as indeed at Bagnaia, the casino garden or 'Barchetto' bears witness to the way in which a garden evolves over time. The additions and accretions seem to have a beauty of their own that transcends the work of one generation.

Chenonceaux

22–23   Somewhat earlier than the gardens at Bagnaia and Caprarola is the château of Chenonceaux and the gardens associated with Diane de Poitiers and Catherine de Médicis. The first phase of construction dates from 1551, when Henri II granted the palace as a gift to his mistress. The second phase dates from 1560 when Henri's wife Catherine took possession, her husband having received a fatal wound to the eye while jousting. Du Cerceau's bird's-eye view of 1559–65 shows a variety of features, now mostly lost: the flower gardens to the bottom right; behind them the circular trelliswork of the so-called Fontaine du Rocher; two gardens on the far bank of the river Cher; and Diane de Poitiers' garden on the north bank to the bottom left. Diane's garden was surrounded by a moat and a massive rampart wall and still survives intact, though the planting has changed. Diane's accounts furnish us with detailed information on how the large rectangular garden was planted. As Kenneth Woodbridge suggests: 'These give the most complete picture we have of gardening practice in mid-sixteenth-century France'.

Diane de Poitiers' garden was essentially for fruit and vegetables. But it was laid out ornamentally and embellished with violets, lilies and musk roses. The ramparted rectangle of around $2\frac{1}{2}$ acres was subdivided into four smaller rectangles by two main cross *allées*; and then into twenty-four equal plots by narrow walks with trees at every junction. A visitor in the spring of the late 1550s would have been assailed by the white blossoms of plum, cherry and pear, by the blush-pink flowers of the dwarf apple and by the sprouts and shoots of currants, artichokes, cabbages, onions, melons and peas. This was not merely a functional kitchen garden, however, for parts were laid out in various figures or knots and in a labyrinth, the nature of which we can only notionally visualize today. It may not have been quite so elaborate or fanciful as the famous twentieth-century *potager* at Villandry, but certainly there was no separation of flowers from vegetables.

The rampart or *levée* has stood the test of time. It was made of earth reinforced by a wooden frame and faced with stone. In April 1555 a flood carried away part of the construction, but it was repaired and replanting took place in 1557 under the supervision of the Archbishop of Tours' gardener. Today it looks impregnable. The planting, however, in the plan-form of a Union Jack, with

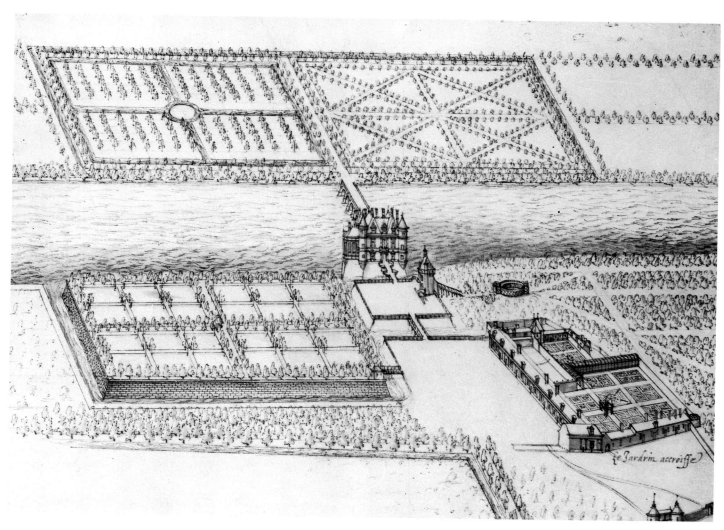

Detail of a drawing by J. A. du Cerceau showing the château and gardens of Chenonceaux. This is now our only visual record of the way the gardens were planted.

cotton lavender broderie, standard hibiscus and yews clipped like Christmas puddings is of a later taste – not without its own appeal. The marvellous atmosphere of the garden owes as much to the backdrop of a dream-like palace floating on water and to the dense encircling forests of venerable trees.

Chenonceaux was the scene of various entertainments under Catherine de Médicis. Descriptions of these festivities vivify our sense of the gardens, taking us beyond Du Cerceau's sketch and beyond the melons and currants ripening in Diane's summer garden. The first entertainment was in 1560. It was a spectacle of entry for the young king François II and his queen Mary Stuart. The temporary theatrical décor consisted in the following: a triumphal arch decked with ivy; giant herms spouting water; oak trees embellished with multi-coloured torches; and in the park all kinds of green architecture – turf theatres, tunnels, arbours or *berceaux* and pall-mall *allées*. Verses and inscriptions written for the occasion were thinly disguised political statements aimed at the memory of Catherine's rival, Diane de Poitiers. The fête extinguished her flame.

In 1563, the garden saw fireworks, a water fête, a picnic and a masque. But the most extravagant display was in 1577. The setting was the Fontaine du Rocher in the trelliswork shown by Du Cerceau. The occasion was again political – the capture of La Charité from the Huguenots by Catherine's youngest son, François, Duc d'Anjou. Catherine's entertainments flourished also at Fontainebleau. On one occasion in 1564, a water fête included sirens singing songs by Ronsard, Neptune in a car with four sea-horses and a climactic battle. In the event, Catholic knights led by the dauphin captured an enchanted island occupied by the Huguenot Prince de Condé, defiant amongst devils, a giant and a dwarf.

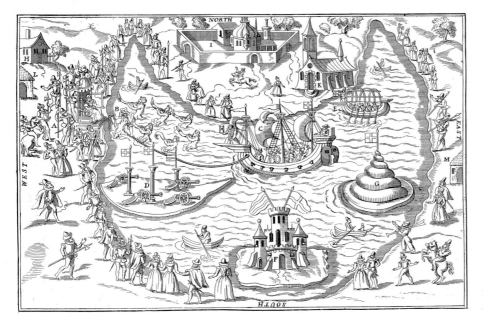

The emblematic lake at Elvetham, dug for Lord Hertford's festive celebration of Elizabeth I in 1591, from John Nichols, *The Progresses of Queen Elizabeth*, 1823.

England: Chastleton and Packwood

The fashion for water festivities spread from Italy and France to England. At Elvetham, for example, Lord Hertford organized a lavish spectacle in 1591 in celebration of Queen Elizabeth, who was identified with Cynthia, the moon goddess. A large lake in the shape of a crescent moon was excavated in the park. Within the lake were three islands: one was decked with trees in the form of ships' masts; one was dominated by Neptune's fort – in defence of England; and the third was the Snail Mount, a twenty-foot spiral of privet. In the climax of fireworks, Neptune's fort prevailed over the evil Mount just as England had prevailed over the Spanish in the Armada of 1588. That such political theatre constituted part of the English Renaissance garden, and that such naturalistic settings existed alongside formal layouts seems extraordinary to today's garden visitor familiar only with Ernest Law's 1920s knotwork at Hampton Court.

Planting, like other elements of the garden, might also have had a symbolic dimension. This is best illustrated by the record of planting by Robert Smythson

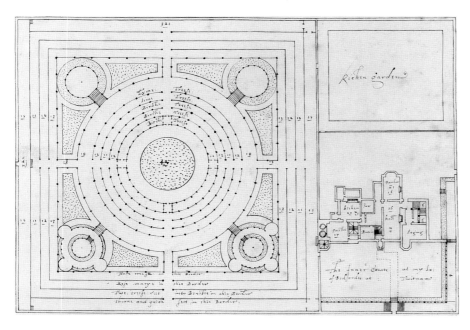

Robert Smythson's record of the planting in the Countess of Bedford's garden at Twickenham Park *c.* 1609. The central circle seems to be of grass. In the corners are mounts ascended by steps.

The garden of Chastleton House, originally laid out in the early seventeenth century, but replanted around 1828.

in the Countess of Bedford's garden at Twickenham Park, c. 1609. The Countess, Lucy Harington, who married the 3rd Earl of Bedford in 1594, was at the centre of a cultural group that included John Donne and Ben Jonson. She was also herself a radiant figure in a gardening galaxy. Her grotto at Woburn Abbey survives as testament to her activities as garden-maker. Of Twickenham, however, nothing now remains.

The garden was in the form of a square and was surrounded by walls 321 feet long. This square was reinforced by a series of hedges set out rather like a maze, each between 11 and 13 feet from the next. The outside one was quickthorn; the second 'trees cut into Beastes'; the third rosemary; and the fourth fruit trees. A rather strange assortment. Within the inner square was a circular arrangement, also somewhat like a maze. This consisted of trees planted in concentric circles (also around 12 feet apart), three of birch on the inside and two of lime on the outside, with what appears to be a grass circle at the centre. In the spandrels between the square and round forms were four mounts ascended by steps. These might have been finished with pavilions, for they were clearly platforms from which to view the whole design. As Roy Strong has pointed out, the contemporary visitor would have looked down upon an emblematic version of the pre-Copernican universe: the grass circle was the earth, circled by the moon, Mercury and Venus (birches), the sun and Mars (limes) and Jupiter (fruit trees); the beyond represented Saturn.

Such planting has vanished entirely. Two gardens, however, suggest something of the original preoccupation with planted geometry: Chastleton House in Oxfordshire and Packwood House in Warwickshire. In the case of Chastleton, what we see today appears to be a replanting of around 1828 on the

View of the 'Sermon on the Mount' at Packwood House, Warwickshire. Best seen from above, the yew trees are supposed to represent Christ surrounded by the listening crowd.

basis of the original layout of 1602–1614. In 1614 the house was completed for Walter Jones, a rich wool merchant who acquired the land from a Gunpowder Plot conspirator. The concentric rose beds around a sundial (reminiscent of the early nineteenth-century rose garden at Chiswick House) and the topiary and yew hedge are only distant echoes of Lucy Harington's plantings, but the horticultural geometry is derivative of the Mannerist style of Jacobean England.

A similar instance is the garden at Packwood. This wonderful place of intricate brickwork and abundant herbaceous borders is dominated by a monumental configuration of clipped yew trees; akin to ancient megaliths. The giant yews, said to be laid out according to the Sermon on the Mount ('Christ on the Mount overlooking the evangelists, apostles, and the multitude below . . .' as Reginald Blomfield described it in 1892), are in fact a mid-Victorian recreation of a Mannerist garden from before the Civil War. The proportions and the simple abstract forms are far from the original – whatever that may have been. But as Roy Strong points out, the 're-creation seems to capture the atmosphere of this type of religious emblematic horticulture'.

Engraving of the redesigned layout of the botanic garden in Padua, early nineteenth century. Each bed contained a different herb. In the background is the great basilica of S. Antonio.

One folio of the manuscript of planting plans for the flower garden of Francesco Caetani, Duke of Sermoneta, 1625: This page shows a single bed from the centre of the flower garden; the positions for the individual flowers are enumerated, 1 2 3 etc., and then listed on the opposite page.

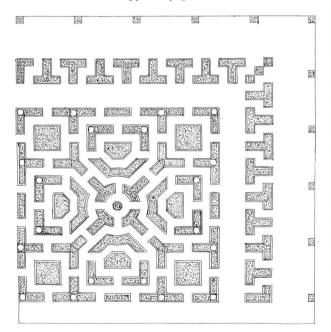

A hand-drawn copy of the plan in G. B. Ferrari's *Flora . . .*, 1638, showing one quarter of the layout for the flower garden. One of the central beds corresponds to the planting plan above; the square beds were subdivided with a peony in the centre.

Flower planting

In Italy as elsewhere, original flower gardens have disappeared from Renaissance sites. Only in the botanic garden in Padua, as redesigned in the eighteenth century, or in the layout of Buonaccorsi, near Ancona, does the tradition live on. At Buonaccorsi we find tiny beds in stars and diamonds, framed by stone edging; the flowers follow their own caprice and spill over the regular configurations. The origins of the layout in Buonaccorsi remain obscure. That it is depicted in a painting of the mid-eighteenth century may merely indicate an unusual survival from earlier times through what Georgina Masson called the 'conservatism of Marche garden design'. Today, the flowers are no longer the once fashionable anemones and tulips. But this does not detract from the wonderful atmosphere of the place, the fine quality of the stonework – obelisks, statues and flower beds – and above all the beauty of a tenacious survival.

It should be said that stone, brick or wood were not always the favoured edging materials for the Renaissance flower bed. Beds were often bordered with herbs (*erbette*) as can be seen in the frescoes of Villa Lante and Villa Farnese and in Utens's lunettes. Box was avoided until the French influence of the seventeenth century, though it was used as an underplanting with myrtle and strawberry tree in the *bosco*. Its odour was considered unpleasant and this sense seems to have outlived the Renaissance. It is always claimed that Queen Anne got rid of the box broderie at Hampton Court in the early eighteenth century from distaste for the smell. Yet it is surely one of the perennial pleasures of a visit to today's Italian garden to encounter the redolent scent of box baking in the sun.

A delightful painting of a flower garden outside the town of Hamburg in the early seventeenth century conveys better than any other single image the profusion that was possible in the chequer-board pattern of a Renaissance flower garden. The design is rather pedestrian, never moving beyond the unit of the square, but the planting effects are dazzling. Each small compartment is bordered by a low clipped herb. The interiors are filled with different combinations of plants. These are sometimes solid masses of tulips, sometimes mixtures – a crown imperial, for example, at the centre of one bed with smaller flowers around it. In the right-hand side absolute symmetry prevails, in the left-hand side a degree of deviation is permitted, though it is scarcely apparent. The variations in the height of the flowers and shrubs, however, soften the otherwise repetitive pattern of the beds. Indeed, quite improbably, a mature tree is represented as poking out of one square; this is the idealized portrait of planting practice.

Unlike the traditions of sparse planting which, flourishing in parts of Northern Europe, was illustrated by Crispin de Passe, the predominant effect in

Italy came from close planting. Yet even in the close method (as the Hamburg painting implies), sometimes a single type or colour of plant was favoured in an individual bed, sometimes a mixture; variation within regularity was important. This division between 'massing' and 'mingling' (as the two systems later became known) was to continue through until the nineteenth century. We shall encounter this dichotomy again in a very different Italian Garden at Chiswick House in the Regency and Victorian periods.

To understand how gardens like Buonaccorsi were originally planted we need to look beyond such pictorial evidence to specific planting plans of the period. The flower garden of Francesco Caetani, Duke of Sermoneta, near Cisterna provides the best example; the planting is recorded in manuscripts from the 1620s in sufficient detail to allow for reconstruction. According to Giovanni Battista Ferrari's book of 1638, in which the Caetani planting was praised, the compartments at Cisterna were bordered not with *erbette* but with the hard-edged *pianelle*. He said that a mixture of two or three kinds of flower with one predominant colour were allocated to each bed to produce the effect of an 'orderly carpet of flowers'. This resembles 'massing' and we might imagine the whole composition then like a floor of coloured marble or like the inlay of furniture. The planting plans themselves of 1625, however, suggest a more complex picture and a vastly greater mixture of different flowers. There were some 2,329 plants in the garden by this stage. In time the figure grew to an astounding 62,095, of which nearly half were anemones.

The arrangement of flowers in each bed, though following orderly rows, varied considerably. While spacing ranged from 5 inches to 1 foot (7 to 30 centimetres) in the interior beds, the outer ones were crammed full of seedlings in whose foliage the flowers appeared as speckled flecks of colour. The flowers themselves dominated the inner beds, sometimes in 'mixtures', sometimes in 'masses', depending on the plants available and the rarities on show. There were flowers in pots or vases at every junction. The larger square beds seem to have been subdivided: for example, a peony at the centre, double anemones in the four quarters, the colours being respectively scarlet, white, red (single), and white with peach in chequer pattern.

The Duke had a predilection for double anemones, now virtually extinct as a group. The peach anemone was the double *Anemone persichina*. With the name 'Casertane' came an appearance to match: 'crimson border'd with brimstone colour, the plush deep scarlett'; 'Gayetane' was quaint in that 'the first flowers are white and purple, the last dove-coloured and peach'. No wonder in correspondence, contemporaries often concealed the true name of the plant to avoid the prying eyes of a spy or informant.

It would be wrong to see these flower gardens as purely ornamental. They were designed not just as patterns to be viewed from the house, but also to gratify the senses of smell and taste. Liébault listed a group of flowers for cutting and a group of flowers grown for their scent or flavour. Those that might be taken into the house included pinks, stocks, lily of the valley, columbine and lily; while those that might end up in cooking were the traditional herbs – rosemary or lemon-balm, for example. Georgina Masson has also pointed out how flowers as objects of scientific interest and as rarities were associated with museums of curiosity or *Wunderkammern*. In Italy this might include a theatre, *manège* and even hunting preserves; and areas for sport such as *palla maglia* (pall-mall). The garden of rare flowers belonging to the Chigi family in Rome was associated with one such museum of curiosity. Later in the seventeenth century it became the setting for an extraordinary *festa gastronomico-musicale*. The same year, 1668, a similar outdoor banquet took place at Versailles. This brings us, however, to a new episode in the continuously evolving traditions of formal gardening.

A flower garden outside the town of Hamburg, by an
anonymous painter in the first half of the seventeenth
century, from the 'Horti Anckelmanniani' in Berlin.
This chequer-board design belongs within the
tradition of 'cut-work' flower gardens; the flowers,
closely grouped, are disposed in both 'mixtures' and
'masses'.

The terraced stairway of the Villa Garzoni at Collodi near
Lucca, now known as Villa Gardi. The original architectural
structure of the seventeenth century is well preserved but the
ornamental planting is more recent.

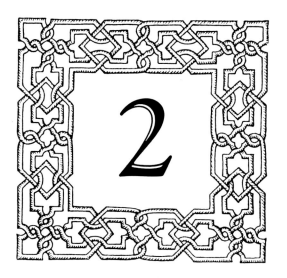

Baroque Gardens

*The Age of the
Parterre and Bosquet*

IN ITALY fresh impulses in garden design were apparent by the beginning of the seventeenth century. The Villa Montalto in Rome exemplifies one new direction. Between 1585 and 1588 Sixtus V, successor to Gregory XIII, had acquired almost 160 acres of land for his villa and park. The gigantic size of the park and the dominance of the landscape over the incidental features of architecture distinguished Montalto from the tight, enclosed geometry of the Renaissance garden in which the villa was the organizing focus. This expansive quality was further enhanced by Cardinal Montalto in the early years of the seventeenth century. Other villas in Rome – Borghese, Ludovisi and Doria-Pamphili – shared park-like characteristics; what David Coffin has called the 'new, expressive landscape design'. Although these Roman park villas have suffered from later urban redevelopment, their spirit survives through the subsequent evolution of the French seventeenth-century style of André Le Nôtre.

The traditions of the Renaissance terraced garden, however, were far from lost; they continued into the seventeenth century, notably at Villa Aldobrandini near Rome and the Villa Garzoni near Lucca. At Aldobrandini, built between 1598 and 1603, the architectonic quality apparent at Caprarola was further elaborated in the splendid Baroque nymphaeum. Moreover, the transition from this monumental formal feature to the informality of the woods was more sudden than before. As Georgina Masson wrote in this connection: 'The evolution of the Baroque Italian garden from that of the Renaissance can best be described as a gradual blurring of the outlines or – as Luigi Dami did – a softening of the edges. The basic principles are still the same and near the house man's order still reigns, but as the garden recedes from it the architectural features gradually disappear, giving way to less violent contrasts of light and shade as the clipped alleys merge into the natural growth of the woods and the surrounding landscape. It is the logical development of the process that began at Villa Lante and in it one can perceive the beginnings of the taste for the picturesque'.

At the Villa Garzoni (now known as the Villa Gardi) at Collodi, laid out in the second half of the seventeenth century, the massive terraced stairway and cascade was as imposing as at Aldobrandini. Significantly, however, the layout projected to one side of the villa on a tangential axis, the villa no longer acting as the focus of the design. Moreover, the use of a box parterre on the lowest terrace indicated the growing influence of French taste.

The emergence of box broderie at Anet, Fontainebleau and Saint-Germain-en-Laye has been mentioned previously; this was around 1600. But how did the parterre develop from these first essays to its supremacy in Europe? And how did the French formal style of the seventeenth century emerge with such sovereignty?

Claude Mollet had referred to the parterres of Anet and Fontainebleau as *compartiments en broderie*. He did not mean by this, however, the style of flowing plant-like forms later associated with Jacques Boyceau and André Le Nôtre. He meant simply the idea of composing the parterre as one unified pattern in box rather than as an ensemble of separate patterns in herbs. His early designs remained heraldic and emblematic; they lacked the finesse and delicacy of the mid-seventeenth century. It was Jacques Androuet du Cerceau who first anticipated these later organic forms in one small section of a fantasy plan; they came out of the grotesque decorative tradition. However, Marie de Médicis' embroidery patterns at the palace of the Luxembourg (1630s) seem to have been the first executed instance of what was later to be the supreme style of planted decoration.

The *parterre de broderie* at the Luxembourg was surrounded by balustraded terraces (somewhat reminiscent of the amphitheatre in the Boboli Gardens at Marie's childhood home, the Pitti Palace) and lay in close proximity to the palace. Thus the custom of laying out *broderie* directly beneath the windows of the garden façade was already established; this had developed out of the traditions of knot-gardening at Fontainebleau and Hampton Court. In 1644 John Evelyn recognized the 'circular knots' as a 'parterre . . . of box . . . so rarely designed and accurately kept up, that the embroidery makes a wonderful effect to the lodgings which front it'.

The embroidery of the early- to mid-seventeenth century was not exclusively confined to 'vegetable' forms. Integrated with stylized acanthus leaves might be masks, birds' heads or dragons in the grotesque tradition of ornamentation. At the Luxembourg the letter M and a crown were interwoven symbolically into the fabric of the parterre. This needlework style gradually developed into the more abstract patterns of the late seventeenth century. Such patterns remained, however, derived from natural objects, whether palm leaves, pinks or bryony tendrils. Moreover, for all the swirls, the *parterres de broderie* designed by Boyceau and the sons of Claude Mollet remained snugly tucked within the traditional rectilinear framework – often a square or rectangle divided into four quarters. In time, André Le Nôtre was to loosen this framework so that the whole composition reflected the filigree of the interior boxwork.

At the Luxembourg flowers were absent. The contrasts of box against the coloured materials must have sufficed. In the parterres of André Mollet, various sand colours were used. Such early parterres were typically bordered by an edging of box or double box, only later by the flower borders known as *plate-bandes*.

Marie de Médicis' broderie at the Luxembourg palace has vanished – what Wilfried Hansmann describes as one of the highpoints of French parterre design before Le Nôtre. The plans, illustrations and accounts are all that are left. Amongst these, Evelyn's comments on planting and pastimes are especially noteworthy. Following descriptions of a tortoise pool and snow conservatory, he evokes vividly the diverse activities associated with French gardens of the mid-seventeenth century. His account continues: 'You shall see some walks and retirements full of gallants and ladies; in others melancholy friars; in others studious scholars; in others jolly citizens, some sitting or lying on the grass, others running and jumping; some playing at bowls and ball, others dancing and singing; and all this without the least disturbance, by reason of the largeness of the place'.

If the grand traditions of the Luxembourg and Liancourt (1640s) are lost, along with the way of life they allowed, some architectural fragments – especially grottoes – have survived at the contemporary Wideville, Richelieu and Tanlay (1630s–40s). At the charming garden of Brécy near Bayeux in Normandy, a miniature terraced layout captures still a little of the world of the Mollets and Alexandre Francini before the advent of France's greatest master of garden design, André Le Nôtre.

Despite influences from France and Italy, the Dutch created a distinctive style at Het Loo and in many other great gardens of the seventeenth century. Erik de Jong, for instance, has emphasized the importance of 'a sense of enclosure, an

Design for *parterres de broderie* probably for the Luxembourg Palace by Jacques Boyceau. The executed parterre, although altered in implementation, has been attributed to Jacques Boyceau on the basis of this design which appeared in his posthumous *Traité du jardinage*, 1638. The broderie is typical of the early Baroque style and may be contrasted with Le Nôtre's work at Vaux (p. 75): the delicate filigree with emblems and the rectilinear framework gave way to bolder patterns and a looser outline; in time the double box border was to be replaced by the *plate-bande* or flower border.

Seventeenth-century view of the water parterres and canal at Chantilly. Some sense of the original animation in the life of the French Baroque garden is conveyed by this image. It also demonstrates Le Nôtre's skill in the use of ornate *plate-bandes* around the borders of the parterre; these have now been lost, but the structure of the layout remains well preserved.

inward-looking orientation'. This style developed in response to the countryside of canal and dyke; in adherence to persistent traits of Flemish Mannerism; and in reflection of strong horticultural traditions. It was expressed through the tendency to compartmentalize – what John Dixon Hunt has called the 'essentially piecemeal and incremental nature of Dutch gardens'. Yet, for all the richness of the traditions, scant evidence remains in the gardens as preserved today. Nothing survives of Honselaarsdijk. Little also remains of the original Huis ten Bosch (1645–52), Hofwijck (1640), Zorgvliet (1640s–80s), Clingendaal (1680) – to name just a few of the great gardens from this period. At Rosendael the magnificent shell gallery (1720s) sits in a landscape park begun by J. D. Zocher in 1836/7. Of the original Dutch planting style only the superbly restored Het Loo bears testament today.

In a tradition extending back at least to the time of Crispin de Passe (1614), designers in the Low Countries had demonstrated a tendency to display flowers as individuals rather than as units within the pattern of the parterre. It is clear from one illustration of Het Loo by L. Scherm (c. 1700) that in the royal gardens

Planting plan for the Grand Trianon, 1693. This type of close planting in the French style was taken as a model for the restored *plate-bande* at Augustusburg, Brühl, though using modern flowers. The result can be seen in the colour plate p.64.

the flowers were set out in isolation along a single row within the borders or *plate-bandes*. If they stood out clearly as specimens, overall unity was provided by the symmetrical disposition; each half was the mirror image of the other. From afar the flowers read as part of the pattern; on the ground each columbine, peony or lily was presented as an individual portrait.

To understand the contrast with the alternative French tradition of *plate-bandes* as it developed under Le Nôtre one has only to look at the anonymous planting plan of 1693 for the Grand Trianon at Versailles. Although intended for a much more intimate setting, its structure is indicative of wider practices. The spring display is represented by tulips, narcissi and hyacinths planted at four-inch intervals in six rows, each a foot apart. The summer display is a more complex grid pattern of perennials at one-foot by eighteen-inch intervals; for example, lilies, sweet williams, Greek valerian and dame's violet. Something of the effect of this pattern has been reproduced in Germany at the gardens of Augustusburg at Brühl, although using modern plants rather than the original species.

If the French style was pervasive in the German domain, both Dutch and indigenous traditions were by no means negligible, as the Great Garden of Herrenhausen in Hanover demonstrated. The lost garden of Gaibach (from 1677) also revealed influences from Holland: the termination was like Het Loo; the sunken oval basin like Heemstede; and the emphasis on the kitchen garden suggested strong horticultural impulses. It was, however, less compartment-alized, more unified than its counterparts to the north. At Schleissheim near Munich the system of canals reflected Dutch models. Yet, both at Schleissheim (1715/17) and at Brühl near Cologne (1728), Dominique Girard, 'garçon fontanier' at Versailles until 1715, created magnificent parterres following the methods of his teacher, André Le Nôtre. The parterre at Augustusburg, Brühl, like so many in Germany, was subsequently restored, this time in the 1930s, while that at Schleissheim was remodelled in the nineteenth century, with the *parterres de broderie* being replaced by lawn after the Second World War. At the opposite end of the spectrum, the diminutive but charming garden of Weikersheim (from 1708) retains through its sculpture a complete iconographical programme for the period.

Two sites in England suggest the same range of scale as Schleissheim and Weikersheim in Germany; these are Wrest Park in Bedfordshire (from c. 1671) and Westbury Court in Gloucestershire (from 1696). Often described in terms of

Design for the Grosser Garten, Herrenhausen, by M. Charbonnier, early eighteenth century. The new layout represents a synthesis of Dutch and French styles, looking back to Charleval, Honselaarsdijk and Mollet's *Jardin de plaisir*. The Italian-style theatre and the *parterres à l'angloise* reflect other diverse influences.

The Amphitheatre with its Fontana Miranda (seen, left, in an engraving of *c.* 1665) – now only partially preserved at Kleve in Germany – forms part of what was once Johan Maurits van Nassau-Siegen's extensive designed landscape. In this landscape a series of artificial viewing mounts were furnished with trophies symbolizing peace after war (e.g. Mars and Minerva); a drawing by J. van Call of *c.* 1680 (right) shows the Mars Column. It seems that an optical device was installed in the exedra at the top of the amphitheatre to enhance the perspective towards the plain below. (Compare the view today, looking over the statue of Minerva to the pools and canal.) The Fontana Miranda was an exhibition wall to display the wonders of nature and art – including apparently four monkey-puzzle trees brought back by Johan Maurits from South America.

respective French or Dutch styles, both displayed distinctly English characteristics – the simple grass parterre at Wrest, for example, or the alternation of clipped holly balls and yew pyramids in the hedges at Westbury Court. Like so many gardens of the seventeenth century in Britain, they are no longer purely of the period, having been altered and redesigned. Yet they illustrate more of the nature of original planting than other seventeenth-century sites: Hampton Court has lost the intricacies and proportions of its parterre; Melbourne Hall and Bramham both retain the structure but not the details of original plantings; and Chatsworth, for all the cascade and fountains, has lost its onetime glorious parterres and bosquets. Despite recent studies of the Italian influence on English gardens from 1600 to 1750 and several publications on the gardens of William and Mary, a comprehensive work on formal traditions in Britain after 1660 awaits its author.

The remains of the extraordinary garden of Johan Maurits van Nassau-Siegen at Cleves on the border between Germany and Holland are a reminder that not all formal gardens of this period followed the models of Versailles or Het Loo in having parterres or bosquets on terraced land. Cleves also brings to attention a complexity of imagery that is entirely lost for today's visitor to this garden of pools and perspectives.

Cleves was not, however, an isolated phenomenon. In France, ordered gardens of increasing scale and complexity – Liancourt, Richelieu, Vaux-le-Vicomte and Versailles – were challenged by sites that took advantage of irregularities, notably Saint-Cloud (from 1620s) and Rueil (from 1630s). Kenneth Woodbridge has written that 'Rueil was in the European tradition which allows the garden to be a proper place for fantasy'; the obscenities of the Hell-mouth grotto were 'an incitement to disorder'. The tradition had been influenced by Italy. While in Rome in 1581, Montaigne had already noted how the Italians made use of irregular terrain to create diversity. The fusion of the regular and irregular at Villa Lante and Caprarola and the seeming disorder of the fantastical Bomarzo represent diverse tendencies within this spectrum. Equally, in Germany, Joseph Furttenbach's *Architectura Civilis* (1628) illustrated an ideal garden in which order or formality was juxtaposed with disorder or informality. In France, however, this tension between art and nature, licence and control, as expressed at Rueil and Saint-Cloud, then disappeared in the prevailing geometry of André Le Nôtre's style until re-awakened in the Picturesque movement of the eighteenth century.

Villa Aldobrandini

A visitor to the town of Frascati, arriving on the train from Rome and taking a few 49–53 steps up from the station, is soon confronted by the imposing site of the Villa Aldobrandini; its massive broken pediment juts out into the hills and sky. Designed by Giacomo della Porta and built by Carlo Maderno in the short space of five years from 1598, Villa Aldobrandini survives as the most complete house and garden of the many handsome villas that originally graced the hills of Frascati.

For some sixty years prior to 1598, the location had been a favourite retreat for cardinals and popes; it was associated with Cicero and ancient Tusculum. The shuffling game of 'musical chairs' that resulted from the *villeggiatura* produced continual rebuilding and enlargement in this blessed spot. When the nephew of Pope Clement VIII, Cardinal Pietro Aldobrandini, acquired his villa, he was determined to emulate the gardens of Caprarola and Bagnaia. As so often in Italian gardens, the provision of water by aqueduct was crucial; it was celebrated in the cascade and nymphaeum, still the marvels of this stupendous garden.

Today's visitor will be overwhelmed by the lovely setting and the garden rising out of the hillside directly to the rear of the villa. The original approach was up the centre of the steeply sloping land to the front. Articulated by terraces and ramps, the layout of horizontals and diagonals echoed the lines of the architecture; orange trees decorated the terraces. Four hundred years later, the central axis has grown together into a massive allée of clipped ilex surrounded by grass and trees. The regiments of orange trees have gone.

From the front terrace, the visitor is conducted by the side of the villa into a quincunx of gnarled plane trees. The corresponding group to the west are underplanted with circles or hoops of hydrangea. The wonderful abstract pattern created by these hoops is compelling, but far from the aesthetic of della Porta and Maderno. A plan of 1647 shows that the area beyond was devoted to intricate parterres or knots. These appear to have been in the form of the traditional Renaissance squares. That such flower gardens continued late into the seventeenth century in Italy, despite the influence of French boxwork, is attested by the anonymous manuscript of planting plans at Dumbarton Oaks in Washington D.C. In this rare design book we find the 'cut-work' patterns of circles and stars – like the stars of Menkins, only one hundred years later.

Two of the spectacular features in the garden of the Villa Aldobrandini, Frascati. Below left: Falda's view of the rustic fountain *c.* 1683, from *Le Fontane di Roma*. Above: view today of the nymphaeum and towering ilex hedge, and a close-up of one of the alcoves.

A folio from a manuscript booklet of planting beds for an unspecified Italian villa garden of the late seventeenth century. This booklet of designs indicates that traditional 'cut-work' flower gardens in patterns of stars and circles continued to flourish at certain sites in Italy despite the growing influence of French boxwork – at Villa Garzoni, for example.

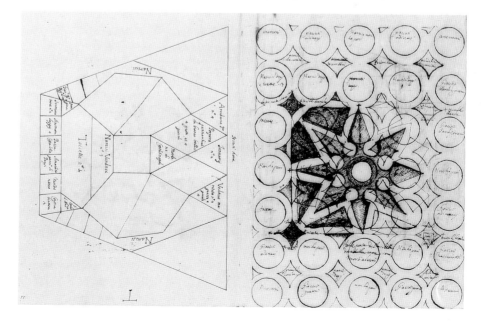

In and around the garden's main feature – the semicircular nymphaeum – the spirit of the original has been well preserved. This splendid structure, which unites house and garden, had a practical function. Located on the north side, its semi-underground rooms provided a cool retreat in summer. The interiors were animated by water, sculpture, *trompe l'oeil* and Ovidian mythology.

Above all it was these animations that impressed seventeenth-century visitors such as John Raymond and John Evelyn. Raymond described in detail the 'Parnassus whereon set the nine Muses with severall winde Instruments that sound by art. Underneath this hill are Organs, which plaid divers tunes so distinctly, that wee conceiv'd some Master was playing on them, but looking we saw they went of themselves, the cause of all this wee afterwards saw; In the midst of the roome, there being a Hole out of which winde issueth, so violently, that for halfe a quarter of an houre it beares up a Ball'. Evelyn commented also on the 'many devices to wet the unwary spectators'.

This was the Hall of Apollo. It was decorated at the time with frescoes by Domenichino, depicting scenes from Ovid's *Metamorphoses*. Here was the story of Daphne and Apollo, for example. The god Apollo had been aroused in love by Cupid's lustful golden arrow – shot from Parnassus. He pursued Daphne. But she had been struck by Cupid's loveless leaden arrow. Praying for respite, she was transformed into the laurel tree and thus evaded the pursuit. The Parnassus itself has recently been restored.

Outside, the nymphaeum walls were equally alive with forces: the centaur's horn roared; Atlas's spiky globe spouted water, while beneath him in rubble the giant Enceladus struggled; a make-believe storm 'imitated Rain, Hail, Snow and Thunder'. Alcoves, inhabited by the centaur and Pan, were fashioned in tufa and pumice to suggest natural rock. Above the nymphaeum itself, an elaborate cascade sustained the imagery: what John Dixon Hunt has called the 'metamorphic play with the elements of art and nature'. Evelyn described this as 'seeming rather a great River than a streame, precipitating into a large Theater of Water representing a exact & perfect Raine-bow when the sun shines out'. Even without the effects of water today, the architecture and sculpture is of such expressiveness that transformations still occur in the mind.

At the top of the cascade are two columns, out of which water is forced in spouts; trickling down, its natural flow is imitated by artful snake-like spirals. Mosaic patterns in red, grey, yellow and white are interspersed between the twists and turns. In the view back towards the villa, the columns frame the central hall; from the villa, the garden is framed. The axis is enclosed by the high ilex hedges, which echo the hemispherical shape of the nymphaeum. If Falda's engraving is accurate then it would appear that these hedges were originally in two sections, above which the crowns of various trees poked their fluffy heads. The same effect can still be found in the Boboli gardens to this day. Amongst other evergreens, laurustinus (*Viburnum tinus*), alaternus (*Rhamnus alaternus*), phillyrea (*Phillyrea latifolia*) and myrtle (*Myrtus communis*) make up the mosaic of the lower storey, while ilex (*Quercus ilex*) composes the upper storey. Now at Aldobrandini, one massive ilex wall dominates.

Falda's engraving of the upper fountains at Aldobrandini indicates how sudden the transition was between the grand formality of the nymphaeum and the rustic formality of the *bosco*. The planting in this area represents a strange fusion of art and nature – a regular parterre and clipped hedges combined with irregularly spaced trees and informal woodland. These distinctions are now lost in the rather overgrown remains, but through Falda we can visualize the original transitions and declensions of planting. For all these alterations to parterre, hedges and groves, the Villa Aldobrandini remains a perennial source of pleasure for visitors to Rome: it is a garden of extraordinary power and beauty.

In the garden of Cardinal Pietro Aldobrandini's villa at **Frascati**, built originally between 1598 and 1603, Giacomo della Porta and Carlo Maderno developed further the architectonic quality apparent at Caprarola. The splendid Baroque nymphaeum dominated the site, and a strong central axis was sustained above and beyond it through a cascade to the upper fountains. This created a dramatic and sudden transition from the grand formality of the nymphaeum to the rustic formality of the *bosco*. Through growth and decay, the original planting that subtly echoed this transition has been lost or replaced. However, in the animated sculpture of the nymphaeum and in the recently restored interior of the Hall of Apollo, the vitality of the original conception may still be enjoyed to the full. In this view the back of the villa is seen from the remains of the rustic fountain.

Villa Aldobrandini

The garden at Villa Aldobrandini is situated on a steep hillside to the south of the villa. The approach from the town of Frascati was originally up the centre of a formal layout to the north.

F OUR hundred years after it was laid out, the central axis has grown together into a monumental allée of clipped ilex (*opposite*) surrounded by an informal setting of grass and trees. For today's visitor, passing to the side of the villa, the first impression of the garden is a quincunx of gnarled plane trees (*right*); those to the west are underplanted with hydrangea. The imposing broken pediment surmounts the north façade (*above right*). At the top of the cascade water originally trickled down columns (*above*), its natural flow imitated by artful snake-like spirals.

ARRIVING at the central feature, the nymphaeum, the visitor is still overwhelmed by the power of the composition and the richness of the ornamentation. Inspired by Ovid's *Metamorphoses*, the architecture was animated by water: Atlas's spiky globe spouted, while the giant Enceladus struggled below (*above*), and the Centaur's horn roared (*below*). In the interior of the nymphaeum was the Hall of Apollo; the Parnassus has recently been restored in all its polychromatic glory (*right*).

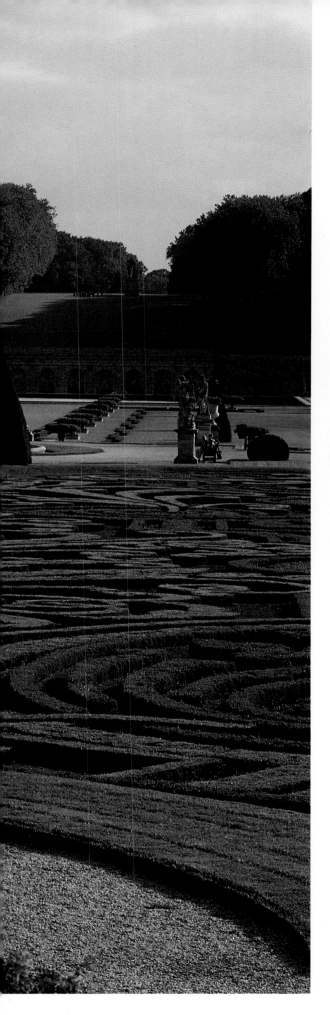

Vaux-le-Vicomte

The garden we experience today at Vaux-le-Vicomte is only partially the work of André Le Nôtre. Originally designed in the reign of Louis XIV, Vaux was completed in 1661 but dismembered from 1665; after a long period of neglect, it was re-created from the end of the nineteenth century by the landscape architects Lainé and Duchêne. The original planting has been radically altered.

THE three contrasting types of parterre that Le Nôtre designed have been transformed: the soft and colourful *parterre de pièces coupées pour des fleurs* has been replaced by grass, while the *parterre de broderie* (in the foreground, *left*) is a much more massive version of Le Nôtre's delicate, organic interlace. It is only in the *parterre à l'angloise* that something of the original effect is sustained by simple areas of lawn (*above*). A seventeenth-century engraving (p.75) shows the garden without the topiary of yew cones and spheres that line the main vista (*left*), and that are a later addition. In spite of changes, the power and beauty of the whole remains: the lovely château in its water moat; the sense of infinite space; the calculated surprises that await the visitor; and the woods that have grown tall with age.

Versailles

The gardens created by André Le Nôtre for Louis XIV at Versailles from 1661 formed a model of garden design for many generations; the complex iconographical programme and the variety of effects produced by water, garden ornament and planting dazzled the courts of Europe. So protracted is the evolution and so diverse is the meaning of the original that no one history can comprehend its full extent. Like theatrical sets, much of the garden's décor has vanished with the activities it supported – above all in the bosquets. The ornamental planting of the existing parterres bears only partial relation to the work of Le Nôtre. Yet for all this, Versailles retains through its sculpture, garden structures and fountains a powerful numinous quality.

THE South Parterre (*above right*) is a coarser version of Le Nôtre's original design with flower borders and topiary in a later style, while the North Parterre (*left*) is planted with massive box compartments full of modern annuals. The Parterre de Latone (seen on either side of the main avenue *opposite*) consists of lawns with borders of modern bedding plants.

THE original iconography of Apollo the Sun God is preserved in the relationship of the two fountains on the central axis (*opposite*). In the foreground is the Bassin de Latone (Latona was the mother of Apollo; fleeing from the wrath of Juno, she was insulted by peasants whom Jupiter turned into frogs – an image of regal power over dissent) and beyond it the Bassin d'Apollon, representing the rising sun. The sphinx (*above left*), now relocated, once added to this theme of authority and obedience.

THE colonnade of 1685–9 by Jules Hardouin-Mansart (*opposite*) and the Bassin de Bacchus (*above*), one of four fountains symbolizing the seasons, are among the surviving ornaments that once enlivened the bosquets at Versailles. This woodland zone, which may now appear dull and lacklustre, originally contained extraordinary fountains, a labyrinth and theatrical settings. Recent replanting of the bosquet within enclosing palisades (*right*) has brought a welcome rejuvenation to this area.

Het Loo

Designed for William III of Orange and his wife Mary from 1684/5, the gardens of Het Loo were meticulously restored between 1977 and 1984. Their splendour today comes close to the original condition. The restoration has recaptured the authentic proportions and the exquisite decorative embellishments of the Dutch Baroque style. Whether in the spouting blue and yellow Fountain of the Celestial Sphere (*above*) or the trelliswork and cascade, whether in the Shell Grotto or in the flower-studded parterres, intricacy, animation and colour have returned to Het Loo.

THE parterres of Het Loo demonstrate the repertoire of planting effects achieved in the Baroque period. Diverse patterns of grass, gravel and box are unified by the surrounding flower borders or *plate-bandes*. These exemplify the Dutch planting style, distinct from the French in the wide spacing of individual flowers. The use of climbers on poles and simple topiary in juniper and yew also characterize the original planting, illustrated by Scherm *c*. 1700 (see p.80). The central axis (*above*) has been brought back to life through every detail of flower and fountain.

The Lower Garden contains two types of planting: the *parterre à l'angloise*, which here combines English love of turf with French love of boxwork; and the *parterre de compartiment*, a composition of broderie symmetrical about both axes (*left*, foreground and background). In the Queen's Garden (*above*), traditional 'feminine' flowers of the virgin such as columbines and lilies are combined with orange trees in tubs.

61

THE Queen's Garden at Het Loo was connected to Mary's apartments by the delightful Shell Grotto (*opposite*), now beautifully restored with lustrous shells and marble chips; a detail of the ceiling (*left*) shows how art and nature were combined. An aviary in one corner allowed birds to fly freely between the interior and the birdcage outside. Now splendidly refurbished, the Grotto is animated by the sound of bird-song and splashing water. Shells were also used in the Venus Fountain in the Lower Garden (*above*); the tritons are casts from Cibber's Sea-horse Fountain (1688–91) at Chatsworth, and the swans from ones by Jan van Nost at Rousham in England.

German Baroque

Many German Baroque gardens represent a synthesis of French, Italian and Dutch influences: Herrenhausen reflected first Venetian and old German traditions, then traditions ranging from Charleval to Honselaarsdijk; at Gross-Sedlitz inspiration came from the steps and cascades of Italy and the fountains of France. In the art of parterre design French influences prevailed – in the work of Dominique Girard for example, who was active at Augustusburg, Brühl, and at Schleissheim and Nymphenburg near Munich.

The parterre at **Brühl** (*above*), first restored in 1933–35, remains one of the best examples of late Baroque broderie; the *plate-bandes*, although composed of modern annuals, are planted in an approximation to the pattern shown in the Grand Trianon, Versailles, of 1693 (see p.43).

The elegant steps (*above*) known as 'Stille Musik' at **Gross-Sedlitz** (after the tritons playing music along the balustrade) survive from the many arenas for festivities at the court of August the Strong.

THE restored planting at **Herrenhausen** (*above*) is a free interpretation of past traditions of *parterre de broderie*, while the borders at **Nymphenburg** (*right*) are more modern than historical; a *parterre à l'angloise* with flower borders was located on the main axis around 1715–20. The influence of the French eighteenth-century designer Dézallier d'Argenville's quest for 'naturalness' had brought a reduction in the use of topiary and the ascendancy of grass and flowers.

GIRARD's parterres reveal a range of tendencies apparent in garden design by the early eighteenth century. In his plan of 1715/17 for **Schleissheim**, he favoured the *parterre de pièces coupées pour des fleurs* in the central position over broderie. The restored parterre (*above*) follows the model of Girard's original flower beds. However, set against a background of grass instead of gravel, and furnished with bright bedding plants, the parterre is no longer strictly authentic. A canal (*right*) replaces the original pall-mall court.

Chantilly

First created by Le Nôtre from 1662/3 for Louis II de Bourbon, Chantilly epitomizes not merely an authentic (if only partial) survival of the great master's work but also a grand formal garden that absorbed later formal and informal additions. In the eighteenth century Louis-Sébastien Mercier referred to Chantilly as 'the most beautiful marriage ever made between art and nature'. Of these later additions, much has been lost but the delightful Hameau of 1774/5 survives in its Picturesque setting.

THE dominant axis at Chantilly passes to the side of the château, whose romantic silhouette (*above*) forms part of the landscape. Taking advantage of the change in level, Le Nôtre laid out a massive ramp of approach, from the top of which the gardens first become visible (*right*). The axis continues through two identical water parterres (1666), across a gigantic canal on the cross axis (1671/2–81), and up to a grass amphitheatre – originally a formal *vertugadin*. Although no longer vibrant with court festivities and the colours of glorious flower borders, the structure of this splendid layout retains its essential beauty (see p. 43).

Wrest Park and Chatsworth

Of the many great formal gardens laid out in England between 1660 and 1740, few survive in anything like their original condition. At Hampton Court, for example, the structure and planting of the parterres and wilderness have been almost entirely obliterated. At Melbourne Hall and Bramham Park, original elements exist but without the intricacies of earlier planting.

CHATSWORTH in Derbyshire provides an example of how landscape improvers sometimes retained formal features: the Canal Pond and the Cascade of *c*. 1700 were left intact by 'Capability' Brown and were incorporated into the revived formal layout of the nineteenth century. At Wrest, Brown followed an even more *laissez-faire* policy in respecting the axial arrangement of canal and pavilion along with the essential outlines of the flanking wilderness or bosquet. That central axis (*above*) was later strengthened by the new house and 'French' garden of the 1830s. The effects of this process can be observed in these contrasting views: at Chatsworth, the Canal Pond of 1702/3 with Paxton's Emperor Fountain of 1843/4 (*left*), and the canal and Thomas Archer's pavilion (1709–11) at Wrest, glimpsed through the figures of Earl de Grey's 'French' garden of the 1830s.

ARCHER's pavilion (*above*) is seen against the backdrop of Earl de Grey's new house of 1834–39. At Wrest, the planting of the bosquet, now under restoration, is especially interesting. John Rocque's plan of 1737 shows how increasingly meandering paths were added to the straight allées; these woodland walks led to hedged enclosures that were embellished with seats, urns and columns. A few survive such as the Duchess's Square (*left*), although in somewhat altered condition.

Westbury Court

First established between 1696 and 1705, Westbury was completed after 1715. Now restored, it presents an exquisite re-interpretation of the original layout, furnished with its Dutch-style summerhouse and canals. Archival records around 1700 point to the alternate yew pyramids and holly balls that stood proud of the hedges lining the main canal. Parts of the garden were devoted to fruit and vegetables. In the restoration a more decorative approach was adopted.

THE parterre (*right*) was based on one shown in the engraving by Kip of *c*. 1707/8 (reproduced on p.86), a kind of 'cut-work' flower parterre. The planting of marigolds, grasses and purple sage, however, has followed the taste of our times. In contrast, along the walls and in the small gazebo garden (*top and above*), espalier fruit trees and a delightful selection of period flowers gives Westbury an authentic feeling.

70

Vaux-le-Vicomte

The contrast with Vaux-le-Vicomte to the south-east of Paris could not be 54–55
greater: the vast scale and the dramatic use of planted pattern. Approached along
the road from Melun on a misty autumn day, Vaux still seems to rise as a
magnificent spectre from the humble woods and fields around.

The first of André Le Nôtre's masterpieces, Vaux was designed during the
1650s for Nicolas Fouquet, Louis xiv's minister of finance. It brought together
the team of architect Louis ii Le Vau, artist Charles Le Brun and garden designer
André Le Nôtre. They were to continue their collaboration at Versailles, after the
king had confiscated Fouquet's property, peeved by his minister's presumption
in upstaging him at the notorious fête of 17 August 1661.

It was Fouquet's intention, on the completion of Vaux, to offer it to Louis xiv
– but for a price. However, the king had already been set against his minister by
his mistress, Louise de la Vallière. Louise, having gained the affections of the
twenty-three-year-old monarch, was irritated by Fouquet's attempts to manipu-
late her. If Louis xiv had vented his rage unhindered, Fouquet would have been
arrested in his own garden during the festivities and during his moment of
triumph. The queen mother, Anne of Austria, intervened to spare him the
ignominy but not the eventual imprisonment.

We can imagine the scene of 17 August 1661 by studying Israel Silvestre's
engraving and by relating what he depicts to contemporary accounts. As in the
engraving, the gardens were enlivened by figures in glorious costumes, moving as
though choreographed through the sequence of events. Unlike today when a
serene repose has settled over the garden, the scene was vibrant with the play of
fountains. The king was conducted to view every angle of the immense layout:
the parterres in the foreground, the cross axis of the so-called Grille d'Eau and the
gigantic grotto and cascade to the rear. After a lavish banquet, a performance of
Molière's *Les Fâcheux* was organized. The stepped cascades of the Grille d'Eau
(to the left in Silvestre's engraving) provided the setting. As a conceit, Molière
had been set up to feign ignorance of the king's visit; he was in his ordinary
clothes and apparently without actors or sets. Once Louis commanded the
spectacle to begin, however, a shell opened to reveal a Naiad or water-nymph. As
the prologue unfolded, trees burgeoned into life and statues became animate.

With the coming of twilight, the château assumed a blazing metamorphosis;
lanterns had been placed along the cornices. The grotto was illuminated. The
velvet sky was emblazoned with fleurs-de-lys. A giant whale was in motion on
the canal; fireworks spouted from the whale's back. To the sound of drums and
trumpets, a battle commenced. As the king departed, a final and unexpected
pyrotechnic climax was organized from the dome of the château. The vaults of
heaven were alight.

It was some three weeks later, on 5 September 1661, as Fouquet left the
precincts of Vaux, that a musketeer by the name of D'Artagnan made the arrest.
After a three-year trial, Fouquet was sent to the fortress of Pignerol where he
languished until his death in 1680.

Between 1665 and 1666 the property at Vaux was stripped of its assets;
thousands of shrubs and trees were transported to the royal gardens. And
although in time Fouquet's wife was able to regain possession, her resources were
depleted; the gardens were neglected, the statues and fountains were sold off. In
1705, on the premature death of her heir, the Comte de Vaux, Madame Fouquet
discharged her responsibilities. Vaux went to Marshal Villars. There began a
period of obscurity. But the memory of the garden was kept alive – the place
where Madame de Sévigné had stopped on the way to Paris, 'with the idea of

The traditions of grand gardening in the France of
the 1630s and 40s – Marie de Médicis' Luxembourg
and the Du Plessys' Liancourt – have entirely
vanished today. Of the many fine gardens made for
the new financial elite in the first half of the
seventeenth century only fragments survive.
However, at the charming garden of **Brécy** in
Normandy a miniature terraced layout still captures
something of the world of the Mollets and Alexandre
Francini. The decorative stonework of urns and
pediments corresponds to the Mannerist ornament in
Francini's *Livre d'Architecture* (1631), and the
broderie has been re-created on the model of André
Mollet's *Le Jardin de Plaisir* (1651).

bathing in the ornamental waters and partaking of two fresh eggs'. Finally, in the 1870s the industrialist Alfred Sommier acquired the property. He commissioned the landscape architect Lainé to 'restore' the gardens. In turn his son Edme Sommier asked Achille Duchêne to complete the work on the parterres. Duchêne, however, avoided slavish imitation of the original as represented in Silvestre's engravings.

Thus the splendour of Le Nôtre's Vaux was short-lived: the four years between its completion and its first dismemberment. This seems especially remarkable when it is recalled that in the process three villages were levelled, that thousands of labourers moved earth with spade and wheelbarrow and that on their behalf a hospital was built in a nearby village. The engravings of Silvestre capture something of the original design, but they fail to convey the atmosphere of Fouquet's spectacle, both in its making and in its theatrical debut. What we see today is a strongly modified version of Silvestre. To perceive the differences involves an exercise of the mind.

The first leap of the imagination is to think of Silvestre's engraving in colour. We are looking down from the palace on men with their long coats of blue, red and gold, with their voluminous wigs, their plumed hats and elegant canes; on women in colourful lace-edged dresses with fans fluttering, and on dogs unleashed and restless. They walk on sandy-coloured paths. Behind, are three ornamental parterres: in the centre, the *parterre de broderie* of dark green box on a coloured base; to the right, the ravishing *parterre de pièces coupées pours des fleurs* in all the hues of the rainbow; and to the left, the *parterre à l'angloise* of grass and sand. If the foreground is shimmering with colour, the background fades to the greens of grass and trees and to the blues and greys of distant hills.

Of these parterres, the central one is somewhat familiar from previous discussion on the origins of *broderie*. Unlike the Mollets or Jacques Boyceau at the Luxembourg, however, Le Nôtre had broken the rectilinear framework at the ends; one swirl of box even extended on to the path. True to the old tradition, the parterre was enclosed by a double row of box rather than by a flower border or *plate-bande* as later became the fashion. There were no clipped shrubs around the parterre, so that all was flat like a carpet; only the fountains gave a vertical accent. The filigree interior was full of abstract spirals as well as forms derived from plants: diverse flowers, seeds and tendrils. If there were contrasts of colour, these came from the red, black and white (or yellow) of earths, brick, iron filings, coal and sand. Today's dominant background of red is far from the original base of sand.

Colour rather than pattern was the essence, however, of the flower parterre to the right. Le Nôtre is not normally associated with flowers, but at Vaux he must have used annuals and perennials with *élan*. This *parterre de pièces coupées pour des fleurs* was not, however, Le Nôtre's invention; it was derived from the discrete flower compartments of the Renaissance garden – previously encountered at Hamburg, Buonaccorsi and Cisterna.

In the early Baroque period flower gardens were usually surrounded by an arbour or balustrade; enclosing structures provided additional support for climbing plants as at Liancourt in France. Although by the 1650s the flower parterre at Liancourt is shown integrated into the overall layout, its position was still relegated to the side of the château; the broderie took pride of place. At Vaux-le-Vicomte, however, Le Nôtre took a novel approach in promoting the flower parterre to the main garden alongside the supreme *parterre de broderie*.

Le Nôtre's *parterre de pièces coupées pour des fleurs* was without enclosure. Its overall structure was articulated by fountains and by circles of grass; it was symmetrical along the axis. We may visualize the individual beds as filled with the brightest flowers and studded with flowering shrubs and topiary. In spring,

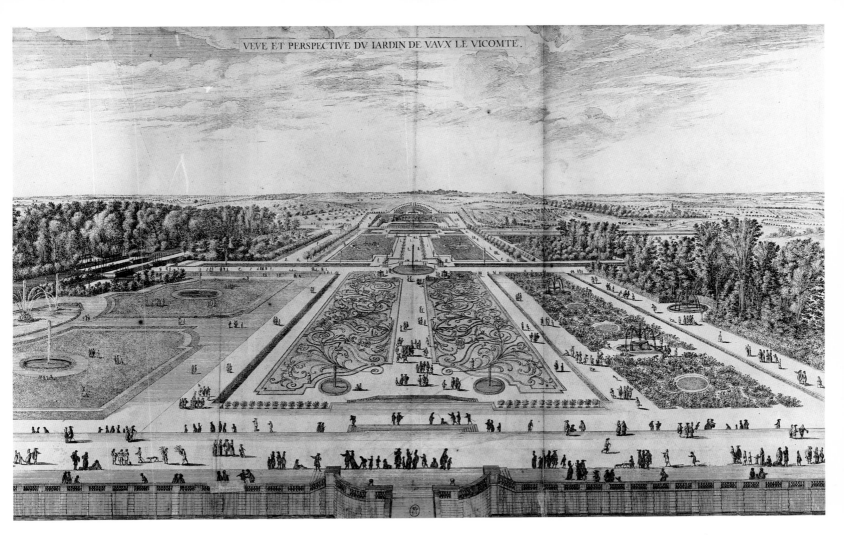

VEVE ET PERSPECTIVE DV IARDIN DE VAVX LE VICOMTE.

Israel Silvestre's engraving of Vaux-le-Vicomte, showing the garden as it was in 1661. A comparison with the colour plate on p.22 makes clear the changes in planting.

tulips, hyacinths and narcissi would have predominated, in summer the rich range of perennials and annuals – perhaps scarlet poppies or blue and pink larkspurs, amethyst honesty or yellow and red coxcombs. The disposition of flowers being symmetrical, the overall effect from afar would have resembled the dyes of a colourful fabric.

The counterpart to the left side was the *parterre à l'angloise*. This type of parterre was named after the English on account of the dominant lawns. Silvestre's engraving indicates how the perspective from the château at Vaux was thus balanced but by no means symmetrical; the English parterre was much wider as well as plainer than its counterpart. Le Nôtre seems to have chosen almost the simplest form available to him: lawn set off by sand. More complex variants allowed for the lawn to be cut into shapes and to be mixed with flower beds or even broderie. The ornamentation at Vaux was provided by the fountain in the shape of a crown; it lay just within Silvestre's view. Once again, the parterre was entirely flat and without the clipped yews that characterized other designs of the period and that were added when Vaux was restored.

Today, this plain grass parterre comes closest to the original. Seen from the immediate terrace above, as the evening sun dips in the west, the crown scintillates in its basin. The shadows are long, cast by bold yew pyramids, cones or balls that punctuate the three parterres. The whole is unified by this topiary and by velvet grass which now covers the flower parterre and indeed the major surface area at Vaux. The restored box filigree in the interior of the *parterre de broderie* resembles the pattern but not the graceful finesse of the original. Especially when highlighted by the sloping rays of the sun, the box relief is massive and monumental rather than delicate; the colours are grass-green, brick-red, coal-black and gravel-white.

The same combination of lawn and clipped yews is sustained beyond the three main parterres over the cross axes as far as the grotto. If Silvestre is accurate, such geometric figures never existed at Fouquet's Vaux. Cypresses or junipers lined the edges of the grotto and an alternation of cypress and cedar (or fir) ran up the Grille d'Eau. Once again, the present yews seem to compensate for the loss of vertical accent provided by the fountains; these must have unified the original design. Mademoiselle de Scudéry described some of these fountains as 'like a crystal balustrade'.

Much of the original sculpture by Michel Anguier and Lespagnandel was removed in the sales. Only the carvings integral to the architecture were left: the huge herms of the grotto, for example, or the masks and bowls of the Grille d'Eau. A series of herms designed by Nicolas Poussin were transported to Versailles in 1684. Two of the ten can be seen either side of the niche by the flower parterre in Silvestre's engraving. The subjects of Pan, Faunus, Hercules, Pomona, Minerva, Bacchus, Ceres and Flora were traditional symbols of gardens and fertility. Thus at Vaux, in addition to the altered planting, there is a loss of an iconographical component; the copy of the Farnese Hercules that overlooks the garden is a lonely though magnificent reminder of this.

Today, we may miss the flower parterre, the herms and the roar of water at the cascade which seemed to the seventeenth-century visitor 'like a glass column'. But the power and the beauty of the whole remains: the lovely château in its water moat; the sense of infinite space; the calculated surprises of level that await the visitor on foot and that neither descriptions nor illustrations can adequately convey; and the woods that have grown tall with age.

Versailles

56–59 Vaux was and is still a garden of open spaces. At Versailles, Le Nôtre made a garden of open and enclosed spaces. The interiors of the woodland zone at Vaux were barely exploited. At Versailles, however, Le Nôtre developed the intimate 'rooms' of the bosquet as well as the grand spaces of the parterre.

By comparison with Vaux, Versailles witnessed a prolonged gestation. It developed over decades from 1661 and was altered on numerous occasions and in numerous ways – even within the lifetime of its master, Louis XIV, who died in 1715. The subsequent alterations are equally complex and continue to the present day; restoration of the bosquets is now in progress. Thus there is no one point at which the gardens could be described as complete; in this sense, as at Vaux and indeed many historic sites, much of Versailles resembled theatre sets, conceived for specific occasions and sustained only as long as the festivities or activities demanded it or the finances permitted it.

Louis XIV's first extensive work in converting Versailles from a hunting lodge to a residential palace (after 1682, the official centre of court and political life under his monarchy) took place in the 1660s and early 1670s. The talents of Le Vau, Le Brun and Le Nôtre were co-opted. During this early period we must imagine the palace without the familiar wings added by Jules Hardouin-Mansart in 1682/83.

Beneath the queen's apartments on the south side and above the massive sunken orangery, the so-called Parterre de l'Amour was laid out by Le Nôtre in 1662. While this was later redesigned as a *parterre de compartiment*, the parterre beneath the king's apartment to the north remained a constant from its first season in 1663; even today, although replanted, it survives in the original form. Its shape is unusual: two symmetrical parts laid out in five segments of grass bordered by flowers and clipped shrubs. It was thus a *parterre à l'angloise*, but

Étienne Allegrain's painting *c.* 1690 of the north parterre at Versailles (above), contrasted with the parterre today (opposite). Le Nôtre's parterres were planted in diverse decorative styles. The north parterre was a *parterre à l'angloise* (consisting in two *pièces de gazon en compartiment*) framed by *plate-bandes* of flowers; these contained elaborate topiary cut like chess pieces and probably flowering shrubs interspersed between.

much more elaborate than the one at Vaux. The painting of the north parterre by Etienne Allegrain *c.* 1690 depicts both planting and personalities. Louis XIV and Le Nôtre, with long wigs and plumed hats, stand in the centre surrounded by a constellation of court figures; the women are off to the side, their hair piled high to the fashionable wire 'palisades'. Behind is the parterre. The flowers seem to be planted densely in a single row and interspersed with yew cut like the figures of a chess board – king, queen and bishop.

It comes as a surprise to find such fanciful topiary associated with Versailles. Previously encountered at Italian gardens from the Villa Medici to the Villa Garzoni, topiary was totally absent at Vaux. The forms used by Le Nôtre are in fact derived from Italian prototypes: Francesco Colonna's *Hypnerotomachia Poliphili*. Its presence at Versailles suggests that the art of topiary, far from being the exclusive tradition of the Dutch and English, has its origins in Italy and France.

Today, the overall structure of the north parterre survives. But the topiary has been replaced by simple yew cones and the flower borders by massive box strips containing bright modern annuals. At the lower level, as a decorative complement to the Bassin de Latone, there was originally a *parterre de pièces de gazon coupées*, which involved strips of lawn cut into the shape of palmettes or shells and scrolls. Today, plain lawns and garish bedding flowers have replaced these. Thus as the modern visitor looks down from the Galerie des Glaces the effect of the whole is of simplicity: a unified composition of lawns and clipped evergreens, where once box filigree and yew topiary contrasted with colourful *plate-bandes* and grass palmettes.

As with the gardens of the Renaissance, Versailles was a place to visit on political and festive occasions; and sometimes just for reasons of interest. John Locke's first visit to Versailles in 1677 was in the company of the king himself. Louis XIV liked to walk rather than to go by coach. This was unusual in court circles, however, as his German sister-in-law Liselotte recalled: 'people here are as lame as geese, and apart from the King . . . I don't know anyone who can walk twenty paces without puffing and panting'. Given the fact that there was not sufficient water in the 1670s for all the fountains to run at the same time the king's tour was always planned ahead. As Ann Friedman has pointed out, the route 'needed to be carefully choreographed, with the fountain operators signalling to each other with whistles'. Later in life, Louis had to resort to a sort of bath chair. But his written account of how to visit the gardens – a guidebook, of which there are six manuscript versions from 1689–1705 – remains for today's visitor on foot an essential way of visualizing the original gardens. The paintings of J. B. Martin and Jean Cotelle and the engravings of Perelle, Silvestre and Le Pautre supply the missing visual links.

After the first five stations on the route – the parterres, the Bassin de Latone and the orangery – the majority of the king's tour was within the bosquet or wooded zones. Today's visitor tends to concentrate on the central axis, passing the Bassin d'Apollon on the way to the great canal, where once mock battles took place. By contrast, the woodland seems dull and lacklustre, since few of the original settings remain intact. Yet it was in the bosquet that the gardens of Versailles excelled; there were extraordinary fountains, sculptural conceits, a labyrinth and garden theatres.

If the labyrinth represented a space for intimate exploration, other bosquets were intended for spectacle. The enormous range of effects can be illustrated by comparing several images: that by Le Pautre of the banquet at the Fontaine de l'Etoile and those by J. B. Martin of the bosquets of the Arc de Triomphe and the Trois Fontaines and La Salle des Antiques respectively. Kenneth Woodbridge described the fête that took place in 1668 at the Fontaine de l'Etoile in the following manner: 'On that occasion, the central basin was disguised, leaving a single jet shooting up from a rock. Round it were five large tables supported on gilded caryatids, loaded with different delicacies: a mountain concealing cold meats in its hollow, a palace made of marzipan and other sweetmeats, tiers of vases filled with liqueurs. After the king and ladies had eaten, the tables were abandoned to the followers, and the destruction of these beautiful arrangements provided further amusements to the court.'

The bird's-eye views by J. B. Martin show the repertoire of water effects achieved at Versailles: a large basin for gondoliers, numerous fountains, rills and cascades. They also suggest something of the original planting. The bosquets consisted typically in trees of a medium height enclosed within hedges that were trained up trelliswork palisades. These were mostly of hornbeam (though sometimes apparently of maple, if Locke is trustworthy) with clipped yew and box planted in front of them. All kinds of scented and colourful plants might be brought out on display in porcelain pots, producing a polychromatic effect far from the muted palette of today.

Locke provides us with further details of the main walks: 'The alleys of the garden are large, laid with sand instead of gravell [on] which coache & horses goe, & are raked over every day to destroy the ruts & keep them even. On each side of these great alleys are litle alleys of about 9 foot wide for walkers, separated from the great alleys by a hedg or wall of beech trees, set close to geather in a line, & 20 or 30 foot high & green from top to bottom, kept shorne even on both sides soe that they are not above half a foot or a foot thick, but green from top to bottom'.

Thus, documents from the Versailles of Le Nôtre confound the received notions of the French formal garden – as a place of gravel walks and simple architectural plantings. Versailles had sand paths and topiary, and the gardens were full of colour and intricacy. Indeed, if one adds up all the things Locke observed in addition to the allées and bosquets – the menagerie, for example, with its elephant that 'eats 50 lb. of bread per diem a 16lbs. of wine with rice'; or the Pavillon des Parfums with draws and mesh of 'treble lute strings' containing orange flowers 'to perfume gloves or anything else' – it is apparent that much of the garden's original vitality has been lost. Major alterations during the eighteenth century account for the transformation of many bosquets; present replanting recalls the effect this must have had on the appearance of the gardens.

Jean Cotelle the Younger, view of the Labyrinth at Versailles. The labyrinth was begun around 1666 and esentially finished by 1673–4; it was replaced after 1775 by the present Bosquet de la Reine. It contained thirty-nine fountains illustrating Aesop's fables, which were linked by complementary themes associated with the 'labyrinth of love'. The animals in the fountains were made of metal and painted naturalistically. In the foreground Cotelle adds a fanciful scene of Diana the Huntress with her nymphs.

Two views of the bosquets at Versailles by J. B. Martin. Left: a view after 1688 of the Bassin de Neptune from the north, looking over the Bosquets of the Arc de Triomphe and the Trois Fontaines, both laid out in 1677–8. Right: a view of La Salle des Antiques, made in 1680–3, but replaced by the later Salle des Marroniers. The twin Bosquets du Nord are currently under restoration – a first stage in a twenty-year programme for replanting the bosquets and parterres at Versailles. The original planting and décor will be re-established to their appearance around 1700.

Yet, for all this, Versailles retains through its sculpture, garden structures and fountains a powerful numinous quality – first captured in Eugène Atget's memorable photography and still ineffable today.

It is interesting to note as a postscript that on his other visits, Locke came as an ordinary tourist; members of the public were allowed to enter provided they showed decorum in their dress and provided they acquired a ticket. The guarantee of entry appears to have been more fragile in Paris than in Rome under the *Lex Hortorum*. Attempts to close the Tuileries garden to the public in 1680, for example, were foiled after gardeners assured Colbert that the public did no damage. At Versailles during the replanting campaign of the late eighteenth century, there were complaints about the Swiss guards failing to control the 'nurses . . . base footmen and scullions . . .[and] all the children of commoners [who] come there to play their games'. Yet, for one hundred years the royal garden had been full of people, aristocrat and common citizen alike.

A banquet being prepared at the Fontaine de l'Etoile, Versailles, from *Les Plaisirs de l'Isle Enchantée . . . du Roy à Versailles*. The engraving by Le Pautre of 1678 records the festivities of 18 July 1668.

Engraving of the Fountain of Venus at Het Loo from L. Scherm's 'Het koninklijk lusthof 'Het Loo', *c.* 1700. It illustrates the wide spacing of the individual flowers in the *plate-bandes*; the climbers are attached to tall stakes or poles spaced at intervals.

Het Loo

60–63 If we visualize Versailles, then, as a place of throngs, we must think of the Dutch palace of William and Mary at Het Loo as a place of retreat. Built as a pleasure-house to be enjoyed between William's military campaigns, it was a base for quiet pursuits and hunting expeditions and only occasionally for larger festivities.

Unlike Versailles, it was not the centre of government and court life. Indeed, after leaving to become queen of England in February 1689, Mary never returned to Het Loo. And although a king in England, William's status in his own land remained unchanged. In 1672–74, he had been appointed stadholder of five of the seven provinces that formed the Dutch Republic, but this did not confer on him the rights of king; he was able to draw on neither vast revenues nor the army of 36,000 that Louis XIV employed at Versailles. The gardens at Het Loo, for all they may have seemed grand by the standards of the Dutch Republic, were really as modest as the king's tastes. As K. H. D. Haley points out, despite French cultural influences, whether in clothes or in books, William is 'said to have liked plain English cooking'. And it is recalled that when the Spanish ambassador in London came across the king in his palace he nearly mistook him for a servant.

The restored *plate-bandes* today. In a tradition going back to Crispin de Passe's *Hortus Floridus*, 1614, the flowers are spaced in intervals to highlight the individual specimen.

The visitor to the restored gardens of Het Loo today has the curious privilege of seeing a site that William and Mary never fully enjoyed themselves. The first stage of construction was from 1684/5 and resulted in the Lower Garden close to the palace; the essentially Renaissance layout of eight square beds corresponded to William's earlier status as Prince of Orange. The second stage from 1692 to 1694 produced the Upper Garden, more Baroque in its structure, and coinciding with William's elevation to king of England.

Mary died in 1694 and was thus unable to accompany William on his visits to the completed project during the period before his own death in 1702. However, she commissioned from Walter Harris a guide to the gardens. This was published after her death as *A Description of the King's Royal Palace and Gardens at Loo* (1699); it proved invaluable in the restoration of the gardens, which took place between 1977 and 1984.

The *parterre à l'angloise* of the Lower Garden at Het Loo. Lawn and box are here combined with a climber to give vertical accent. Along the boxwork is a strip of sand – the *bande-de-propreté* – allowing the clippings to be removed after trimming.

A series of fifteen copper engravings by L. Scherm of c. 1700 and views by other artists help to give some visual support to Harris's account of 1699 and the plan by C. P. van Staden of c. 1692. As a result of careful research into original planting, today's visitor is able to enjoy, between frequent April showers, beds full of glorious tulips – 'Beauty of Volendam', 'Lac van Rijn' and 'Zomerschoon' –; and in the warmth of July or August the sight of roses and honeysuckles climbing up poles placed rhythmically between juniper cones and yew pyramids. At any time of year the restored parterres are the most glorious examples of the Baroque art of planting design.

The Lower Garden consisted of two types of parterre. The four central ones were of broderie, but were known as *parterres de compartiment* because of their symmetry about both axes (*parterre de broderie* being symmetrical only along the main axis). The outer four were *parterres à l'angloise*. Although Jacob Roman's design of eight squares in 1684/5 recalls the traditions of the Renaissance, the box motifs reflect the new Baroque style of Daniel Marot. As a Huguenot, Marot fled France in 1685, coming to work at Het Loo around 1691; the ornamentation of the parterres probably dates from then. He no doubt also influenced the design of the parterres in the Upper Garden. All eight lower parterres, as well as the upper parterres, are unified by surrounding borders of flowers or *plate-bandes*. As at Versailles, the flower border had come to replace the older type of edging in box.

One of Scherm's views shows the *plate-bandes* along the central axis. The planting is distinctive in a number of ways. First, there is no sign of topiary of the kind used by Le Nôtre at Versailles. Thus the traditional association of topiary with Dutch taste is not supported by Het Loo, where simple cones or pyramids prevailed; these have been restored in juniper and yew. Secondly, vertical emphasis was provided by climbing plants on wooden stakes, placed rhythmically between the evergreens. In the restored planting, these include honeysuckles, roses and flowering peas; they clamber up poles painted a bluish green. Thirdly, the plants were placed at considerable intervals along a single row rather than massed together. This tendency contrasts with the French tradition of density and may have resulted from the value placed on individual exotics during the seventeenth century, when tulip bulbs were traded for vast sums. Whatever the motivation, the aesthetic is very pleasing. The individual specimen reads clearly in the rich black soil – like the flowers of Jan Brueghel the Elder or Jan van Kessel against a dark background – yet the whole border is unified by the symmetry of the planting pattern; each half is the mirror image of the other.

To one side of the palace lay the princess's garden (after 1689 the Queen's Garden), to the other the prince's garden (after 1689 the King's Garden). The former was connected to Mary's apartments by a delightful shell grotto, studded with precious materials; a garland of pink shells, for example, on a background of powdered lapis lazuli. It was animated by birds and water. Around the box broderie of the small enclosed garden were more *plate-bandes*. These have been restored with the traditional 'feminine' flowers of the virgin such as columbines and lilies. In the early summer, the carmine peonies, pink dittany, blue and red double columbines and purple mullein seem to recall the colours of Mary's bedroom. So too in the King's Garden the red hot pokers (*Kniphofia uvaria*) and blue meadow cranesbill (*Geranium pratense*) evoke the walls of William's bedroom in orange damask trimmed with blue fringes – the Orange-Nassau family colours.

While William's flower garden was attached to the bowling green (a male preserve, and, as an especially popular English game, appropriately looked after by an Englishman), Mary's garden contained rare potted exotics and was connected to an arbour. In midsummer, the walk inside the curving green nave is as enchantingly cool and mysterious as the parterres outside are blissfully warm and colourful. One of the additional pleasures of visiting Het Loo comes from the sight of gardeners maintaining the geometry of box arabesque, yew pyramids, juniper cones and the hypotenuse of grass slopes. While stooping figures clip the box patiently by hand, as in William's day, the grass slopes are cut by a gigantic machine whose rollers are specially made for the task. The pop-up sprinklers that water the slopes also use modern technology, but in William's time the sprinkling system had already been invented.

When the working day ends, and the crowds thin out, the parterres seem magically perfect. The bees are still busy in the honeysuckles, the Fountain of the Celestial Sphere still spouts forth water – the tinkle resonant against the crunch of dry gravel – and the figure of Narcissus still gazes lovingly on his reflection caught in time.

Gardens of Germany

64–65 Although today the garden of Augustusburg at Brühl between Bonn and Cologne exemplifies one of the only surviving late Baroque parterres in the French style, the restoration of 1933–35 (and 1947) is not entirely authentic. For in the *plate-bandes* it is modern flowers that are arranged according to the system illustrated in the planting plan for the Grand Trianon of 1693. In spring, red tulips, white narcissi and blue hyacinths take up the pattern; in summer, red salvias, mauve ageratum, yellow calceolaria and white impatience. Moreover, in the 1930s the original sculpture of the flower borders was replaced by yew pyramids. Yet, set off by the pleached lime hedges and water basins, the broderie and flower borders are a splendid evocation of Dominique Girard's ostentatious work at the favourite residence of Clemens August von Bayern, archbishop and Kurfürst in Cologne.

Girard's plan of 1728 indicates a *parterre de broderie mêlée de massifs de gazon*. This was an elaboration of the conventional broderie parterre, in that box filigree was mixed with swirling bands of lawn. The effect has been reproduced in the restoration and set against an appropriate whitish background. The idea of incorporating grass strips goes back to the time of André Mollet and is illustrated in A. J. Dézallier d'Argenville's *La Théorie et la pratique du jardinage* (1709), but it was not an essential component of the *parterre de broderie* during the period of Le Nôtre. The fact that clipped evergreens were missing from the original plan indicates the influence of Dézallier d'Argenville's maxim: 'faire céder l'art à la nature'. For although topiary was still to be found as late as the mid-eighteenth century, simple flower borders increasingly became the rule – as the contemporary parterres of Nymphenburg and Nordkirchen demonstrate. The same tendency to 'naturalness' also brought the grass parterre to prominence, as at Nordkirchen.

This promotion of flowers is apparent in the fact that Girard placed the *parterre de pièces coupées pour des fleurs* in the central position of his design for Schleissheim, relegating the traditional favourite, the broderie, to the sides; that is, the reverse of Vaux-le-Vicomte. Girard's plan was drawn in 1715/17 for Clemens August's father, Max Emanuel von Bayern, as part of a scheme initiated at the end of the seventeenth century to link the pleasure and hunting lodge of Lustheim to the main palace. What we see today is the product of an extraordinary evolution in which the canal system, intended for transport from Munich, was repeatedly developed or renewed – the last time in 1962.

Schleissheim is for today's visitor a superb complex: the architecture reflected in canals where swans drift. It is, however, a much simplified version of the original concept. The flower parterre corresponds to the design by Girard, yet

Detail from Dominique Girard's plan of 1715–17 for Schleissheim. The *parterre de pièces coupées pour des fleurs* is in the central position in the design.

M. Diesel's engraving of the 'Jeu des Passes' court at Nymphenburg, *c.* 1722.

Johann August Corvinus, engraving of the festivities under August the Strong at the Japanisches Palais in Dresden, 1719. The occasion was the marriage of the Kurprinz and the climax of the evening came with the fireworks accompanying the drama of Jason's winning of the golden fleece.

the beds, being set in lawn rather than in gravel, are filled with gaudy modern cultivars; the flanking *parterres de broderie* have vanished entirely. Along with the loss of Girard's *parterre de broderie*, the bosquets have suffered severe depredations. Sadly this is true of the bosquets of other contemporary gardens such as Nordkirchen, Brühl and Nymphenburg. At Brühl there was, for example, an 'Indian' pleasure house for escape to private dinners and gallantries; there was a pheasantry, a turtles' enclosure and exotic birds; and inevitably there was a pall-mall court – a favourite game of the archbishop's father, Max Emanuel. It was he who invented the game 'Jeu des Passes', and at Nymphenburg he possessed a court for skittles too. In addition to these everyday pastimes, we may imagine the grander occasions for fireworks and mock battles – best depicted by J. A. Corvinus at Dresden under the rule of August the Strong.

August's love of festivities – from horse ballets to concerts – was expressed through the gardens in and around Dresden: the Zwinger, Pillnitz and Gross-Sedlitz. The occasion commemorated by Corvinus was the wedding of the Kurprinz to the daughter of Emperor Joseph I in 1719. The theme was Jason's quest for the golden fleece, in which, as will be recalled, Jason sailed with the crew of the *Argo* to Colchis. In the drama at Dresden, Jason was shown defeating King Aeetes of Colchis, and with Medea's help, fighting the fire-spitting bull and

Detail from a painting of Graf Carl Ludwig and his family by G. A. Eger, 1773, showing the garden and orangery as completed at Weikersheim in the early eighteenth century. The elaborate broderie is depicted around fountain basins that originally embellished the four quarters; the basins were sunken and set off by grass steps.

Opposite: view of the two-part orangery at Weikersheim by Johann Christian Lüttich (1719–23) (above); and (below) one of the 'Callot' caricatures of court staff – the Wachtmeister or watchman – and one of the obelisks of the four winds.

vanquishing the dragon guarding the golden tree. Fireworks and cannon-fire formed the climax. Thus the traditions of the water fête – Chenonceaux, Fontainebleau and Elvetham – were recalled over a century later. The one-time splendour of these grand German gardens is captured in such images.

The influence of French formality on the small scale is represented by the charming garden of Weikersheim to the northeast of Stuttgart. For all its modest proportions, the garden remains the best surviving example in Germany of a complete Baroque sculptural programme. The garden was designed in several phases from 1708 to 1725 for Graf Carl Ludwig von Hohenlohe. Begun by Daniel Matthieu, the project culminated in the dramatic two-part orangery by Johann Christian Lüttich (1719–23), through which the central axis of the garden is projected out into the hilly countryside beyond. In the background of a delightful portrait of the family, the layout is shown as finished, a simple structure but richly decorated with statues. These were mostly by Johann Jakob Sommer and sons.

The Graf or his designers were rather unimaginative in choosing Hercules to represent his image. They also followed the conventions of Baroque iconography in the disposition of the figures surrounding the central group – Hercules fighting the Hydra. Yet the ensemble is magical. It is made especially affecting by the presence of caricature portraits of court staff along the balustrade before the palace: the drummer with his beer paunch depicted in mid beat or the watchman ready to unsheath his sword. The presence of these so-called Callot figures (after Jacques Callot 1592/3–1635) provides an ironic counterpoint to the grandeur of the mythological scene: the Graf as a demigod, the new Hercules, is in the company of the gods of Olympus – from Apollo to Zeus – with outer support from the four winds, the four seasons, the four elements and other allegorical figures making up the cosmos.

Originally each of the four quarters contained a basin which was framed by broderie. As elsewhere, the planted decoration has fallen victim to time. Now the sculpture is set off by lawn, bright flower beds and clipped evergreens. This cannot, however, detract from the beauty of the composition as a whole – the sight of the obelisks of the four winds piercing the sky against the red roof and ornate gables of the palace. Weikersheim nestles in the comfort of a little town, ensconced in its own quiet valley away from the bustle of bigger places.

Westbury Court the Seat of Maynard Colchester Esqr.

Westbury and Wrest

Engraving of Westbury Court by J. Kip *c.* 1707/1708 from Robert Atkyns, *The Ancient and Present State of Glocestershire*, 1768. Behind the house is the canal, with the summer-house at the end.

68–71   In England, the gardens of Westbury Court in Gloucestershire and Wrest Park in Bedfordshire reflect the same diversity of scale as Schleissheim and Weikersheim in Germany. At one end of the spectrum lies the small-scale layout of Westbury Court. An engraving by Kip (c. 1707/1708) shows Maynard Colchester's garden in the early phase of development from 1696 to 1705. Beyond the old Tudor mansion we see the water garden with its tall Dutch-style summerhouse of red brick aligned on a canal that is flanked by evergreen hedges. The area to the rear of the Kip engraving was apparently redesigned after 1715 by Colchester's nephew in the form of a T-shaped canal with adjoining gazebo.

What today's visitor encounters is an exquisite re-interpretation of the original, following restoration in the early 1970s. Due to the loss of the house and the adjacent land shown in the foreground of Kip, the restored garden is now concentrated around the two canals and the high pavilion. This was rebuilt using parts of the dismantled structure which had been badly damaged. The documentation of planting is especially interesting; a reference in 1702, for example, to '4 perimyd hollys, 12 perimead yew, 6 lawrestinus headed, 6 headed phillereys . . .' What Kip shows as hedging along the main canal was clearly

86

planted in yew; from the top of this hedge a characteristic English combination of yew pyramids and holly balls poked their heads.

Although more elaborate topiary was to be found in English gardens, notably Staunton Harold, Levens Hall and Oxford college gardens, these pyramids, balls and cones seem to have suited the English taste for predominantly plain grass parterres. At Westbury, the emphasis was on horticulture and productivity; while espaliers were grown along the walls, the area in Kip's background appears given over to fruit and vegetables, the 'beans, pease, seeds etc.' listed in the accounts. In the restoration these utilitarian aspects have given way to a rather decorative approach, in which the plants are at times more typical of the period than the planting design itself.

Westbury is a wonderful sight in spring, when the brick walls are sprinkled with white and pink blossoms of espaliered apples and pears: Golden Reinette, Wyken Pippin, Chaumontel and Jargonelle. These are underplanted with bulbs, especially tulips of the period: the feathered deep maroon of the 'Black Parrot', the yellow and red of 'Keizerskroon' or the pink and yellow of *Tulipa saxatilis*. The enclosed garden of the gazebo is given over to a rich display of flowers; after the spring bulbs and double wallflowers come the roses and honeysuckles, the marvel of Peru and love-lies-bleeding. In place of the original vegetable garden and orchard, a parterre has been laid out. This is based on the one shown in Kip's engraving close to the house. With its simple geometric beds, it recalls the earlier traditions of Renaissance 'cut-work' parterres or knots, far from the *parterres de broderie* or *parterres de pièces coupées* of France. The planting of grasses and purple sage along with cherry trees (which are missing in the original) follows the taste of our times.

Looking out over the meadows from the summerhouse or through the grills of the *clairvoyées*, it is possible to imagine the setting is Holland, especially on days when low clouds scud across the Severn estuary. With its canals and pavilions, Westbury shares something with lost gardens like Charlecote in Warwickshire; a Dutch flavour, now almost entirely obliterated by later generations.

The evolution of the design for Wrest Park, more French in flavour, is immensely complicated. The first phase under the 11th Earl of Kent (1645–1702) established the long canal and parterres with mazes depicted in Kip's

Bird's-eye view of Hampton Court showing Daniel Marot's elaborate hemispherical parterre and the three radiating avenues in the form of a *patte d'oie* (literally 'goose's foot'), from *Britannia Illustrata*, 1720.

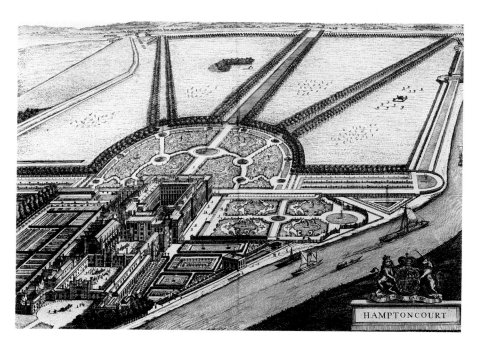

engraving c. 1705. What is striking in comparison with France or Germany is the simplicity of the grass parterres on the main axis; they are embellished with borders, clipped evergreens and exotics in tubs. Although more elaborate *parterres de broderie* existed in England – from the innovative design for Hampton Court to the old-fashioned Mollet-style patterns at Bretby – variations on the theme of plain grass predominated. At Chatsworth, for all the complexity of layout, the main parterre was a *parterre à l'angloise* composed of *gazon coupé*, or grass cut into forms and set off by sand. It is also noteworthy in the early Wrest that a bosquet or wooded zone is lacking; the area to either side of the canal remained a deer park.

A second phase came with the 12th Earl (1671–1740), but in a series of steps rather than in one campaign. The anonymous perspective of the early eighteenth century shows the following: the simple parterre enlarged at the expense of the mazes; the central canal terminated by Thomas Archer's pavilion of 1709–11; and a new woodland zone around the canal. The circular or elliptical plantation on top of Cain Hill, beyond the tangential canal, is an interesting extension of the formal garden out into the landscape. John Rocque's plan of 1737 shows the final state of the alterations under the 12th Earl: the parterre has been simplified to a grass bowling green, the tangential canal has been extended into an encircling waterway and the bosquet is full of both straight and increasingly meandering paths as well as garden rooms with buildings, ornaments and seats.

Below: bird's-eye view of Chatsworth by J. Kip and L. Knyff, 1699.

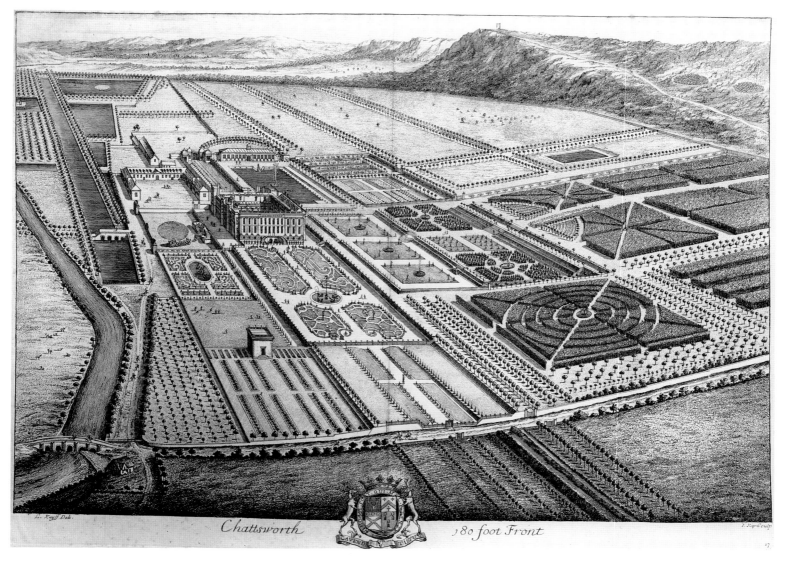

Chattsworth   *180 foot Front*

Above: unsigned view of Wrest Park in the early eighteenth century. The plain grass parterres, the bosquet, canal and Archer pavilion (1709–11) dominate the centre of the view; to the left is the plantation on Cain Hill.

What we see today, under careful restoration, are elements of this early formal layout, notably the splendid canal and pavilion with fragments of the bosquet. The water and woods retain a serene beauty, whether on hazy mornings in summer or in the frosty light of winter. These formal elements are overlaid with landscape features from the period of 'Capability' Brown and with a second formal garden of the 1830s. Here is a remarkable continuity of evolution, but these later alterations belong to other times and other chapters.

The Alcove Seat in the Lady Dutches's Walk

A detail from the plan by John Rocque of 1737 shows the Alcove Seat built in 1726 along the 'Lady Dutches's Walk'. Right: a view along one of the allées of the bosquet today.

Three examples of garden spaces that maintained the
tradition of formality in the mid-eighteenth century. Above:
view of the Neues Schloss of the Eremitage, Bayreuth, by J.
T. Köppel *c.* 1755. Below left: the menagerie at Villa Crivelli
Sormani-Verri from *Delizie della Villa di Castellazzo*, 1743.
Below right: the flower garden and aviary at Kew Gardens
from *Plans, Elevations, Sections . . . Kew*, 1763, by
William Chambers.

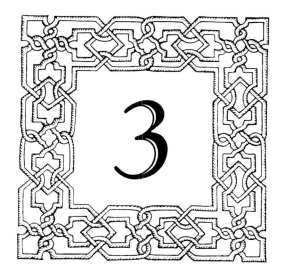

Eighteenth-century Themes

*The Marriage of the
Straight and the
Serpentine*

D URING THE EIGHTEENTH CENTURY, formal traditions in garden design survived in Europe and North America despite the increasing dominance of the landscape garden. While parterres, terraces and canals were often replaced by undulating lawns and irregular lakes, this was by no means an abrupt and uniform process. The transition from the formal to the informal was gradual, complex and sometimes only very partial. Indeed, many Baroque layouts in Italy, Germany and France remained immune to wholesale conversion; and even in England some sites like Castle Bromwich Hall outlived the Picturesque movement, being revitalized as geometric gardens in the nineteenth century.

The rapidity and thoroughness of the transition, both in England and elsewhere, depended on many things: the social status, wealth and attitudes of the owner, the geographical location and nature of the site, the scale and setting of the garden (whether rural or urban), and the susceptibility of the designer and client to new fashions spreading out over local and national boundaries from the epicentres of the landscape movement on a few estates in mid-eighteenth-century England.

The survival of formality sometimes reflected persisting ideological and social requirements. Many traditional forms and functions retained their validity, especially in court circles on the Continent. Although completed in the second half of the eighteenth century, the iconography of the gardens at both Veitshöchheim in Germany and Caserta in Italy continued to express the theme of progression from the wild to the civilized; through linear narrative the role of the owner's family in this accomplishment was celebrated. At Caserta, Ovid's *Metamorphoses* continued to provide imagery. The return of the Golden Age recurred as a theme at both Veitshöchheim and at Schwetzingen, even though at Schwetzingen Kürfurst Carl Theodor showed that the same theme could be adapted to an informal setting and circuitous route after 1777.

The traditions of entertainment were sustained through formal features such as garden theatres, menageries and *volières*, as well as areas for sport and intimate recreation. The hedged theatres of Veitshöchheim (1767–68) and Villa Rizzardi (1796) bear witness to enduring Italian models (cf. Villa Marlia, second half of seventeenth century); the ruined antique theatre in the Eremitage at Bayreuth (1743) reflects the adaptability of forms to growing sentimental impulses. Around Le Nôtre's water parterre at Chantilly new features, at first regular and then irregular, were laid out from the 1730s to the 1770s; amongst these the 'Bosquet du Jeu d'Oie' for the game of 'goose'. In English gardens, bowls seems to have retained its favour well into the eighteenth century. In German gardens pall-mall continued its popularity. Here the courts were over 2000 *Schuh* long and the players were transported to and fro in little pleasure coaches like the electric carts of a modern golf course.

The persisting formal traditions in Britain were expressed in various forms. Tom Williamson has illustrated through an important pioneering study of geometric gardens in the county of Norfolk, how many gardens contained formal features until late into the eighteenth century – walled enclosures, axial avenues

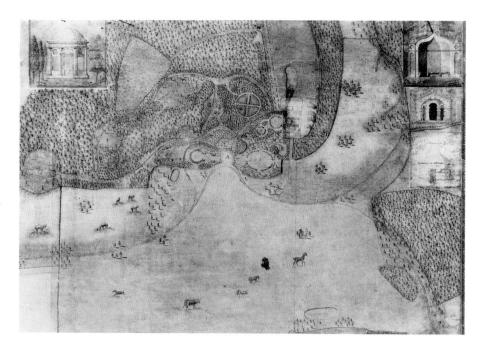

Detail from the plan of improvements at Wormsley by Richard Woods, *c.* 1779, showing circular and elliptical gardens, set within an irregular landscape park. Below: two more circular schemes, Thomas Wright's plan for a rosary at Beckett Park of the early 1750s and a circular planting plan for the flower garden at Hartwell House, 1799.

and regular groves. He wrote: 'walled gardens and other geometric features were continually altered and refurbished – often at great expense – right through the middle, and often into the late decades, of the eighteenth century, as for example at Intwood and Ditchingham'. The retention of such features was due as much to utilitarian as aesthetic impulses: the desire, for example, of the local gentry to cultivate fruit trees inside walled gardens. Town gardens often remained more regular than irregular: the Francis Douce garden of 1791 in Gower Street, London; or the recently restored garden of 4, The Circus, Bath, of 1760.

Many of 'Capability' Brown's contemporaries were happy to mix geometric elements with naturalistic elements or to work alternately in both manners. Richard Wood's design for Wormsley, Bucks, of c. 1779 shows, for example, a series of circular and elliptical gardens within an irregular park. Thomas Wright's plan for Badminton, Avon, of 1750 was in a mixed style, while that for St James's Park, London, in 1766 was remarkable for its symmetry. Wright's rosary of the early 1750s for Beckett Park was as complex as the interlace of a medieval rose window.

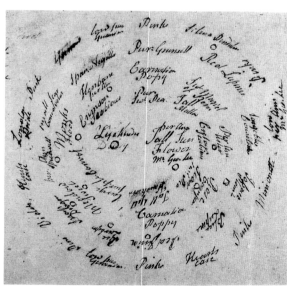

It was in the flower garden, above all, that old traditions survived most persistently; the circular planting plans of 1799 for the flower beds of Hartwell, Bucks, make this abundantly clear. While such residual geometry was contrary to the general pattern of naturalistic improvement, it indicates how the distinction between the formal and informal was less clear-cut than the propagandists of garden history subsequently allowed. Brown was able to work around the cascade at Chatsworth, and the canal at Wrest; William Emes left the terraces of Powis Castle untouched. Indeed, Uvedale Price's criticism of Brown's lakes shows how contemporaries perceived that some formal characteristics were absorbed into the landscape style: 'the character of . . . formality alone is changed. The old canal, for instance, has lost, indeed, its straitness and its angles; but it is become regularly serpentine, and the edges remain as naked and as uniform as before'.

The studies of Ingrid Dennerlein and Iris Lauterbach have illustrated how the traditions of the French formal style persisted throughout the eighteenth century in France despite the challenge from landscape exponents at Ermenonville and the Désert de Retz. Evolving out of styles that dominated the first half of

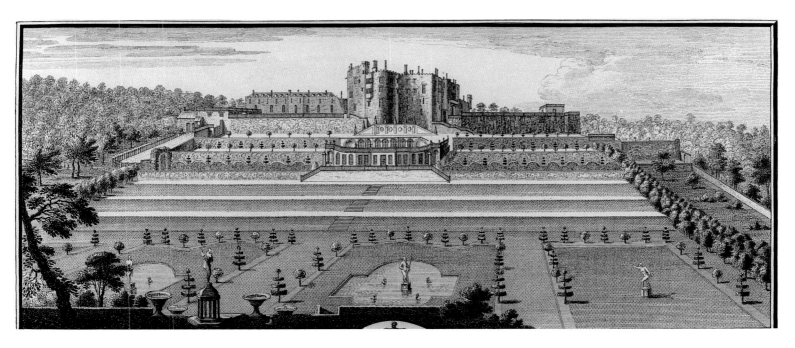

View of Powis Castle by Samuel and Nathaniel Buck, 1742, from *Buck's Antiquities*, 1774. In the foreground is the top of the cascade, in the middle ground the parterre. A plan by T. F. Pritchard suggests that by 1771 the cascade may have been dismantled along with the topiary on the lower ground, but the water basins survived (probably until *c.* 1809). When William Emes was consulted in the 1770s he left the terraces untouched and they were revitalized and replanted in the early twentieth century.

the eighteenth century (now known as Régence and Rococo), the geometric garden at the end of the Ancien Régime was increasingly confined to the smaller Hôtel gardens of Paris. Interestingly, in the parterres of Jean-François de Neufforge (*Supplément au recueil élémentaire d'architecture*, 1772–1780), Renaissance patterns reappeared. Elaborate formal layouts, however, did not vanish from the larger sites. At Chantilly, for example, new features were created on either side of Le Nôtre's water parterre: the 'Ile d'Amour' and 'Ile des Jeux' from 1765; the labyrinth from 1770; and the 'Jardin de Sylvie' of the later 1770s – an interesting hybrid of regular and irregular elements. In the eighteenth century, Louis-Sébastien Mercier called Chantilly 'le plus beau mariage qu'ait jamais fait l'art et la nature'.

Wilfried Hansmann has written with great insight about planting traditions in the parterres of France and Germany during the first half of the eighteenth century. One tendency generated from England (but already apparent to some extent in France, Germany and Holland) was towards simplification. At Cliveden, Bucks, for example, plain grass was chosen in preference to broderie in 1723/4 – what the owner Lord Orkney called a 'quaker' parterre. At Rambouillet

Detail of plan of Chantilly published in Le Rouge's *Détails des Nouveaux Jardins à la Mode: Jardins Anglo-Chinois, c.* 1775–88. In the bosquet zone to the right of Le Nôtre's layout are a range of features including a pinwheel labyrinth, derived from Dézallier d'Argenville, and the elliptical spiral course for the game of 'goose'; the 'Ile d'Amour' and 'Ile des Jeux' lay to the left of the water parterre.

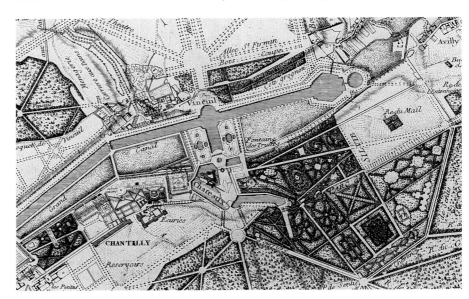

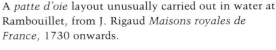

A *patte d'oie* layout unusually carried out in water at Rambouillet, from J. Rigaud *Maisons royales de France*, 1730 onwards.

Engraving by Hendrik de Leth of five radiating allées at Waterland published in *Het Zegenpralent Kennermerlant*, 1729–32. These allées were focused on various features, from an urn to an arch, to boats passing on the lake.

in France and Waterland in Holland (1710s–1720s) the parterre had lost its traditional importance, as grass, water and bosquet gained dominance over boxwork; the same was true of Chiswick House. At St Paul's Walden Bury in Hertfordshire (c. 1730s) and Canon in Normandy (from 1727 and from 1768), intersecting allées formed the core of what were essentially woodland gardens. They developed out of a tradition extending back to the 'wood walks' of Cassiobury in the seventeenth century.

In traditional palace gardens, the influence of England was registered in the increasing use of the *parterre à l'angloise* – for example, in J. C. Schlaun's plan of 1725 at Nordkirchen. Ease of maintenance and natural appearance helped promote the cause of the grass parterre. Paradoxically, an alternative tendency towards elaborate flower borders also arose out of the quest for naturalness; natural herbaceous plants increasingly replaced artificial topiary within the *plate-bandes* of the parterre. A painting of Nymphenburg in the 1720s and the plan of Schwetzingen in 1753 demonstrate these two tendencies combined in one; these were grass parterres with flower borders. Indeed, during the Rococo period flowers became the preferred decorative element; the flower parterre was sometimes promoted to a central position over the *parterre de broderie*.

In the German sphere, complex geometric layouts appear to have suited the needs of court society until late into the eighteenth century, when the ideas of the Enlightenment inclined *Landgraf* and *Kurfürst* in the direction of informality. The formal layouts of Schwetzingen (1750s to 1770s), Veitschöchheim (1760s to 1770s) and Schloss Solitude (1770s) all indicate the persistence of formality during a period when landscape gardens such as Wörlitz were already gaining influence. In Italy diverse traditions of the Renaissance, Baroque and Rococo continued to have validity. Jean Gianda's plan for the Villa Crivelli Sormani-Verri (1740s), Luigi and Carlo Vanvitelli's layout at Caserta (1750s to 1780s), and Luigi Trezza's design for the Villa Rizzardi (1780s to 1790s) suggest the range of geometric styles flourishing across the Italian peninsula. That the garden of Buonaccorsi was illustrated in an anonymous painting of the mid eighteenth century, implies that the traditions of the Renaissance flower garden had never vanished entirely.

Detail from J. L. Petri's plan for the parterre at Schwetzingen, 1753. The grass parterre with flower borders conformed to Rococo taste; broderie was reduced to a decorative element from its dominant position in the *parterres de broderie* of Le Nôtre. (The whole plan is reproduced on p.128.)

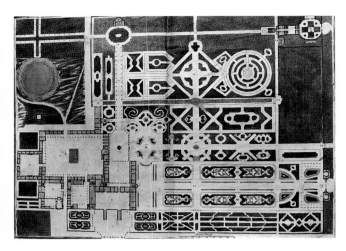

Jean Gianda's plan for Villa Crivelli Sormani-Verri published in *Delizie della Villa di Castellazzo*, 1743.

Above right: an anonymous painting of the garden at Buonaccorsi in the mid eighteenth century.

Detail from 'The South West Prospect of the Seat of Colonel George Boyd at Portsmouth, New Hampshire', anonymous 1774.

In many instances both on the Continent and in North America, the formal was accommodated within the informal. At Schwetzingen after 1777, a landscape garden was attached to the geometric layout; at Wilhelmshöhe in the 1780s, the Baroque cascade was incorporated into a romantic park; at Caserta, an English garden was made in the 1780s alongside the axis of canal and cascade; at Beeckesteyn near Haarlem an irregular garden was stitched into the regular garden by the 1770s; and at William Paca's house in Annapolis a terraced 'knot garden' seems to have coexisted with a miniature English pleasure garden from the 1760s.

By the first half of the eighteenth century, gardens in Colonial North America had progressed from simple beginnings (e.g. Bacon's Castle c. 1680) to considerable sophistication as the grand geometric layouts of Crowfield and Middleton Place in South Carolina indicate (1740s). Geometry, however, remained a dominant force to the end of the eighteenth century, despite the emergence of landscaped grounds such as William Hamilton's Woodlands (1780s) – what Thomas Jefferson called 'the chastest model of gardening . . . out of England'. Indeed, in a recent study of garden-making amongst the gentry in the Chesapeake area, Barbara Wells Sarudy has written: 'Order, control, and regularity dominated the garden designs of eighteenth century Marylanders'. Charles Willson Peale's painting of Mount Clare (c. 1775) and the anonymous painting of Colonel George Boyd's seat at Portsmouth in New Hampshire in 1774 suggest the range of formal effects achieved on the smaller estates.

For all the progressive landscaping displayed in parts of the late-eighteenth-century estates of Thomas Jefferson at Monticello and George Washington at Mount Vernon, geometry continued to play a vital role in the garden. Allan Brown has recently shown how the structure of Jefferson's retreat at Poplar Forest was determined by precise mathematical proportions. What he calls that 'fondness for regular forms' – influenced by study of the ancients and Palladio, and shaped by his direct experience of geometric gardens in the France of the 1780s – informed Jefferson's design for Monticello: 'Even when indulging in romantic naturalism at Monticello, geometric discipline was maintained, as the precise grid he devised for creating the serpentine walk demonstrated'. Regularity and irregularity were often inseparable in the eighteenth century.

Interestingly, traditions of public access did not necessarily improve in England as the landscape garden replaced the 'autocratic' formal garden. On the contrary, by 1828 Prince Pückler-Muskau could complain of the 'illiberality of modern Englishmen who shut up their gardens and estates more closely than we do our sitting-rooms'. Yet in Italy, the Borghese gardens were open twice a week in the 1770s – even to Englishmen who, according to Lady Miller, played cricket and football to the interest of the Roman ladies.

St Paul's Walden Bury

97–99 The history of St Paul's Walden Bury in Hertfordshire is somewhat obscure. The house was built around 1730 for Edward Gilbert and the main framework of the garden would seem to date from that time. Despite later replanting and changes this century, the layout remains close to the late-geometric styles of early Georgian England. St Paul's Walden Bury also shares characteristics with contemporary gardens in France and Holland. Now entirely lost, they once constituted a distinct style which Ingrid Dennerlein, following historians of interior decoration, was to call Régence – a term denoting the Regency following Louis XIV's death in 1715. Developing out of the Baroque, Régence was associated with the work of A. J. Dézallier d'Argenville. His maxim 'faire céder l'art à la nature' evoked the new quest for naturalness within the French formal style.

Today's visitor to St Paul's Walden Bury, the birthplace of the Queen Mother, is affected by the quaint alliance of straight allées with undulating English countryside. For this geometric bosquet garden was laid out on swells and dips rather than on flat terrain. Each allée is terminated by a structure or by sculpture: a temple or figure within the garden, a church beyond the garden. Enjoyable in every season, the layout is most dramatic after the fall of leaves. In winter the figure of Diana, frozen in motion, echoes the twisting branches above; two wrestlers writhe against beech hedges limp with bronzed leaves. In the early days of spring, when the twigs are tipped with green and the grass studded with cowslips, this underlying formality may be enjoyed to the full with the anticipation of warmer days to come.

What strikes the eye familiar with the parterres of Vaux-le-Vicomte, Het Loo or Brühl, is how the woodland garden runs up almost to the back door of the brick mansion. The immediate setting of the house is a rectangular lawn, framed by pleached limes. This may once have contained a flower garden, but the space is relatively small compared to the diamond-shaped area given over to bosquet. Three radiating allées project away from the house in the form of a *patte d'oie* or goose's foot. Reminiscent of an Italian street plan – the Piazza del Popolo or Palladio's illusionary streets of the Teatro Olimpico – the *patte d'oie* entered garden design during the seventeenth century. By the 1730s it had become a central device of Régence and early landscape gardens: Chiswick House in England, Waterland in Holland, Rambouillet in France. Following the eye down the central axis at St Paul's Walden Bury, the allée dips and rises to a rather meagre Hercules, almost a quarter of a mile away. The vista to the right captures the tower of the village church; the vista to the left leads to Diana, the goddess of hunting, accompanied by her prancing dog.

There are many similar cross-walks. The octagonal Organ House of 1735 forms one original focal point. Others have been added later, such as the temples by James Wyatt (1775) and William Chambers (c. 1770). These were brought to St Paul's Walden Bury from Copped Hall and Danson Hill respectively, around 1950 and in 1961. The only garden room or 'cabinet' in the bosquet contains an open rotunda set on a little amphitheatre hillock; this is faced by the figure of the discus-thrower behind a small formal pool. Here Geoffrey Jellicoe's interpretation of the past merges discreetly with the original.

The planting of St Paul's Walden Bury has certainly altered over the years. The original hornbeam hedges were replaced by beech after 1932 and the drifts of daffodils that surround the lake belong to a later aesthetic. For all this, the layout retains its essential character. A garden of grass walks, hedges and woods, St Paul's Walden Bury demonstrates the satisfaction of a composition based around variations on a theme. This achievement was matched by the mid-eighteenth-century garden of Élie de Beaumont at Canon in Normandy.

At St Paul's Walden Bury in Hertfordshire, intersecting allées formed the core of what was essentially a woodland garden. Under diverse influences, elaborate parterres began to be eliminated entirely from English gardens by the early years of the eighteenth century. At Cliveden, a plain grass surface was chosen in 1723/4 in preference to boxwork, and around the same time at Chiswick House and St Paul's the grove or bosquet was brought up close to the house, thus reducing the formal area of lawn. St Paul's survives in good condition today, although refurbished this century by Geoffrey Jellicoe. This view of the bosquet 'garden room' – embellished with rotunda, pool and sculpture – illustrates Jellicoe's discreet addition of flowing steps.

St Paul's Walden Bury

THE *patte d'oie*, the three diverging vistas that were a feature of earlier Baroque gardens, was used at St Paul's to create a series of framed views from the house. One of them focuses on the church beyond the garden (*opposite*), others on figures of Hercules and Diana within the garden (*above left* and *below left*). The octagonal Organ house (*above right*) terminates a lime allée. The garden is especially beautiful in winter; the figure of Diana echoes the twisting branches above, while two wrestlers writhe against beech hedges limp with bronzed leaves (*below right*).

Sanssouci

Sanssouci – literally 'without care' – was created between 1744 and 1764 as a retreat incorporating a terraced vineyard garden. This provided fresh fruit for Frederick the Great, who always had bowls by his side brimming full of grapes, peaches and figs. During the nineteenth century the layout was affected by alterations to the surrounding park.

THE six terraces, reached by a series of curved flights of steps (*right*), were beautifully restored in 1982–3. In the mid-eighteenth century each terrace contained twenty-eight niches with movable glass doors to protect the grapes and figs in winter. On green trelliswork between the niches grew espalier cherries, apricots and peaches. Towards the edge of the terraces, yew pyramids were alternated with potted citrus fruit and pomegranates; between them more fruit trees were trained in a low 'hedge'. These planting techniques have been reinstated at Sanssouci and complement the delightful little palace (*above*). On the lower level, the *parterres de broderie* were originally embellished with borders of spring bulbs and scented summer roses, jasmine and stocks. This planting has now been lost and the central basin altered. Yet the impact of the lyrical composition remains dramatic and sensuous.

Veitshöchheim

The supreme Rococo garden to survive in Germany, Veitshöchheim owes much of its reputation to the sculpture of Ferdinand Tietz, whose humorous and playful representations of children, putti and dancers seem to capture the essence of the style. Yet, of the layout as completed in 1763–76, only parts are original: much of the statuary has been replaced by copies, and missing are Rococo colour and intricacy – especially of planting. For all this, a beguiling spirit still pervades Veitshöchheim.

AMONG the structures and sculpture to issue from the hand of Tietz, the Chinese pavilion of 1768 is perhaps the most enchanting (*above*). This was a place for leisurely alfresco meals. The guests sat on sandstone stools beneath red and green palms that supported a canopy whose under-side was blue; pineapples tipped in gold garnished the whole. This was located in the densely wooded zone of dark firs. A middle zone consisted in more open bosquet, full of fanciful enclosures. Here Tietz created magical figures celebrating music, dance and the hunt as essential ingredients of court life (*right*). On the dominant axis was the rondel, whose trellised *berceau* led symmetrically to garden pavilions. These pavilions survive today, but the planting of hornbeam – like the reflections of opposing mirrors – is the taste of a later generation (*opposite*).

THE eastern boundary of Veitshöchheim was devoted to a grotto, belvedere (*below*) and cascade; the latter is now missing. The iconography of Fürstbischof Seinsheim's garden was constructed around the progression from this realm of nature through court festivities to the highest aspirations of the arts – symbolized by Parnassus, Apollo and his Muses. The westernmost section of the bosquet is dominated by a large basin and Mount Parnassus, where Pegasus, originally gold and with a fountain glockenspiel ringing inside, rears up from its peak (*right*). Tietz carved Olympian gods and allegories of the arts and seasons to fill the niches of the surrounding hedge. Today the weeping willows, planted *c.* 1825, give the setting a romantic tinge.

Schwetzingen

The complex evolution of Carl Theodor's garden at Schwetzingen from the formal layout of the 1750s–70s to the informal landscape of Friedrich Ludwig Sckell (from 1777) is marvellously conserved today through a restoration over several decades. Rococo parterres and bosquets are interwoven with features that look back to earlier French styles and forward to the English style. Carl Theodor's garden also demonstrates how iconographical themes such as the return of the Golden Age could be translated from the idiom of the formal garden to the circuitous narrative of the landscape garden to suit both a new style and a new ideal – the Enlightenment.

THE parterres at Schwetzingen (*above*), restored in the manner of J. L. Petri's plan of 1753 (p. 128), combine the virtues of the *parterre à l'angloise* with the Rococo predilection for flower borders. The use of contrasting colours of gravel in the interiors of the broderie also conforms to Rococo taste. By the end of the eighteenth century, Carl Theodor's garden expressed in diverse forms the return of the Golden Age, symbolized by Apollo and his lyre (*right*).

THE garden of Schwetzingen was extended by Nicolas Pigage from 1761–66 towards a canal on the cross axis; river gods of the Danube and Rhine were later placed to emphasize the central axis (*below left*). The aviary (*below*) was laid out around 1770 and focused on the sculptured owl mocked by birds from above. It forms part of an enchanting trelliswork *berceau* leading from the bath house to the *trompe l'oeil* painted landscape, now known as the 'end of the world'.

IN the Temple of Apollo of 1761–76 (*right and previous page*), the symbolism of the Sun God and the Muses was adjusted to new concerns: the Enlightenment. Apollo was meant here to represent the light of reason. Likewise, in Sckell's landscape garden, the mosque of 1778–87 (*above left*) was meant to embody tolerance; science and agricultural progress were celebrated in other temples.

Wilhelmshöhe

**The splendid grounds of Wilhelmshöhe that
overlook the city of Kassel represent a 'happy
synthesis of three generations' of garden design
between 1700 and 1800. The dominant force in the
layout is the cascade and Octagon, surmounted by a
giant Hercules. Forming a mere third of the original
composition as presented by Guerniero in 1705/6,
this formal feature was integrated into the
increasingly Picturesque landscape of the late
eighteenth century.**

Today, the view from the palace is over formal
bedding and informal lawns to a lake, beyond
which the trees seem to part before the imposing
cascade and Octagon (*left*). To the right lies a classical
temple that recalls the beauties of Stowe or
Stourhead; a vista leads the eye up the slope to the
aqueduct (*above*), dating also from the period of
Jussow's romantic landscape. On certain afternoons, a
water spectacle may be enjoyed, beginning at the
cascade, passing beneath the Devil's Bridge to the
aqueduct and culminating in the fountain near the
palace. It is a progression from the formal to the
informal and back to the formal.

Canon

This essentially woodland garden was created by Élie de Beaumont between 1768 and 1783 taking advantage of an earlier geometric layout of 1727. The central axis to the west of the house consists in a grass parterre with statues and busts and a rectangular water basin enclosed by pleached limes; an avenue stretches beyond into the distance.

THE main cross axis is terminated at one end by a crimson Chinese kiosk (*below*), from where there is a delightful view down the allée to the Temple de la Pleureuse. Between the straight allées, sinuous paths through the bosquet lead to other garden structures – a pigeon house or the ruins of a château – reflecting Élie de Beaumont's knowledge of English Picturesque.

Chiswick House

The garden at Chiswick House is often associated with the birth of the landscape style, the Picturesque; here by the 1730s William Kent created a serpentine river and informal groves. Yet, much of the formal structure established by Lord Burlington survived even beyond his death in 1753.

THE amphitheatre (*above*), illustrates how the tradition of geometric orangery gardens was perpetuated at Chiswick, even if softened by the use of grass instead of masonry terraces. The temple, amphitheatre and obelisk in a circular pool were also meant to evoke Italy and ancient Rome. Orange trees in tubs, probably fifty-two in number like the weeks of the year, suggest further iconographical levels. This area, along with Burlington's *exedra* and grove, are currently under restoration.

Caserta

The dramatic axial layout of canal and cascade at Caserta near Naples demonstrates the persistent appeal of formal traditions in Italy until late into the eighteenth century. Planned by Luigi Vanvitelli in the 1750s for Carlo III, the great 'river-road' was only completed in the 1780s under the direction of Luigi's son, Carlo Vanvitelli. He was responsible for the sculptural programme based on scenes from Ovid's *Metamorphoses*. With the arrival of the English gardener John Graefer in 1786, a Picturesque garden was added to the side of the cascade and canal. The progress of informalization continued into the 1820s, but without destroying the integrity of the axis.

THREE views of the sculpture illustrate the central imagery of the 'river-road' that runs for over a mile between the palace and the hills in ever steepening falls (*overleaf*). At the foot of the Grand Cascade are figures that enact the story of Diana turning Actaeon into a stag (*top right*). Their motions are echoed at the next fountain by the putti that float around Venus and Adonis, lovers depicted before rather than after the hunt (*left*). Below this comes the Fountain of Ceres (*above*), and further still, the Fountain of Aeolus. The theme of progression from the wild to the civilized, from hunting to agriculture and settlement, is echoed in the style of these fountains. The romantic garden (*right*) offers a contrasting scene.

North America

In Colonial and post-Colonial North America geometry remained a dominant and innovative force in garden design. At George Washington's estate at Mount Vernon, the symmetry of bowling green and the regularity of flower and vegetable gardens counterbalanced the expansive deer park overlooking the Potomac. At William Paca's garden in Annapolis, underlying geometry informed the structure of a miniature landscape garden.

The William Paca Garden

DATING back to the middle decades of the eighteenth century but destroyed by later building, the garden at Annapolis was entirely reconstructed in the 1970s following archaeological and archival research. The upper terraces, best seen from the house (*left*), contain parterres modelled on English and Tidewater American patterns. The central axis leads to a pavilion situated within an irregular garden with its pool and bridge (*above*) – all re-created from details in a painting of *c*. 1772 and from excavations.

Mount Vernon

W HEN Benjamin Latrobe visited Mount Vernon in 1796 he commented on the 'extremely formal serpentine walk' along the bowling green and a 'parterre' in the flower garden 'in the form of a richly flourished Fleur-de-lis' (below). He added the pejorative remark – 'The expiring groans I hope of our Grandfather's pedantry'. Although George Washington's house was situated to take advantage of romantic views over the Potomac (above), it was flanked by neat little gardens – restored this century. In the flower garden is a miniature greenhouse for tender exotics (above right) and quarters, both rectilinear and curved (below right). These are filled in spring and summer with a profusion of flowers that Washington would have known.

Chiswick House

While the Hertfordshire garden is poorly documented, the same cannot be said 113 of Chiswick House in London. Lord Burlington's villa and gardens have been the subject of numerous studies and various interpretations. His collaboration with William Kent is often seen as the beginning of the Picturesque style, since a serpentine river and scattered groves were introduced to Chiswick in the 1730s; the sloping lawn between villa and water became the model for the later landscape style. Yet the changes were very modest in scale. What is unmistakable is how much of the Chiswick grounds remained formal even beyond Lord Burlington's lifetime: the symmetrical forecourt and rear garden; the circular orange tree garden; and above all the axis of the *patte d'oie* leading into the regular/irregular bosquet.

The evolution of the Chiswick garden is extremely complex. The crucial period lies between 1705, when Lord Burlington inherited the old Chiswick House illustrated by Knyff and Kip (1707), and 1753, when he died aged fifty-nine. There is some uncertainty over his first improvements, which predate the building of the villa as an adjunct to the old mansion around 1727–29. What is certain is that by the time the villa had been connected to the old mansion through a link building (c. 1732–3), the gardens contained the following features: a forecourt lined with terms and regularly spaced cedars to the south; a geometric maze with formal plantings and water basin to the west; a regular grove immediately to the north; and beyond this, an orangery garden, a grass amphitheatre and a radiating *patte d'oie* leading into the bosquet. Of these, only the maze was removed entirely by 1753 to make way for the view to Kent's serpentine river. Although the groves were loosened, this had no major impact on the predominantly formal structure of the Burlington layout. Indeed, on the rear axis of the villa, part of the grove was replaced between 1733 and 1742 by a symmetrical configuration of trees and sculpture terminated by an exedra. This was undertaken while Kent was active at Chiswick.

The forecourt appears to have been laid out according to the principles of Alberti's *De re aedificatoria*, which had been translated into English by Giacomo Leoni in 1726. Burlington had cedars planted, for example, on the 1:3:9:27 architectural module recommended by Alberti. These may have been semi-mature trees removed from the nearby Sutton Court; the last survivor even made it into the twentieth century. Recent archaeology confirmed the presence of roots in these precise positions and large cedars imported from Italy have now been replanted, four to either side. The same system may have helped determine the spacing of the cypresses and cedars to the rear of the villa. John Donowell's engraving of 1753 shows them disposed between urns and sphinxes leading up to a semi-circular termination – the exedra. This was in the form of a scalloped yew hedge, in which classical figures were placed between lions, terms and urns. The influence of Italy was apparent once again – from the Villa Mattei to Robert Castell's reconstructions of Roman gardens in *The Villas of the Ancients Illustrated* (1728). This rear garden has recently been replanted with cedars and cypresses, bringing Donowell's image back to life.

The exedra replaced part of the grove which had been planted in a regular pattern around 1719. Like St Paul's Walden Bury it came close to the house – ten feet, if one visitor's account is trustworthy. What remained of the grove after clearance can be seen to the right of the Donowell engraving. Recent surveys have attempted to reconstruct the precise positions of the grove trees (these range from high-tech computer-aided graphics and resistivity survey to low-tech dowsing). A regular quincunx pattern seems probable and restoration will follow.

The amphitheatre garden, with its Ionic Temple, was designed to contain

As illustrated in a plan of 1772 (see p. 132) by its creator, Johann Georg Michael, **Beeckesteyn** was an extraordinary mixed marriage: the Baroque wooed by the Picturesque. After a visit to England in the early 1760s, Michael altered the original layout for the owner Jacob Boreel. To the geometric structure he added irregular fields, woods and water, but still within a rectilinear boundary. 'Restored' in the 1950s, Beeckesteyn is now as much a product of our times as a relic of the original.

orange trees in summer in the manner of Dutch models of the seventeenth century: Zorgvliet, Heemstede and Zeist, for example. The form at Chiswick was a segment of a circle rather than a full circle, with three grass terraces descending to a round pond at the centre. The temple, the amphitheatre and the obelisk in the middle of the pool were evocative of ancient Rome; the orange-tree tubs, probably fifty-two in number like the weeks of the year, were suggestive of further iconographical levels. These were transported from the orangery on the east side of the grove after the frosts of every spring.

Pieter Andreas Rysbrack's painting of the *patte d'oie* c. 1728 illustrates clearly the inheritance of earlier planting traditions. The radiating allées provided three main vistas and several subsidiary vistas. The central allée to the so-called Pagan Temple is the most interesting. It was divided into one wide and two narrow walks, in a manner similar to what Locke had encountered at Versailles, but on a much more modest scale. While the main walk was 'open', the side walks were 'closed' by overarching branches to provide shade. In contrast, the walk to the Casina was enclosed between simple high hedges. To the left in Rysbrack's painting, a gardener clips the hedge with shears; while a figure emerges out of the shady bosquet walk. What we see today is a faint version of the original; the embellishments largely removed, the yew hedges only partially restored in the 1950s. A visitor must make the journey to Schönbrunn in Vienna to see hedgework still managed in a manner that would have been familiar to Lord Burlington.

Burlington used his villa and garden as a centre for the arts; concerts and theatre took place there. He was a patron and sponsor, supporting the philosopher Berkeley, writers like Pope and Swift and artists like Kent; at different times Gay, Handel, Kent and Guelfi all lived with the Burlingtons in Piccadilly. Given Kent's love of food, the grocery bills must have been large; his

Pieter Andreas Rysbrack, painting of one half of the *patte d'oie* at Chiswick House *c.* 1728. When John Donowell illustrated the same feature in 1753, the formal planting was still maintained although modified in places.

John Donowell, the exedra seen from the north perron of Chiswick House in 1753.

letters are full of allusions to 'potted hare' and venison – 'The doe you sent was extremely good, the more you send the better'. When the actor Garrick married the dancer Violette, it was Lady Burlington who provided the dowry. The garden, like the villa, was both a museum of architecture and a setting for the arts. If the contemporary views are indicative, however, the grounds at Chiswick were given over to the quieter pursuits of fishing, bowling and walking rather than to the larger spectacles of the Baroque world.

Many of the formal features at Chiswick survived the landscape improvements of the 1780s, when the fifth Duke of Devonshire employed 'Capability' Brown's former assistant Samuel Lapidge. Indeed, what might be called this 'informal interlude' was short-lived. Within three decades, a formal revival had occurred with Lewis Kennedy's Italian Garden of 1814. Today's visitor sees a garden in transition – parts restored, parts awaiting restoration. Yet even now the forecourt, exedra and amphitheatre recall Burlington's evocation of the gardens of the ancients through cedar, cypress and orange tree.

Sanssouci

Burlington's reputation as an architect spread throughout Europe. In 1751 100–101 Frederick the Great asked the Italian philosopher Algarotti to show him pictures of Lord Burlington's work. Frederick had an equally wide interest in the arts. As a child he had defied his father's rages and corporal punishment, reading forbidden books and playing the flute with his servant. There was some complicity on the part of his mother and older sister Wilhelmina. As a monarch he employed C. P. E. Bach amongst fifty musicians; when Bach's father came on a visit to the Prussian court in 1747, it was the king who provided the theme for his composition *The Musical Offering*. What Frederick created at Sanssouci, however, as a retreat from court ceremony was far from the intimacy of Chiswick House.

Sanssouci – literally 'without care' – was created between 1744 and 1764. If the king provided the overall concept, Georg Wenzeslaus von Knobelsdorff oversaw the planning. The stimulus came as much as anything from Frederick the Great's passion for fresh fruit; he always had by his side bowls brimming full of grapes, peaches and figs. The garden of Sanssouci consisted in a series of six terraces dedicated to the production of fruit; they were set out in a rippling plan form. Each terrace wall was around ten feet high and contained twenty-eight niches with movable glass doors to protect the grapes and figs in winter. So that

the king could enjoy the earliest grapes of the season, the niches were warmed in spring by coal fire. On green trelliswork between the niches grew espalier cherries, apricots and peaches. Towards the edge of every terrace a counterpoint of yew pyramids and potted citrus fruit and pomegranates repeated the alternation of niches and trelliswork. Topped by the delightful little palace, the whole composition was as rhythmic and lyrical as the flute music composed at his court.

At the foot of the terraces stretched a large parterre ornamented with broderie, flowers, sculpture and water. The centre was dominated by a basin of elongated quatrefoil shape, decorated with a golden Thetis group and surrounded by four *parterres de broderie*; the outer four parterres were of grass. The *plate-bandes* were filled with tulips, narcissus, hyacinths, crocus, iris, crown imperials, auriculas, wallflowers and anemones in spring; lilies, stocks, asters, mallows, jasmin and roses in summer – the musky scents of June and July. Rows of chestnuts and walnuts enclosed the garden and the palace was ensconced between little groves of larch, firs and robinias – labelled 'larch heath' on J. D. Schleuen's engraving of c. 1760–70.

While the broderie was clearly French in inspiration, the whole composition defies easy categorization. It was not, however, unique. A similar terraced garden once flourished at the Cistercian monastery of Kamp on the lower Rhine. It was built around 1740. Today, that site exists only as a remnant, but Sanssouci survives with splendour after a restoration in the 1980s. The parterre and quatrefoil basin have not survived unaltered, but the restored terraces of stone and glass, vine and stone-fruit radiate the joys of Frederick the Great's passion for pomology.

Engraving by J. D. Schleuen of the vineyard garden of Sanssouci, *c.* 1760–70. A modern view is shown on p.100.

Veitshöchheim

Veitshöchheim, near the vine-clad hills of Würzburg, is regarded as the supreme   102–105
surviving Rococo garden. To a large extent, this reputation stems from the
sculpture of Ferdinand Tietz (1765–68), whose humorous and playful representations of children, putti and dancers seem to capture the essence of Rococo taste.
On a warm summer evening, enchanted by Tietz's Chinese pavilion with its
garnish of pineapples, the visitor is transported far away from suburban streets
that have encroached on the fringes of the garden. What we see today, however,
is only partially the creation of the Prince-Bishops of Würzburg. Much of the
sculpture has been copied or altered, and the colouring has been lost; little of the
Rococo planting remains intact. For all this, the visitor cannot fail to be
captivated by the beguiling charms of Veitshöchheim.

A plan of c. 1780 shows the garden of the summer residence as completed
under Fürstbischof Adam Friedrich von Seinsheim between 1763 and 1776; he
had developed an earlier layout begun in 1702/3. While the garden around the
residence with its elaborate parterres formed one unit, the main garden, centred
around a large water basin, formed the other. This may have resulted from
combining the functions of a pleasure garden with those of the former hunting
lodge.

The parterres on the plan are largely in broderie, coloured up with reds,
yellows and greys. The largest *parterres de compartiment* recall the work of
Dézallier d'Argenville. With topiary figures on the axis, the garden has an
altogether old-fashioned look for 1780. Today the corner pavilions survive but
the broderie is modernized and the copper beeches and magnolias belong to a
later aesthetic.

The former pheasantry to the south was already divided into three parallel
strips of bosquet, when it was decided in 1753 to embellish the quatrefoil-like

Plan of Veitshöchheim by Johann Anton Oth *c.* 1780.
Views of the restored garden of today appear on pp.
102–105. Pegasus rears up in the middle of the pool
bottom right.

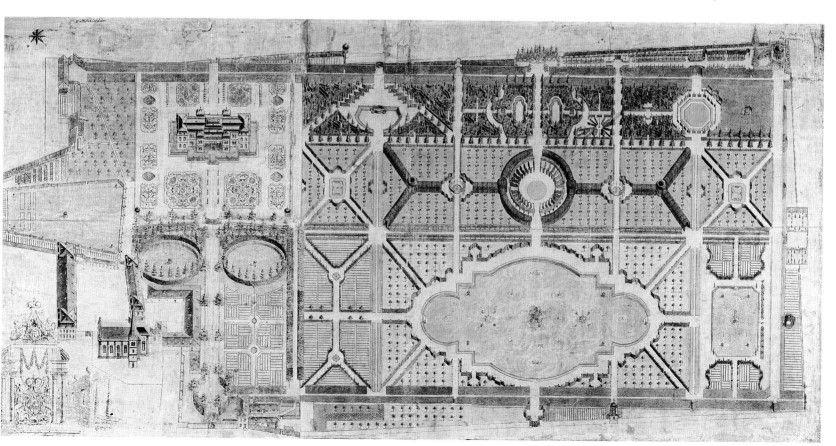

basin with sculpture. The original idea of Hercules binding Cerberus, the hound of hell, was abandoned a decade later in favour of a tried and trusted theme, Mount Parnassus surmounted by Pegasus. Ferdinand Tietz provided an accompanying group of Olympian gods and allegories of the arts and seasons to fill the niches of the surrounding hedge. Although the Parnassus survives intact it has lost its dramatic colouring (it was originally burnished in gold). The weeping willows planted c. 1825 give the whole setting a romantic tinge. The planting of the bosquet quarters is entirely altered. Behind the scalloped hedgework, this largest section on the west side of the garden was originally laid out with fruit trees and vegetable beds.

The middle section beyond a lime allée also contained bosquet. On the dominant axis a circular space was created with a trellised *berceau* known as the 'rondel'. This led symmetrically on both sides into hedged enclosures and to pavilions. In the rondel Tietz placed further magical figures: allegories of the four continents, dancers and musicians, vases with animal groups, trophies with musical instruments and hunting weapons. They celebrated the music, the dance and the hunt as essential ingredients of the court life. Though the sculpture retains a vitality, even as copies, the planting has lost its delicacy. The rondel, which once contained radial hedges forming twenty-eight theatrical boxes for figures, is now dominated by four mighty planes. The *berceau* has been replaced by hornbeam hedges. These create an infinity of spaces beyond trelliswork pavilions – like the reflections of opposing mirrors. But this is the taste of a much later generation.

Beyond a fir allée, the narrowest section near to the eastern border of the garden was more densely wooded. It was divided into three parts, from north to south: a hedged theatre with figures from the *commedia dell'arte*; a central area

Ferdinand Tietz's Orpheus surrounded by wild boar, wild ox, stag and eagle.

One of the animal groups by Ferdinand Tietz representing the *Fables* of La Fontaine.

One of the pavilions at Veitshöcheim enclosed by hornbeam hedges.

with the Chinese pavilions for outdoor eating; and a hedged room with figures depicting La Fontaine's *Fables* – somewhat reminiscent of the animals in the Versailles labyrinth. A thin strip of land on the extreme eastern fringe was turned to advantage with a grotto, belvedere and cascade to complete an extraordinary ensemble of garden inventions in such small quarters. While the original planting with its dark firs was in decline by 1815, the comedy figures having been removed in 1791, the fable animals and Chinese pavilions remain to amuse the visitor. It is sad only that the sense of colour is missing: the comedians painted like enamel, and the pavilions brushed with gold for pineapples, red and green for palms and blue for the sky of the ceiling.

That the appeal of the formal persisted into the Picturesque era is attested by King Max I Joseph's order of 1823 that 'the symmetrical forms of this royal garden' be preserved. From 1776 the garden had been open to the public, but this led to complaints about losses and damage to the garden's furnishings. Despite these and other depredations, despite the removal of figures to the museum in Würzburg in 1927, and despite bomb damage in spring 1945, Veitshöchheim lives on.

The iconography of Fürstbischof Seinsheim's garden recalls familiar themes of the past: the Muses gathered around Apollo on the Parnassus and the return of the Golden Age, in this case after the end of the Seven Years' War in 1763. The flow of meaning moves from the realm of nature in the woodland zone through court festivities to the highest aspirations of the arts – symbolized by Parnassus – in the area of open water. At Schwetzingen near Heidelberg the Golden Age is a central theme of Carl Theodor's summer residence garden, built from 1748–53 onwards. Here original planting and colour have returned through a restoration programme of the 1970s/80s.

Schwetzingen

106–109 From the hills of Heidelberg, where the romantic remains of the Hortus Palatinus are enveloped in chestnut woods, today's summer visitor can travel across the steamy Rhine plain to Schwetzingen, passing fields of corn and tobacco. For such a splendid garden, Schwetzingen possesses a rather tiny palace in a charming pink; even the central passageway is quaintly misaligned on the garden façade, for palace and garden were not conceived at one and the same time.

Between 1748 and 1755 the Kurfürst Carl Theodor had grand curving wings built to either side of the older palace, which had been remodelled between 1699 and 1715. Orangery, festive rooms and theatre were housed within, where Mozart played in July of 1763. The additions provided a motivation for a new parterre. Johann Ludwig Petri's plan of 1753 shows how curving *berceaux* were designed to mirror the wings and complete a circle around the parterre; the reconciliation of central axis with this circle proved an unprecedented challenge. Lime trees were delivered from Haarlem in 1753, basins were laid out in 1754, but the whole was not completed until the mid-1760s.

The four central parterres around the circular Arion-basin were of broderie, but the more dominant four along the main axis were essentially of grass. While these *parterres à l'angloise* had been gaining in popularity since the beginning of the century, Petri added broderie flourishes and flower borders to conform to Rococo taste. Jacques-François Blondel had illustrated a similar scheme in 1738 as a *parterre de broderie melé de gazon entouré de platebandes de fleurs*. At Schwetzingen it was more a case of '*gazon melé de broderies*'.

Petri's plan shows the colouring of the materials between the boxwork: yellow, red and black set on a white base. The idea of filling the interiors of broderie with bright contrasting colours corresponded to Régence and especially Rococo practice. It was the latest style of Louis Liger and Blondel. In contrast, Dézallier d'Argenville, looking back to the practice of Le Nôtre, had written that, while white sand served as a general background with yellow sand sometimes as a base for broderie, only black was suitable for the interiors of boxwork. Such was the scheme at Schleissheim, and at Brühl black highlighting on a white base can be seen today. According to Dézallier d'Argenville, red was used to outline grass strips and grass shells or palmettes when these occurred, but this is now absent at Brühl. Indeed, there was never one universal practice even in the age of Le Nôtre; at Het Loo the Dutch followed their own way with inorganic as well as living materials.

Today, the parterres of Schwetzingen have been restored in every detail: from these earth colours to the flowering *plate-bandes* and from the lime allées to the surrounding *berceaux*. In spring tulips, wallflowers, honesty, forget-me-nots and crown imperials create a carpet of pink, yellow, white, orange, mauve and blue; in summer the palette is composed of the blues of love-in-a-mist and corn-flowers, the yellows and oranges of African and French marigolds, the reds of poppies and the magenta of marvel of Peru.

The flower borders follow the French fashion of density in contrast to the sparse planting of the Dutch; bulbs were placed around 4 to 5 inches apart. The beds rise a little in the centre like the back of donkey or carp, as the French liked to express it; this enhanced the sense of modelling. Far from being flat, the flowers were meant to create a sense of relief against the broderie. At the time of Le Nôtre even the tallest hollyhocks and sunflowers had sometimes been used along the spine of the bed between shrubs and clipped evergreens. But by the eighteenth century the medium-sized flowers were gaining favour as compli-cated topiary went out of fashion. At Nymphenburg in the 1720s, for example, low flowers were in and shrubs were out. At Schwetzingen, a few yew cones

Plan of Schwetzingen by Johann Ludwig Petri, 1753.

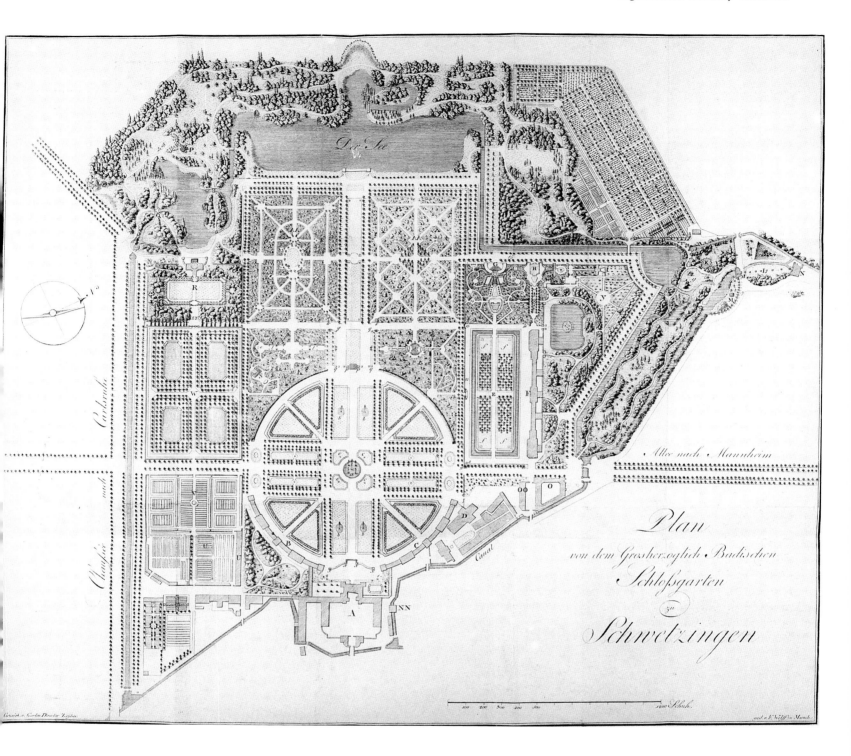

Plan of Schwetzingen from *Nouveau Guide dans le jardin de Schwetzingen*, 1830. (The orientation is the opposite of the Petri plan – north on the right instead of the left). This plan illustrates the addition after 1777 of Sckell's landscape garden to the earlier formal layout; the formal basin (*See*) was only given its irregular shape as late as 1823/4. The natural theatre, Temple of Apollo and bathhouse lie to the immediate right of the bosquet (G and H). Views of these features as they are now can be seen on pp. 106–109.

punctuate the borders but the height of the flowers is kept in the middling range.

Originally these borders would have been filled with three different floral plantings – in spring, summer and autumn. Today this has been reduced to a twice-yearly régime. The practice of rapid successions – every fortnight at the Grand Trianon – could only be sustained by 'plunging' potted plants, an unusual extravagance by the mid-eighteenth century. The restoration, unlike that at Het Loo, is not authentic in every horticultural detail. Many of the flowers – *Cosmos* and *Eschscholtzia*, for example – belong to a later period, yet the impression of profusion and colour is close to the intended effect – like the fusing hues of enamel, wrote Dézallier d'Argenville.

129

After 1761 the garden was enlarged by Nicolas Pigage. As the superintendent garden architect he had worked with the court gardener Petri on the layout of the parterres and *berceaux*. To the west, the central axis was extended between bosquets to a rectangular canal on a cross axis; the vista continued out into the landscape. At this stage, Carl Theodor appears to have been considering a new palace, but it never came to fruition. To the north, an orangery garden, a *volière* and natural theatre followed.

Now meticulously restored, this intimate area is one of supreme enchantment. From a wooden bridge over the canal that surrounds the orangery garden, the visitor enters a space enclosed by arcaded hedgework. Immediately in view is the Temple of Apollo (1761–76), built on a grotto, from which a miniature cascade flows out. Apollo, as symbol of the Muses, strums his lyre. Sphinxes flank the steps into a charming little amphitheatre formed of steep grass slopes and gravel walks; this was once used for outdoor performances. Taking the path to the right, the visitor comes upon the Dutch teahouse with its Delft tiles, and beyond that, the elegant bathhouse with its illusionary perspective now known as the 'end of the world' (c. 1770s).

Looking out from the bathhouse after a cold dip, Carl Theodor's guests must have enjoyed the play of light and shade in the trelliswork tunnel that lay outside, and the sound of fountains and bird-song. For this quaint *berceau* was centred on an aviary. Taking inspiration from the fable of the 'horned owl and the birds' as in the labyrinth at Versailles, an elliptical enclosure contained a pool in which the owl sat, mocked by spitting birds above. We may imagine the guests issuing forth into the fresh air, the men restored to their curled and coiffured wigs, the women in those wide pannier-hoop dresses that must have made negotiating every passageway and seat a matter of extreme delicacy.

Detail of the central *parterre de broderie* at Schwetzingen, illustrating the contrasts of coloured inorganic materials.

The Temple of Mercury (1784–7) seen across the informal lake.

View from the *berceaux* that surround the parterre.

Today, on a hot afternoon in July, the shadow patterns of the trelliswork combine with the fretwork of the pool's white fence and with the emblems of the pebble paving. Birds hop and chirp in their cages and light plays on the minerals and glass of the agate 'resting cabinets' between. At the end of the tunnel all is dark beneath vines except for a *trompe l'oeil* landscape illuminated only by the light of the sun.

Carl Theodor identified himself with Apollo the Sun God and protector of the Muses. But this was no longer the Apollo of Versailles, for here light was associated with the light of reason: the Enlightenment. From the 1770s a series of garden structures was conceived for the expanding garden; these alluded to the ideas of the Enlightenment. The Temple of Botany (1778) paid homage to science, a mosque (1778–87) to religious tolerance and the Temple of Mercury (1784–87) to the achievements of improved cultivation. These were woven into a contrasting theme: stags symbolizing Diana, the realm of the woods and hunting, and river gods personifying the Danube and Rhine, the rivers of Carl Theodor's land. Through his enlightened rule the Golden Age had returned at Schwetzingen.

The iconography was mirrored in the landscape itself. For just as the traditional symbols of the Baroque became symbols of Carl Theodor's Enlightenment, so too the formal layout gave way to an informal one. From 1777 Friedrich Ludwig Sckell, after a study tour of England, developed the French-style garden into a Picturesque landscape to north and west. The rectangular basin became an irregular lake, the far side of the Temple of Apollo became lawns and clumps.

Beeckesteyn

On the outskirts of Haarlem, where Carl Theodor's lime trees were first   120 nurtured, lies the charming country seat of Beeckesteyn. Today's visitor has a first glimpse of the little white palace between brick pavilions that look out over the surrounding fields. On an afternoon in early June, cuckoos repeat the song of countless springs in neighbouring woods. Although restored in the 1950s to a mere outline of its former glory, the garden at Beeckesteyn still tells the story of a mixed marriage: the Baroque wooed by the Picturesque.

A plan by Johann Georg Michael of 1772 shows the layout as altered for Jacob Boreel, envoy extraordinary to the English court from 1761 to 1762. The older, largely geometric garden close to the house was remarkable more for its variety than for its sophistication. It was dominated by a quatrefoil basin on the junction of the central axis and cross axis; these were lime allées. To either side were miscellaneous features. Flanking the house lay glasshouses, a cherry orchard and vegetable plots; between the house and basin were orchards, a pinwheel flower garden, a *potager*, a circular menagerie, and a grove of oaks with meandering paths; while beyond the basin lay further groves including the *bosquet à fleurs*, no doubt an early imitation of the shrubberies that were so fashionable in England from the 1750s.

The plan indicates that the landscape garden beyond the geometric garden, which had been altered by Michael after a study tour of English gardens in the early 1760s, was still contained within a rectilinear boundary. Moreover, with a colonnade sited on the far boundary (modelled on the Corinthian Arch at Stowe), the termination of the central axis remained formal, despite the irregular terrain that lay between. While sunny wheat fields formed the intervening landscape, a hermitage and stream decorated the shady woodland zone to one side. In these aspects, both of style and function, Beeckesteyn recalls the work of Stephen Switzer and Batty Langley in England during the first quarter of the eighteenth

131

Right: plan of Beeckesteyn by Johann Georg Michael, 1772, and (above) views of the pavilion and house, and the crinkle-crankle wall of the 'restored' garden today.

century – a half century later. Yet the architectural allusion to Stowe reflects Michael's aspiration to emulate new, progressive tendencies in English garden design.

The 'restoration' of the 1950s was unable to compensate for the substantial deterioration of the original structure. The basin, allées and meadows provide a simplified setting for the elegant house, but the colonnade and hermitage are gone, the animation of the menagerie vanished, and the fecundity of orchards and *potager* lost. The flower gardens to either side of the house are modern, despite the charming crinkle-crankle walls that line them. For all this, Beeckesteyn is a rare survival like the pastoral music of the contemporary Count Wassenaar. With Michael's plan in hand, the visitor may roam in imagination over groves, orchards and fields once both straight and serpentine.

The William Paca Garden, Annapolis

When Beeckesteyn was being laid out, people, plants and plans travelled three thousand miles back and forth across the Atlantic. There was naturally some cross-fertilization of ideas. William Paca, later signatory to the Declaration of Independence and Governor of Maryland, was one of those who made the crossing in 1760/61; his miniature English garden suggests he was up with the latest fashions in England. William Paca had acquired the land on Prince George Street, Annapolis, in 1763. He was then a young lawyer, having received his education at the College of Philadelphia and at the Inner Temple in London between 1756 and 1761. He may have helped design the house and garden himself. Since, however, no original plan and few contemporary accounts have survived, and since parts of the site had subsequently been covered over by a hotel, the layout had to be reconstructed from archaeological evidence. A painting of William Paca by Charles Willson Peale of c. 1772 was invaluable in the process. It shows Paca against the backdrop of pavilion and bridge.

The upper section of the garden proved to be geometric, while the lower section was informal – a miniature version of the landscape gardens Paca would have seen in England in 1760. In the upper area, excavation located the central walk and the levels of the descending terraces but the pattern of flower beds had been destroyed by the hotel's foundations. In the lower area, the outline of a pond and canal and the foundations for bridges and a pavilion survived undisturbed under nine feet of soil. It was then that the correspondence between painting and site became critical to the restoration. The existence of walls with unusual vertical slits, for example, as depicted by Peale, was confirmed by the excavation of foundations.

Today the visitor to Annapolis sees a garden brought back to life. Looking down on the whole composition from the upper windows of the brick residence, we see the quaint coupling of the formal and informal; four geometric *parterre* compartments on the two upper terraces give way to the serpentine lines of the lower garden. The layout and planting are inevitably an imaginative re-interpretation rather than a replica of the past. With remarkable horticultural precision and diversity, the planting presents an idealized portrait of the original. Yet all is based carefully on lists of eighteenth-century flowers, shrubs and trees; the patterns of the parterres on models of the period in England and Tidewater America. The skilful use of larger trees in the upper garden helps to unify what might otherwise seem a strangely unharmonious composition: the house is not aligned on the central axis and the transition from straight to flowing lines is abrupt. That harmony, however, is also derived from the underlying proportions of the design – the geometry of a rectangle made up of two 3–4–5 triangles that defines the informal wilderness garden as much as the formal terraces above.

118

One of the replanted geometric compartments on the upper terraces of the William Paca Garden, Annapolis. This one is known as the Boxwood Parterre; the others are the Holly Parterre, the Flower Parterre and the Rose Parterre. See also p.118.

Mount Vernon

119 If few visitors left accounts of William Paca's garden, the same cannot be said for the gardens of Mount Vernon. Towards the end of his life George Washington received a visit from Benjamin Latrobe at his home on the Potomac since 1759. Latrobe was one of scores of visitors whose arrival ensured that the Washingtons almost never dined alone. His account of the gardens, like those of his contemporaries, gives Mount Vernon the distinction today of being the best described estate in eighteenth-century Virginia. Latrobe noted the following in his journal of 1796: 'The ground on the West front of the house is laid out in a level lawn bounded on each side with a wide but extremely formal serpentine walk, shaded by weeping Willows, a tree which in this country grows very well upon high dry land. On one side of this lawn is a plain Kitchen garden, on the other a neat flower garden laid out in squares, and boxed with great precission'. To this description he added a pejorative comment on the flower garden: 'For the first time again since I left Germany, I saw here a parterre, chipped [*sic*] and trimmed with infinite care into the form of a richly flourished Fleur-de-Lis: The expiring groans I hope of our Grandfather's pedantry'.

A plan of the grounds at Mount Vernon drawn by Samuel Vaughan in 1787 illustrates the symmetry and regularity that Latrobe found too formal and too precise. In contrast, the east side consisted in a simple lawn. It fell naturalistically to the Potomac, affording a vast panorama over the wooded hills of Virginia. Latrobe sketched this view in 1796 and wrote: 'Towards the East Nature has lavished magnificence, nor has Art interfered but to exhibit her to advantage'.

Today's visitor to Mount Vernon is still able to enjoy the same expansive prospect – a miraculous thing so close to the nation's capital. Beneath the east portico there is the opportunity to rest on the quaint row-seats and enjoy the calm expanse of water, trees and sky. So too in June 1789 the Polish visitor Julian Niemcewicz sat with the Washingtons as the evening light brought the landscape into sharp relief.

The surprise of discovering a seeming wilderness as the visitor steps from the domestic front lawn through arcades clad with honeysuckle has been sustained over two hundred years. Yet the contrast between the west and the east sides of the house has become less dramatic. The trees along the serpentine walk have grown so large and spreading that the original discipline of the composition is obscured. In Washington's time, the symmetry, self-evident on Vaughan's plan, was strengthened on the ground by the house itself, by the perimeter shrubbery and by two mounds that flanked the entrance gate. Indeed, in writing to Vaughan, Washington praised the accuracy of the plan, but pointed to the omission of the mounds and the prospect between – 'an open and full view of distant woods'.

On 19 January 1785 Washington was 'Employed until dinner in laying out my Serpentine road & Shrubberies adjoining'. It was one of those sunny days that make winter in Virginia seem like a perpetual spring. During the ensuing months a great variety of native trees and shrubs were planted out along the serpentine paths: poplars, locusts, pine, maple, black gum, ash, elm, arbor vitae, hemlock, dogwoods, fringe tree, magnolia and sassafras. Pines helped to thicken the plantation and to screen the flower and kitchen gardens to either side. The Polish visitor Niemcewicz must have seen this shrubbery in its fourth season in June of 1789, when the trees and shrubs were still close to eye-level. He commented on the diversity of plants: 'A thousand other bushes, for the most part species of laurel and thorn, all covered with flowers of different colors, all planted in a manner to produce the most beautiful hues'. We may visualize this plantation,

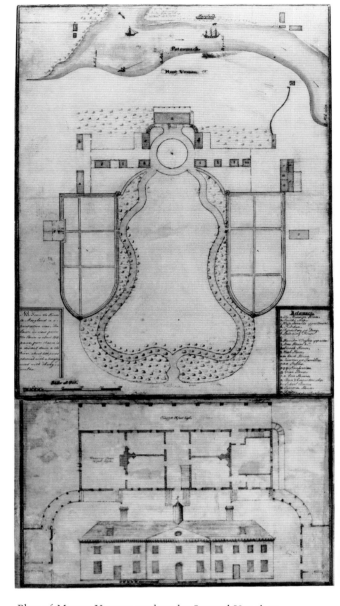

Plan of Mount Vernon gardens by Samuel Vaughan, 1787. To the east (top) the ground falls away to give views of the Potomac river.

View of the restored vegetable garden at Mount Vernon.

for all its variety, as disposed in an orderly manner that echoed the lines of the paths – slopes of regular gradation. For Washington's plan is derived from semi-formal styles characteristic of smaller English gardens of the 1760s, when a degree of symmetry and regularity in plan and planting still prevailed.

Today the contrast between this relaxed entrance lawn and the meticulous flower and vegetable gardens to either side has become exaggerated. Lofty trees overhang the central bowling green and from their rather shaggy crowns the white and red of the house peeps out in bright sunlight. By comparison, the Upper Garden devoted to flowers and the Lower Garden to vegetables – both restored to their original formality – seem the epitome of neatness and order.

To one side of the charming brick greenhouse of 1784 lies the box fleur-de-lys that troubled Latrobe in his account of the flower garden in 1796. Before it lie the beds of flowers that impressed the less cosmopolitan Reverend John E. Latta on his visit in 1799: 'The garden is very handsomely laid out in squares and flower knots and contains a great variety of trees, flowers and plants of foreign growth collected from almost every part of the world'. Today in June the flower garden is full of poppies, irises, peonies, Greek valerian and dame's violet. Orange trees stand in front of the greenhouse. The profusion of colours is offset by the box hedges, the gravel walks and the delightful undulating white picket fence that encloses the tiny garden. Furnished with the same white fencing and a charming gazebo, the vegetable garden to the south is an equal marvel of horticulture. Here in 1789 Niemcewicz recorded 'all the vegetables for the kitchen, *Corrents*, *Rasberys*, *Strawberys*, *Gusberys*, quantities of peaches and cherries'.

Wilhelmshöhe

110–111   On summer afternoons, when the cascade at Wilhelmshöhe is unleashed at 2.30 precisely, the huge landscape that dominates the city of Kassel comes to life. The expectant visitor looks up between the dark spires of spruce to the colossal copper Hercules that tops the Octagon. From there the cascade flows – at first a silver sliver, then a distant sheet, finally a torrent of water. Along the flowery meadows and jagged rocks and in the cascade itself townsfolk and tourists go bare-footed. Meanwhile, the fleet-footed visitor follows the water spectacle down the hill past the aqueduct to the giant fountain before the palace, where the jet of water rises and then falls.

Standing at the foot of the hill, the visitor is amazed that this gargantuan feature forms only one third of the original design. An engraving of 1705/6 records that first conception for the palace and garden; it was then known as Weissenstein. The Landgraf Karl von Hessen-Kassel, having seen the Villa Aldobrandini on a visit to Italy in 1699/1700, commissioned the Roman *stuccatore* Giovanni Francesco Guerniero as architect for Weissenstein. Despite the grandiose scheme for the axial cascade with tangential rides, it appears that the surrounding landscape of trees and scrub was to be left as a hunting park. It was the upper third that Karl had built. Work began on the imposing Octagon in

Perspective view of Wilhelmshöhe (then Weissenstein) by Alessandro Specchi after G. F. Guerniero, from *Delineatio montis*, 1706. Above: view of the cascade and Octagon today, seen also on p. 110.

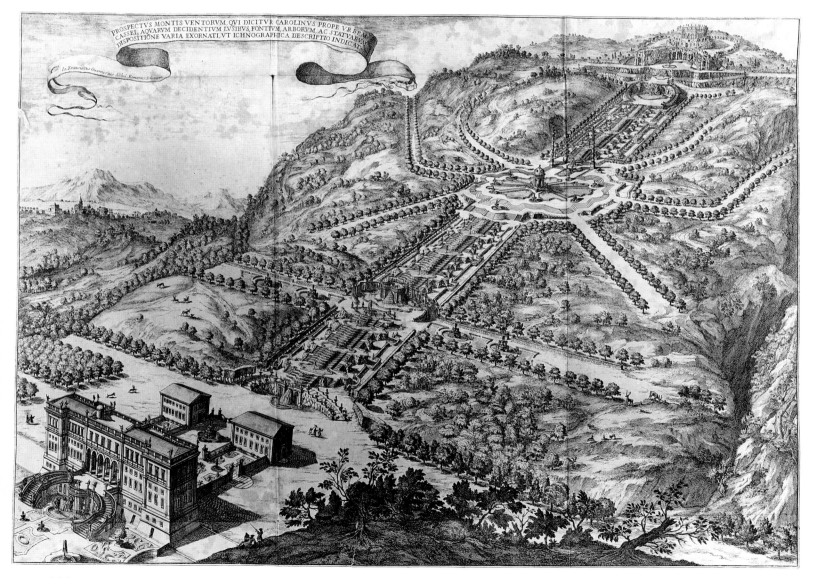

Painting of Wilhelmshöhe by J. E. Hummel, c. 1800 and (below) view of the ruined aqueduct at the top of a craggy ravine.

1701; it was inspired by the pentagonal Villa Farnese. After 1713 an obelisk spire was added to the eastern side overlooking the cascade. By 1717 the Hercules was ready – around thirty feet in height with room inside for some eight people. The architecture seems to rise out of the craggy substructure. As Guerniero wrote in his *Delineatio montis*, the Octagon was 'raised up on the hill not only by art but as it were by nature'.

A plan of c. 1780 shows how the unfinished Baroque layout had been transformed under Landgraf Friedrich II and his English wife Mary into a landscape of diverse Rococo scenes; the neoclassical temple and Turkish mosque were copied from William Chambers's Kew. A rosary of 1765 was noteworthy and the collection of trees, many exotics from North America, numbered over four hundred by 1785. But the major campaign of alteration into an English romantic landscape occurred under Landgraf Wilhelm IX (Elector Wilhelm I), after whom Weissenstein was renamed Wilhelmshöhe (from 1798). A remarkable series of illustrations by J. H. Müntz records that process in action between 1786 and 1796. The court architect was Heinrich Christoph Jussow. From 1786 he rebuilt the old palace in three parts of classical style. By 1791 Müntz shows the completed building, with the neo-Gothic Löwenburg as a contrast on the hillside behind. A painting by J. E. Hummel, c. 1800, captures this transformation in the wider setting of parkland.

The sense of union between the formal and informal is thus reflected in both the architecture and the landscape, a 'happy synthesis of three generations' as Hans-Christoph Dittscheid describes it. The balance between the formal and informal has continued to shift up to the present day following changes of taste. When K. Götze published his *Album für Teppichgärtnerei and Gruppenbepflanzung* in the late nineteenth century, he illustrated the view from the palace. On the so-called bowling green in the foreground was a large formal display of carpet bedding – geometric patterns composed of low plants. This affirmed the central axis up to the cascade and contrasted with the Picturesque landscape of lawns and temples between. Today, beyond the bedding, plain grass stretches to the lake where weeping beech and classical temple recall the beauties of Stourhead. To the right the eye is led up a craggy ravine to the aqueduct, while directly ahead the trees seem to part before the imposing cascade and Octagon above.

Caserta

114–117 Ornate parterres never formed a part of Guerniero's original design. Unlike Brühl or Schwetzingen, Wilhelmshöhe was modelled on Italian rather than French layouts. And although flower gardens appear in the plan of c. 1780, they were to the side of the palace; a grass bowling green lay on the central axis immediately to the west. In contrast, Luigi Vanvitelli's proposal for Carlo III's Palazzo Reale at Caserta near Naples was dominated by French-style parterres and bosquets as much as by the Italian-style cascade. The views in his *Dichiarazione dei Disegni del Real Palazzo di Caserta* of 1756, illustrating the layout as projected though not completed, suggest elaborate *parterres de broderie* flanked by *parterres à l'angloise*. If this hierarchy follows the traditions of the French Baroque, the overall disposition of both parterre and bosquet, as well as the stylistic character, recall the work of Dézallier d'Argenville.

Today's visitor on a day-trip from Naples finds the parterres vanished and the garden dominated by the celebrated canal and cascades; little remains of the work of Luigi Vanvitelli. For although anticipated in the *Dichiarazione*, the magnificent water garden was entirely the creation of Luigi's son, Carlo Vanvitelli, after the death of his father in 1773 (and after Carlo III's departure to Spain in 1759). It was constructed between 1777 and 1783, during 'Capability' Brown's twilight years in England and during Sckell's formative years in Germany. Yet, by 1786 the English style had reached Caserta too, when the English gardener John Graefer was summoned to Italy. That process of informalization was to continue into the 1820s but without challenging the integrity of the magnificent water axis.

On a sultry summer day the walk of several miles from the palace to the top of the Grand Cascade is arduous yet rewarding. At the Bridge of Hercules where the canal begins, the vista extends over still water between towering ilex groves to distant wooded hills. With every few hundred steps, a new feature unfolds: first the Dolphin Fountain, then the Aeolus Fountain, then the Ceres Fountain. At this point the canal has changed momentum, becoming a shallow cascade as the incline increases. The steepening falls continue up to the Fountain of Venus and Adonis, and beyond, to the figures of Diana and Actaeon. Behind them the Grand Cascade leads skywards, becoming a mighty torrent. Looking back down the axis to the shimmering palace, the visitor, until then oblivious of the outside world, is surprised at seeing how settlements have encroached on the very edges of the axis. What was once Carlo III's hunting park has become a thin wedge of open space in the midst of urban expansion.

The iconography of the fountains and cascades of Caserta forms part of a familiar tradition: the primary source is Ovid's *Metamorphoses* and a central theme is of progression from the wild to the cultivated. To either side, at the foot of the Grand Cascade, are groups of figures. They enact the story of Diana turning Actaeon into a stag – for espying her nakedness after a successful hunt in the vale called Gargaphie. Hungry hounds, their rib-cages protruding, are ready for the kill, but Actaeon has become their quarry. While Diana commands, her attendant nymphs recoil in consternation. Their shocked inaction mirrors the dogs' frenzied motions. These were Actaeon's own dogs – Blackfoot, Trail-chaser, Hurricane; they turn on him and his moans, neither human nor animal, are left to echo in the mountains.

The Fountain of Venus and Adonis offers a contrasting scene of lovers enveloped by nymphs and putti – before, rather than after, the hunt. Venus implores Adonis not to pursue fierce game like the boar that lurks with bristling coat to the side of the lovers. The fountain anticipates the story that unfolds in Book X of the *Metamorphoses*: the boar grazed by a spear kills Adonis; Venus

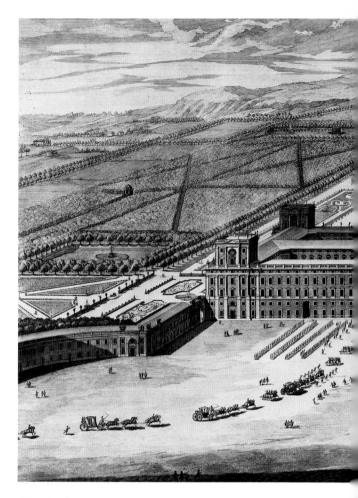

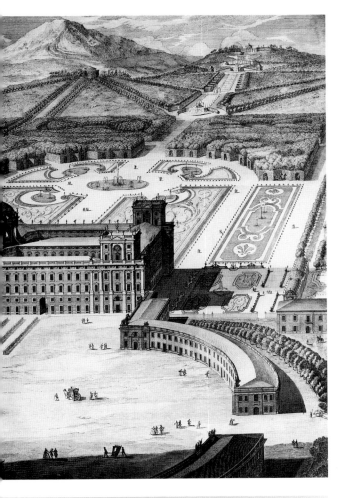

hears the groans and comes down from the sky; from her sprinkling of fragrant nectar on Adonis's blood, a flower springs up – the anemone – its petals red like the skin of a pomegranate.

The Fountain of Ceres depicts tritons, dolphins and river gods grouped around the figure of Ceres. According to Ovid, it was Ceres who provided wheat and law for the world. A medallion bearing the symbol of the three running legs, Trinacria or Sicily, is held by the central group. The theme of agriculture is thereby related to a mythical story set in Sicily: Ceres's daughter Proserpina is abducted by Pluto, personification of the underworld. Jupiter promises to restore Proserpina to her mother only on the understanding that she will spend six months with her husband in the underworld and six months on Earth – like the division of the year into winter and summer.

The Fountain of Aeolus consists in a rusticated and balustraded wall, pierced by alternating arched and square openings. Water cascades through a central parapet, while on rocks beneath, twenty-nine figures personify the winds. For the Fountain of Aeolus was meant to contain the figure of Juno in her chariot commanding the god of the winds to blow Aeneas towards Carthage.

But the money was running out and the fountain remained incomplete; only the winds were finished. In the original story, Aeneas was not in fact aided by winds but blown about by storms; only after Neptune intervened was he able to proceed to Carthage and thence to Campania and Rome, where he founded the Roman people. Thus as Ceres represented Sicily, Aeneas was meant to represent Campania – the Kingdom of the Two Sicilies over which the house of Bourbon ruled. According to George L. Hersey, this was to have been the 'sculptural climax of the river-road'; where mythology was transformed into history, and where the theme of progression from the wild to the civilized reached its conclusion – from hunting to agriculture to urban settlement.

The original planting – the parterres, bosquets and parkland – is almost entirely lost. For we must visualize this extraordinary 'river-road' not as self-contained corridor but as the cultivated part of a much wilder hunting park. Within that park an informal English garden was constructed by John Graefer to the east of the upper fountains. Joseph Banks had recommended Graefer through Sir William Hamilton, the British envoy to King Ferdinand's court. Later Graefer was to become gardener to the Brontë estate in Sicily, laying out the garden at Castello di Maniace for Lady Hamilton's lover, Horatio Nelson. He appears to have brought the camellia to Caserta from England and an original plant still survives to this day. By the early nineteenth century Caserta moved into a further stage of evolution. To the Baroque cascade and Picturesque park the architect De Lillo added a *flora* or formal flower garden on one side of the palace in 1838. The revival of formality, spreading from England after 1800, had reached the southern realms of Italy.

Engraving of projected layout for Caserta by Luigi Vanvitelli, plate XIII in *Dichiarazione . . .*, 1756. The specific influence of Dézallier d'Argenville is apparent in the outer parterres – modelled on his *parterre à l'angloise*, plate 6B in *La Théorie . . .* (1709). Below: view from above the Fountain of Aeolus back to the palace at Caserta, along the vista completed by Luigi's son Carlo.

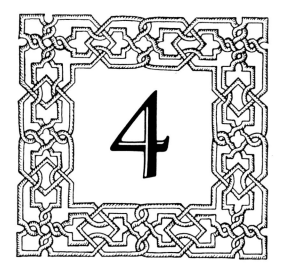

Revivals and Eclecticism

From Broderie and Bedding to Mixing and Massing

The terrace garden at Drummond Castle, undated painting by Jacob Thomson. The planting of the flower border suggests hollyhocks, pelargoniums and stocks between conical evergreens – in an arrangement not unlike the *plate-bandes* of the French Baroque. Today, a dazzling display of roses and miscellaneous topiary has replaced the original planting of this formal revival garden of the 1820s–30s.

THAT FORMAL ELEMENTS of garden design survived in one shape or another throughout the eighteenth century should not obscure the fact that by 1800 the landscape garden had become the dominant force in Europe. In North America, moreover, layouts such as William Hamilton's Woodlands (1780s) indicated a new impulse to informality across the Atlantic.

Yet for all this, there were some signs in England that formal gardens were making a return to centre stage. In 1795 Repton had recommended that a large terrace be created as a platform for Burley-on-the-Hill, Leicestershire: 'I therefore make a compromise between ancient and modern gardening, between art and nature, and by increasing the height, or rather the depth, from the upper terrace to the lower level of the ground, I make *that* the line of demarkation between the dressed ground and the park'. By 1803 Repton had designed a small garden in an old-English style for the lodge at Woburn, Bedfordshire, and in the 1810s elaborate formal layouts followed at Ashridge, Hertfordshire, and Beaudesert, Staffordshire.

When, around 1803, the landscape gardens of Mount Edgcumbe near Plymouth were furnished with 'French' and 'Italian' gardens alongside the informal shrubberies of the 'English' garden, this set a pattern of increasing importance for the nineteenth century – creating gardens according to national style. Lewis Kennedy's design for the 'Italian Garden' at Chiswick House of 1814 forms an early example of self-conscious revival. At Wilton, Wiltshire, in the 1820s, Lady Pembroke and Richard Westmacott remodelled the terrace into an Italian garden of cypresses, parterres and statuary.

Significantly, both sites lacked dramatic terracing and the parterre at Chiswick was rather French in flavour – a simplified version of Dézallier d'Argenville's *parterre de compartiment*. Sometimes, therefore, it was the presence of statues or cypresses that seems to have distinguished the image of the Italian garden from that of the French. More often than not, however, such national styles were based on rather vague differentiation; Repton had suggested that French and Dutch styles were merely variants of the Italian. Moreover, as Brent Elliott has pointed out, after Charles Barry's plans for Trentham, Staffordshire (from 1840), 'Italian' was used as 'an umbrella label for the revivalist styles'; George Kennedy's terrace at Bowood, Wiltshire, of 1851 was at first called 'French' and only later 'Italian'. Yet from the 1880s what had been 'Italian' suddenly became 'Dutch'. This latitude in interpreting national styles of the past was not confined to Britain. Peter Joseph Lenné's plan for the 'Nordischer und Sizilischer Garten' at Sanssouci of 1860 indicates considerable overlap in the style of flower beds, even though sombre northern colouring was meant to contrast with bright Mediterranean hues. Frederick Law Olmsted's first plan for the Italian garden at Biltmore (from 1892) could well have been called French, especially given the backdrop of the château-style architecture.

Yet, by the time Charles M'Intosh was writing in 1837–38 there was some attempt in Britain to codify these national attributes. 'In the true English style . . .', M'Intosh proposed, 'we have neither the Italian terrace, the French parterre, nor the Dutch clipt evergreens'. In the gardens created at Shrubland from 1848 to

1852, the terracing clearly evoked Italian models. Many of William Andrews Nesfield's designs were based on French parterres; that at Worsley Hall, for example, was modelled after Dézallier d'Argenville. In his plans for Kew, moreover, Nesfield implied his topiary was derived from French examples: 'the more you ring the changes on the *spiral*, the *round*, or the *pyramid like Versailles*, the better'.

Most designers, however, identified clipped evergreens with Holland. When William Barron created the 'Mon Plaisir' garden at Elvaston, Derbyshire, on the basis of a plan by Daniel Marot, the topiary of the original was heightened while the parterre was played down. When, later in the century, gardens in Holland like Twickel were 'restored' with elaborate birds and spirals this further deflected attention from the origins of topiary in Italy and France.

Meanwhile, indigenous traditions within British gardens were revitalized in ways unknown to Tudor or Stuart gardeners. In step with this revival of formal styles came the impulse to 'restore' old gardens that had somehow escaped landscape improvement. Levens Hall in Westmorland is perhaps the most striking example. Although the original layout of c. 1700 contained fanciful topiary, this was no longer maintained when visitors came a century later. It was the promotion of a new head gardener, Alexander Forbes, in 1810 that brought a renewal of old practices. To what extent this was replanting or merely reclipping cannot be established; the golden yews certainly date from his time and some of the figures – the crowned lion – suggest his insignia. Yet, most importantly, Levens Hall forms part of a wider fashion of revival, of which the replanting of Chastleton in Oxfordshire in 1828 and the later remodelling of Packwood, in

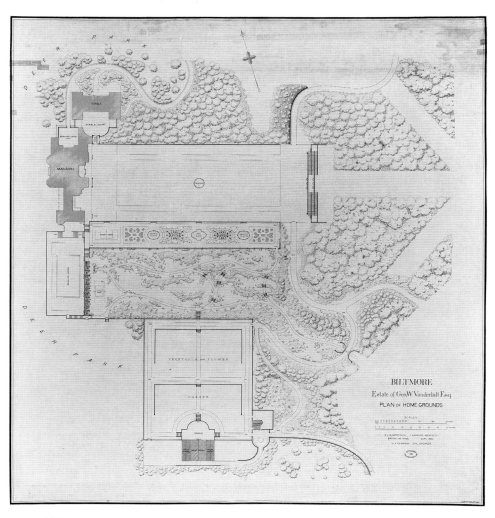

Plan for the Nordischer and Sizilianischer Garten, Sanssouci, by Peter Joseph Lenné, 1860. The Nordischer Garten (top) was planted with dark conifers, while the Sizilianischer Garten was lighter in atmosphere and dominated by a circular hornbeam arbour; to the side were fountains and geometric spaces to display palms. The two gardens were linked aesthetically by the use of bright carpet bedding.

Plan by F. L. Olmsted for the grounds of Biltmore, 1892. In this plan the long thin terrace now known as the 'Italian garden' was furnished with elaborate parterres between pools for fish and aquatic plants; in the plan of 1894 the parterres had been eliminated and the pools enlarged. The resulting effect, as it survives today, recalls the fishponds of Villa d'Este.

E. Adveno Brooke's view in *The Gardens of England*
(1858) of Elvaston Castle, Mon Plaisir – a garden
reconstructed from an original plan by Daniel Marot.

Warwickshire, are other notable examples. These have subsequently been taken
as genuine models of the old English garden of the seventeenth century.

The parterres of Audley End, Wrest Park and Cliveden offer diverse
examples of how the planting traditions of the Renaissance and Baroque were
interpreted in the nineteenth century. At Audley End, Essex, the 3rd Baron
Braybrooke's interest in restoring the Jacobean style of the original house spilled
over into the flower garden; around 1830 a formal parterre was designed to
enhance the period character of the house. In the 1830s Earl de Grey,
acknowledging the French style of the original layout at Wrest, created a parterre
in keeping with the French tone of the new house. Yet at Cliveden in the 1850s,
Charles Barry and John Fleming produced a design for a parterre of interlocking
wedge-shaped beds quite unlike French or Italian models, despite the Italianate
character of Barry's architecture. They used a novel planting palette of clipped
privet and spruce, rhododendrons and azaleas and spring bulbs.

The traditions of planting flowers in Renaissance and Baroque parterres were
radically transformed during the nineteenth century through new plant
introductions, through advances in horticultural technology and through the
theories developed for colour composition. Brent Elliott has written in this
context: 'Botanical exploration of South Africa and North America was yielding
increasing numbers of brightly coloured flowers which first, as tender plants,
made their way into the greenhouse; but in 1826 one of the first articles in
Loudon's *Gardener's Magazine* could describe an experiment at Phoenix Park,
Dublin, in planting such flowers out in beds during the summer'.

In the 1830s and 1840s, a further range of South African and South
American flowers of vibrant hues – *Pelargonium*, *Verbena*, *Calceolaria*, *Lobelia*,
Petunia, and *Salvia splendens* – were hybridized in vast numbers to become the
favoured 'bedding plants'. These tender flowers could be produced in quantities
in the improved glasshouses of the period; they were then 'bedded out' after the
last frosts of spring. With J. C. Loudon's patented wrought-iron glazing bar of
1816 and with Joseph Paxton's 'ridge-and-furrow' construction of the Great
Stove at Chatsworth in 1836–40, glass house technology advanced rapidly;
James Hartley's sheet glass process of 1847 allowed for further improvements.

In the first quarter of the nineteenth century the preferred method of
combining flowers had been according to the 'mixed' system inherited from the
plate-bandes of the seventeenth century and the flower borders of the eighteenth

Paxton's Great Stove or Conservatory at Chatsworth
of 1836–40, now demolished.

century. Such was the system used by Lewis Kennedy in the 'Italian Garden' at Chiswick House in 1814. But by 1830, gardeners like Philip Frost at Dropmore had demonstrated 'the advantage of placing beauty in masses'. The parterre at Audley End seems to have followed the lead around 1833. By the 1840s, 'massing' had replaced 'mixing' at Chiswick House. And at Shrubland in the 1850s, the fan-shaped Panel parterre consisted of calceolarias, pelargoniums and verbenas in blocks of carefully graduated colours.

Andrew Murray was to attribute this shift to experiments in simulating 'the vast flowering prairies of Mexico . . . It was the Nemophilas, the Coreopsides, the Eschscholtzias of these plains that first formed the glowing beds'. Yet the idea of combining flowers in large groups of contrasting colours owed much to theories advanced by Goethe in his *Farbenlehre* of 1810 (translated into English as *Theory of Colours* in 1840) and by Michel-Eugène Chevreul in his *De la loi du contraste simultané des couleurs* of 1839. W. P. Ayres, for example, supported Chevreul's theory of complementary colours when he wrote in 1841 that 'blue and orange-coloured flowers, yellows and violets, may be placed together, while red and rose-coloured flowers harmonise with their own green leaves'.

In Germany in the first half of the nineteenth century there occurred similar developments in 'massing' and in the arrangement of flowers according to colour theory. Klaus von Krosigk has discussed the implications for individual flower beds of the type used in Peter Joseph Lenné's Klein-Glienicke Park in Berlin (from 1816); these were circular beds in lawns, edged with acanthus-leaf clay tiles. Within these typically round or oval beds the flowers were arranged in two or three concentric bands of contrasting colours. Such contrasts were not necessarily of the complementary colours (i.e. yellow and violet or orange and blue); 'characteristic' colours might be used instead (i.e. colours separated by an intermediate one in the colour circle – for example, red, blue and yellow).

This does not mean that the one system based on Goethe and Chevreul remained unchallenged. Donald Beaton dismissed the use of complementary colours, and other theorists such as Owen Jones based the principles of composition around receding colours such as blue and advancing colours such as yellow; some designers looked for inspiration to the work of painters – from Turner to Rubens. The use of graduated colours appears to have been popular at Shrubland Park (from 1848), where Lady Middleton created ribbon beds like 'Berlin wool'.

Nor was the older system of 'mixing' vanquished by 'massing'; herbaceous plants never lost out entirely to the exotic 'bedding' flowers. By the 1850s the mixed herbaceous border had made a come-back, but it was not until several decades later that the herbaceous plants were released into the beds of the parterre. Around 1870 Lady Lothian dismissed Markham Nesfield's proposal for the parterre at Blickling, Norfolk, and replaced boxwork scrolls with beds of herbaceous flowers.

A variety of other effects could be achieved through formal planting. The traditions of the *parterre de broderie* were kept alive by the gardens of embroidery, of which W. A. Nesfield was the leading practitioner. Between box arabesques, coloured infill of spar ranged from yellow to red, white to blue. This increase in the spectrum was not, however, without difficulties; the blue spar used at Stoke Edith proved to be full of lead and the box died off as a result. Nesfield's increasing use of monograms by the 1850s indicated a shift away from the Baroque parterre to Tudor knots. In the 1860s following his impulse, the Marquis of Northampton created a parterre at Castle Ashby of heraldic devices defined not in box but in pelargoniums, lobelias and purple verbenas on a base of white verbenas. This proved extremely hard to maintain, and a solution was found elsewhere in the new style of carpet bedding.

The celebrated topiary of Levens Hall, although surviving in part from the original as laid out by Guillaume Beaumont after 1689, is as much a creation of the nineteenth century. From 1810 the garden was resurrected by the head gardener Alexander Forbes, who added some golden yews and some new figures. Levens forms part of a wider revival of historic styles, of which the replanting at Chastleton in 1828 and the later remodelling of Packwood are other notable examples. Today, the beds of pansies depart yet further from original planting effects.

Formal Revival in England

In the first few decades of the nineteenth century, gardeners were encouraged to think in terms of 'national styles', though these styles were not always based on clear differentiation.

A T **Mount Edgcumbe** (*above*), the gardens were called 'French' and 'Italian'. Louis Kennedy's parterre at **Chiswick** (*right*) was known as the 'Italian Garden', though it was derived from a French pattern-book. At first, the planting of the 'cut-work' beds was according to the traditional 'mixed' system – an assorted mixture of flowers. By the 1840s, this was superseded by the new 'massed' system – single-colour blocks of flowers. Today's pattern of massed planting is more modern. At **Audley End** (*below*) the recently restored parterre, originally from the 1830s, will provide an authentic version of 'massed' planting after a few seasons of growth.

Klein-Glienicke

The pleasure ground of Klein-Glienicke in Berlin was laid out by Peter Joseph Lenné from 1816 in the prevailing taste of English informality; there were meandering paths, undulating lawns and irregular clumps of trees and shrubs. Yet as the garden evolved over the following decades, a range of formal features were integrated into the original – an arbour with sphinxes, a *stibadium* or semicircular, raised seat, and the Fountain of the Lions. Above all, circular flower beds edged with acanthus-leaf clay tiles added a formal note to the planting, even though arranged casually in the midst of silky lawns.

KLEIN-GLIENICKE is now beautifully restored to its condition around 1840. A range of contrasting views expresses well the complex interplay of Picturesque and architectonic elements. A delightful tunnel-shaped arbour (*above*), flanked by sphinxes, provides a link between the Schloss and *stibadium*. The circular pool of the Fountain of the Lions (*above right*) forms an imposing feature in axial relationship to the Schloss. Picturesque fragments of columns rise out of the lawns, seen here against the Froschbrunnen (*right*). In the garden pavilions, antique sculpture is mounted on classical plinths (*opposite*).

Charlottenhof

From 1816 Lenné was responsible for reorganizing the extensive landscape that lay between Frederick the Great's vineyard garden at Sanssouci and the Neues Palais to the west. In 1826 an additional portion of land had been acquired to the south and here Lenné created from the 1830s a complex of gardens around the small palace of Charlottenhof.

THE garden directly attached to Charlottenhof was terminated by an *exedra* covered by a blue and white canopy or *velarium*; there were fountains and rills, and to the north views across meadows to the New Palace (*above*). A surviving pergola and fountain convey something of the original (*left*). Across an informal lake lay the Roman Baths complex. Today the flower garden and lakeside pavilion remain, but without original carpet bedding (*opposite*).

Wrest Park

When the 2nd Earl de Grey inherited Wrest in 1833
he decided to demolish the original house, replacing
it with a new French-style mansion some four
hundred yards to the north of the canal. In the
additional space he designed a matching 'French'
garden.

THE parterre was a much heavier version of
French originals. It consisted in broderie of tulip
and other forms, mixed with swirling bands of gravel
and lawn. With the loss of splendid mature trees and
a simplification in the broderie, the parterre now
awaits further restoration (*opposite*). Beyond the
parterre lay an area of lawn, decorated by a central
fountain and statues; it was quite unlike models of
the French Baroque. A view from the fountain to the
house expresses the individuality of the whole as it
survives today (*above*).

153

Shrubland Park

The terraced gardens of Shrubland were created between 1848 and 1852 by Charles Barry, but only parts survive today.

ONE feature retains its original splendour: the dramatic steps (*above*) overlooking the 'Panel Garden' with its fountain and loggia (*opposite*). Emulating Italian forerunners such as the Villa Garzoni at Collodi, the architectural composition, once starkly dominant, is now softened by clambering plants. The original planting within the fan-shaped parterre of box was calceolarias, geraniums and verbenas of bright but carefully graduated hues. Today *Santolina* and *Pelargonium* offer a simplified version of this bedding scheme. Elsewhere, vases of cascading plants (*right*) continue the traditions of horticultural excellence practised in the Victorian Shrubland.

154

Cliveden

After a fire in 1849, Cliveden was rebuilt by Charles Barry in an Italianate style. The layout of the parterre by Barry and Fleming demonstrated an imaginative new approach to planting. The large interlocking wedge-shaped beds were edged not in box but in clipped privet and spruce. The interiors were filled with azaleas and rhododendrons for the spring, hollyhocks and gladioli for the summer. In the outer borders, Fleming experimented with spring bulbs.

BY 1862 he had discovered that 'mixing' detracted from the 'grand effect' of the design; he converted the planting to 'massing'. Restored in 1976, the massed planting perpetuates these contrasting patterns but the palette is restrained (*above and left*). The Long Garden (*below*) was created by Lord Astor at the end of the nineteenth century. It contains fanciful topiary and figures from the Commedia dell'Arte; the borders were a later addition by Norah Lindsay.

Weldam

Two of the finest products of garden design from the turn of the century are to be found in Holland; yet they are both offspring of the collaborative work of a French designer, Edouard André. At Weldam his design of 1886 was implemented by H. A. C. Poortman, and at Twickel, Poortman developed one of André's proposals in the completed project of 1907.

Bounded by canals, the grounds around Weldam's moated house reflect the traditions of the Dutch seventeenth-century garden (*above*). Yet the plan André produced was full of allusions to the work of Dézallier d'Argenville. One parterre was copied from *La Théorie et la Pratique du Jardinage* of 1709; and his *parterre de broderie* incorporated at its centre Dézallier d'Argenville's version of a *parterre à l'angloise*. Of these originals, only the *parterre de broderie* survives; its massive boxwork and giant evergreen pyramids are characteristic of André's times. Along one side is a spectacular beech *berceau* (*below right*). From the platform at the centre of the maze, there is a view of the charming house and monumental scrolls of yew that replaced a peacock's tail motif *c.* 1900 (*opposite*).

158

Two illustrations of carpet bedding and foliage bedding at Wilhelmshöhe from K. Götze's *Album für Teppichgärtnerei und Gruppenbepflanzung, c.* 1900.

At Twickel, not far from Weldam, another version of the peacock's tail motif is preserved. It stands in the orangery garden around a fountain and is planted out in red and white begonias.

The innovator in carpet bedding in Britain was John Fleming of Cliveden. In 1868 he laid out a bed with the monogram of Harriet, Duchess of Sutherland. The HS pattern was composed of *Arabis*, *Echeveria* and *Sempervivum* on a background of sedum of different colours. In the *Gardeners' Chronicle* of that year this was termed 'carpet bedding'. Clemens Alexander Wimmer has written recently about the spread of carpet bedding across Europe in the 1860s. Amongst the leading practitioners, Edouard André should be mentioned, with publications illustrating his own and others' designs in the period from 1873 to 1885. In Germany, Schleissheim and Nymphenburg were now praised for their carpet bedding.

At the other end of the spectrum, large-leaved foliage plants came to be used as an alternative to flowers in formal beds – *Canna*, *Ricinus*, *Coleus*, *Caladium*, *Diffenbachia* and *Philodendron*, along with rhubarb, maize and kale. These two divergent styles – carpet bedding and foliage beds – are illustrated in a formal context at Wilhelmshöhe in K. Götze's *Album für Teppichgärtnerei und Gruppenbepflanzung*. The central axis down from Guerniero's mighty cascade was re-expressed through a symmetrical arrangement of carpet bedding in the midst of sweeping lawns. To one side, a round bed of large-leaved plants demonstrated the bolder effects of these *Blattpflanzen* in a formal setting. Although an entirely different palette of plants, this stepped planting recalled the planting plans of Hartwell a century before. The ultimate development in hierarchy, however, came with the floral pyramids – composed entirely of pelargoniums, for example – as recommended by Shirley Hibberd in the late 1850s.

Too little has been written about the social functions of the formal garden during the nineteenth century. The public parks of Europe and North America, in which the architectural and landscape traditions of the past were adapted to new social requirements, have stolen most of the attention. Many of the features of the Renaissance, Baroque or Rococo gardens had been assimilated into the public sphere, whether in the form of zoological gardens or areas for sport and recreation, music, dance and theatre. Moreover, contemporary illustrations of the Victorian formal garden – E. Adveno Brooke's views of Bowood, Elvaston Castle, Harewood House or Shrubland Park in the 1850s, for example – show the owners or visitors observing a stiff and uninformative decorum as they stroll, look and parade.

Yet, if accounts of Shrubland Park – 'a very perfect copy of Italian gardening' – are typical, some of the traditions of the past seem to have persisted despite depleted iconographical content and changed social structures. The code of public access, for example, survived the 'illiberal' tendencies Pückler-Muskau had observed in 1828, but opening was limited by Sir William Middleton to Fridays and to those writing ahead for permission. The 'museum of curiosities', as it was described in *The Florist*, was still in evidence, but transformed into a Swiss Cottage containing relics of 'Napoleon the first, the Duke of Wellington, Lord Nelson &c'. And the labyrinth, although without the sculptural programme of Versailles, was still associated distantly with the 'maze of love'. As Donald Beaton wrote in 1856: 'One of the walks leads down by two flights of steps to the Labyrinth, with an Edgington tent, a table, and seats in the centre. A gate allows the sedate, the grave, and the aged to pass straight on to the tent, while the gay, the giddy, and the more thoughtless must try their good luck and who will get first married among the mazes which lead to the turning point in the fortunes of the chase'.

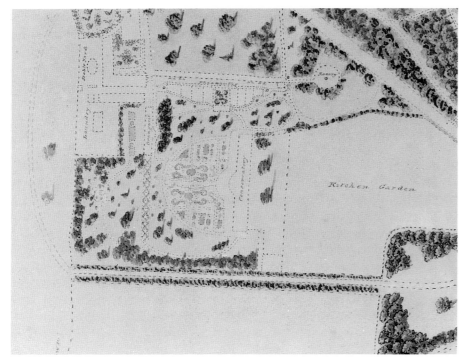

Left: detail from Lewis Kennedy's plan in his *Notitiae* of 1814 for Chiswick House, showing the Italian Garden and Rosary. Below: the plan of the Italian flower garden at Chiswick from Charles M'Intosh's *Book of the Garden*, 1853.

Chiswick House

146–147 When Thomas Jefferson visited Chiswick House on 2 April 1786 he wrote disapprovingly: '*Chiswick* – Belongs to Duke of Devonshire . . . the garden shows still too much of art. An obelisk of very ill effect; another in the middle of a pond useless'. This condemnation of 'too much of art' was a significant statement for a man with a 'fondness for regular forms'. It showed how much of the old structure had survived the Picturesque movement, for although it now seems possible that alterations under the 5th Duke had by then eliminated some of the geometry of the bosquet, as well as the two rectangular basins, strict formality still persisted in the exedra, amphitheatre and orangery garden.

This was, of course, the 'art' of Lord Burlington, which must have looked to Jefferson's eye rather old-fashioned in 1786; it had somehow resisted the improvements of Samuel Lapidge in the early 1780s. Charles M'Intosh recalled in 1853 that the gardens 'so early as 1770, were noted for the purity of the Italian style', and that despite some landscaping, Chiswick House remained 'probably the only residence in Britain which has retained that style in anything like its original purity'.

This continuity in formal traditions is demonstrated still further by the 6th Duke's decision to build a conservatory and 'Italian Garden' between 1812 and 1814 – a very early instance of formal revival. Samuel Ware was the architect of the conservatory: a magnificent structure over three hundred feet long that became home to a fine camellia collection in 1828. The Duke employed Lewis Kennedy to design a semi-circular garden embracing the full length of the glass-house. His proposal for the 'Italian Garden' was presented in January 1814 in the form of 'Notitiae' – a verbose text with splendid watercolours bound in green vellum and akin to Humphry Repton's 'Red Books'.

Kennedy had returned in 1813 from France where he had been laying out similar gardens at Navarre and Malmaison for the Empress Josephine. The design is accordingly as much French as Italian in character, the form being derived from the pattern of a *parterre de compartiment* published by Dézallier d'Argenville in

Parterre de Compartiment

Above: the *parterre de compartiment*, plate 2B in Dézallier d'Argenville's *La Théorie et la pratique du jardinage* (1709; this edition 1723).

Two views of the restored garden at Chiswick House: the rosary and a detail of planting in the 'Italian Garden'.

La Théorie et la pratique du jardinage (Plate 2B). It consisted in a large parterre on a level only slightly lower than the terrace of the conservatory. Divided by a grid of gravel paths, the centre of the semi-circular area was filled with flower beds of various shapes, some like the f-curves of a violin. This was therefore a *parterre de pièces coupées pour des fleurs* in the tradition extending back to the Renaissance and Baroque and exemplified in Dominique Girard's design for Schleissheim one hundred years earlier. The main beds were lined with box and set out on gravel. In contrast, the outer flower beds of mixed geometric forms were laid out on a base of grass intersected by narrow gravel paths.

The planting of Kennedy's flower beds seems to have followed the traditions of the so-called 'mixed' manner in which a mingling of colours was achieved through an assortment of herbaceous plants. This was the system inherited from the French Baroque, described in detail by Dézallier d'Argenville and perpetuated in the flower borders of the landscape garden. By the 1840s, however, the 'mixed' system had been replaced by the 'massed' system, in which, as Thomas Faulkner noted at Chiswick, bold groups of plants were 'arranged according to the colours of their flowers'. This was part of a wider tendency. Joseph Paxton wrote in 1838: 'In modern flower-gardens, the old practice of having a variety of plants in one large bed, and arranging them according to their height and colour, has been entirely superseded, and the system of grouping plants of one sort in small beds substituted for it'.

One influence on the change in taste came from advances in colour theory: Goethe's *Farbenlehre* of 1810 and Chevreul's important work of the 1830s. Contrasts of complementary colours replaced the assortment of hues in the 'mixed' system. A correspondent to the *Cottage Gardener* wrote in 1850: 'There is no doubt that arranging flowers according to their contrast is more pleasing to the eye than placing them according to their harmonies. Consequently, a blue flower should be placed next to an orange flower, a yellow near a violet'.

Advances in glasshouse technology and the introduction of new exotics, many from South America, also played a role. The practice of bedding out tender annuals relied on the production of vast quantities of plants in the improved greenhouses of the early Victorian period: the 13,000 'Verbena, Petuonia [*sic*], Calceolaria, Aenothera, Fuchsia, Salvias, Anagalis' that Faulkner recorded at Chiswick in 1845. We may thus imagine the 'Italian Garden' in mid-summer as full of bright pinks and yellows, blues and reds boldly displayed in separate beds; the softer hues of standard and China roses, arranged in three rows around the semicircle; and the light green of mop-headed robinias contrasting with the sombre greens of the enclosing shrubbery. After the summer display, the beds lay bare over the late autumn and early winter until a carpet of pansies brought the flower garden back to life in the late winter and spring.

Today's visitor to Chiswick may witness the same seasonal rituals and an equally flamboyant display of flowers within the pleasant hemisphere furnished with vases and urns. Even a dullish July afternoon cannot suppress the vivacious beds. Now, however, the pattern and planting owe more to the redesign of the 1880s and to modern horticultural practices than to the traditions of the early nineteenth century. The surrounding hedge dates from the 1950s. In due course, restoration will follow in keeping with the high standards of work on the Lord Burlington grounds; a notional date of 1840 has been chosen and trial beds already tested out elsewhere.

On Lewis Kennedy's plan of 1814, it is possible to see a number of other geometric elements: the orangery garden off to one side of the conservatory and the circular feature marked 'Rosary' to the north west. By then, what was Lord Burlington's orangery had been made redundant by the new conservatory. The 6th Duke had the roof removed and the resulting 'pergola' flanked by yew hedges

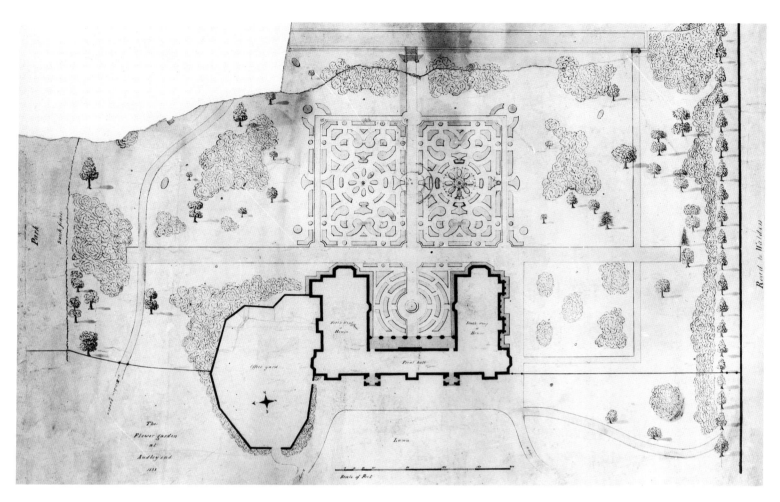

formed the visual link between the old and new gardens. The former orangery garden then became a pheasantry. From the golden and silver pheasants of 1824, the Duke's collection grew to the giraffe, elk, emus, kangaroos, Indian bull and Neapolitan pig seen on the Tsar's visit in 1844. Thus the traditions of the menagerie lived on beyond the Renaissance, Baroque and Rococo.

The rosary forms part of its own formal horticultural continuum in being based around a circle. Thomas Wright's plan of the early 1750s was circular and when Humphry Repton produced his design for Ashridge in 1813, he made his rose garden in the round. Lewis Kennedy's design of 1814 was in fact elliptical, but to the eye it looked a circle. As later recorded in a measured survey of 1895, it consisted of concentric beds, the outer ones in ivy with classical vases, the inner ones with roses. A column formed the central focal point. Recently restored to its condition around 1840 with the pinks, reds and whites of hybrid roses from the gallica, damask, centifolia, alba, moss, Portland and China groups, and with London's pride edging, this rosary will soon become a delight in the early summer months at Chiswick House.

Audley End

146 If today's visitor to the Italian Garden at Chiswick House needs imagination to conjure up a picture of the original, none is required to enjoy the geometric flower garden at Audley End near Saffron Walden; it is as pristine as in its first season over a hundred and fifty years ago. Although the planting will take a few summers to grow in, this recent restoration provides a unique opportunity to see an early Victorian design in its true colours. Through extensive archaeology and

Plan of the flower garden at Audley End by William Press, 1833. Lord Braybrooke may have conceived of a Jacobean-style parterre to match his refurbished house, but the design for the flower garden – probably by William Sawrey Gilpin – owes something to the pattern of the *parterre de pièces coupées pour des fleurs* in plate 6B of Dézallier d'Argenville's *La Théorie . . .*; the concentric circles of the courtyard parterre may be compared to the rosary at Chiswick House and the replanting of Chastleton in 1828.

View of the recently restored parterre at Audley End. The courtyard parterre of beds in concentric circles awaits restoration.

Detail of one of the circular flower beds at Klein-Glienicke Park. In early summer, standard shrubs lend a further note of formality to the geometry of the bed. In midsummer, bedding plants grow into a 'pincushion' of contrasting circles of red, yellow and blue.

careful horticultural research, the layout of 1825–33 has been brought back to life following gradual decline after the death in 1858 of its creator, the 3rd Baron Braybrooke.

The 3rd Baron, who inherited the estate in 1825, was a keen historian. On deciding to reinstate the Jacobean character of the original house, he no doubt conceived of a matching formal garden. A further impulse to revive the Jacobean parterre came from the demise of the Elysian Garden – an informal layout of flowers and shrubs that the landscape gardener Richard Woods had created in the 1780s. Damp and shady, it had become 'unfavourable to the culture of flowers', as Lord Braybrooke recalled in 1836.

A plan of 1833 by William Press records the layout as prepared but not as executed. The design was probably by William Sawrey Gilpin: a main parterre, symmetrical about the axis, and a smaller courtyard parterre with beds in concentric rings. The whole was placed in an informal pleasure ground of shrubbery and lawn. Lord Braybrooke may well have adapted this design to incorporate a central fountain; this amendment was discovered beneath the surface in recent archaeology. A planting plan of one half of the main parterre survives from c. 1833 but is only partially legible. It suggests the 'massed' rather than the 'mixed' system was being used: separate beds devoted to fuchsias, verbenas, eschscholtzias and roses.

The influential flower garden at Dropmore, which belonged to Lady Jane Braybrooke's uncle, Lord Grenville, may well have been a model. It was described by J. C. Loudon in 1828: 'The effect of considerable masses, entirely composed of Geranium, of Celsia, of Heliotropum, of Fuchsia, of Salvia coccinea . . . is striking from its novelty and rarity, and well-worthy of imitation'. At Audley End, the fuchsias and eschscholtzias will soon be dazzling in a glorious display that does justice to the magnificence of the Jacobean house. The return of the flower garden makes this site in the lovely surroundings of Saffron Walden amongst the most appealing in Britain. The pattern of the beds may be enjoyed from the upper storey or obliquely from the Temple of Concord hillside in the landscape grounds of 'Capability' Brown. Strolling down, the visitor may then enter the Elysian Garden with its Tea House Bridge by Robert Adam of 1782, and from thence cross a bridge into the extraordinary formal Rose Garden laid out with otter pool in 1868.

Klein-Glienicke

At Klein-Glienicke Park in Berlin, the informal pleasure ground created by Peter 148–149 Joseph Lenné from 1816 contains circular flower beds in the midst of undulating lawns and meandering paths. These have been restored to their original planting of the early nineteenth century, when first the Prussian chancellor Karl August Fürst von Hardenberg and then Prinz Carl von Preussen owned the estate. The notional date for the restoration is 1840. In spring the centre of one bed is filled with blue forget-me-nots surrounded by pink daisies; another with red primulas surrounded by white daisies. In the summer, red pelargoniums, yellow calceolarias and blue heliotropes form concentric circles. These follow the principles of colour composition that resulted from the work of Goethe and Chevreul.

Rather than using simple complementary colours – those that lie on the opposite sides of the colour circle, e.g. blue and orange – it was possible to combine two or three colours divided by an intermediate one in the colour circle: for example, red, yellow and blue. These were the 'characteristic' colours. White could always be used to set off any colour; it or other light colours were particularly suitable to stand on the outside against the green of the grass. Higher sorts of plant were placed towards the centre to create the effect of a mounded bouquet, rather in the traditions of the Baroque *plate-bande* and Picturesque flower bed or border. The edging to the bed, unlike the box of the *plate-bande* or the more informal pinks and heartsease of the Hartwell plans (1799), was often inorganic like the stone edging of the Renaissance flower beds: sometimes metal or wood, or sometimes clay like the acanthus-leaf edging at Klein-Glienicke.

Today's visitor will be affected by the beauty of the restoration. In addition to the pin-cushion flower beds, the sinuous gravel paths and silky lawns, carefully preserved architectural features lend a note of formality to the otherwise informal pleasure grounds: a pergola with sphinxes, the *stibadium* with caryatid. The style of architects Karl Friedrich Schinkel and Ludwig Persius is detectable in monuments and garden furnishings. From nearby, a boat leaves for the fabulous 'Peacock's Island'. Alternatively, the visitor may cross the Havel and what was once the boundary into East Germany to visit the equally remarkable Charlottenhof.

Ludwig Persius's *stibadium* of 1840 at Klein-Glienicke Park. The raised seat allowed views out over the Havel towards Potsdam.

Charlottenhof

150–151   In 1816, the same year that work began at Klein-Glienicke Park, Lenné produced several plans for reorganizing the landscape around the Rococo vineyard garden of Sanssouci. He had been commissioned to work at Potsdam for King Friedrich Wilhelm III. The largest plan – roughly three feet by six feet – shows the vineyard terraces preserved intact, along with the vista to the Neues Palais or New Palace over a mile away. These formal elements, however, had been incorporated into a radically new informal landscape garden reflecting the influence of the English Picturesque style.

When the early plans were abandoned, a new design emerged. The executed project as recorded in 1836 and 1839 reflected a much stronger emphasis on the underlying geometry. A hemispherical parterre – modelled on one Lenné had seen at Eaton Hall – was placed in front of the New Palace instead of lawns; the central allée replaced a straight but only loosely axial vista; the architectural layout around the vineyard and picture gallery was retained and enhanced; and an entirely new geometric composition was located on land acquired in 1826 as an extension of the landscape to the south. This was the complex known as Charlottenhof or Siam; it included a planted Hippodrome garden, a pheasantry, a circular rose garden and the so-called Roman Baths on the far side of an irregular lake.

The associations with Siam seem strange when linked to the dominant influences at Charlottenhof: the architecture and gardens of ancient Rome. H. Schönemann has explained how the vision of an ideal world was located not merely in the traditions of the Golden Age but also in the view of Siam and the Antipodes as the realm of the 'free'. He wrote of the success that Schinkel and Lenné demonstrated at Charlottenhof in 'representing in an enclosed area the vision of "a new and more perfect system of social order"'.

The Hippodrome garden, first planted in 1836, belongs within a formal tradition extending back (through planted amphitheatres of eighteenth-century England, e.g. Painshill Park) to the Boboli Gardens in Florence and to descriptions of gardens in the ancient world, especially those of Pliny. The planting was meant to evoke stepped seats: jasmine at the front, lilac in the second row, limes in the third, chestnuts in the fourth and pines in the fifth. Tall Lombardy poplars formed the outer walls. There were vine arbours, a *stibadium* and a water table – following the manner of Villa Lante and Pliny; there were benches for resting to the sound of bird-song and fountains; and in the central area a place set aside for dancing beneath the candelabra illuminations of the night.

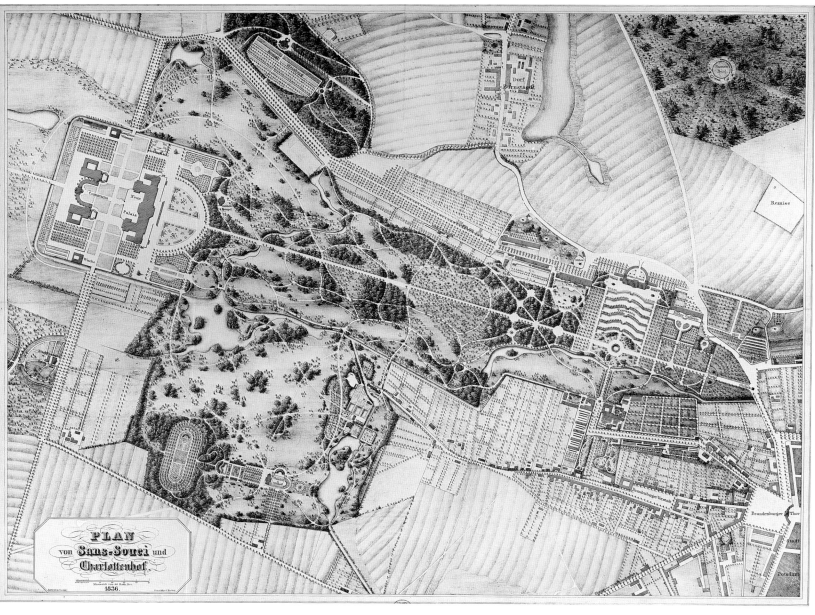

Peter Joseph Lenné's plan of 1828 for Sanssouci and Charlottenhof, drawn by G. Koeber in 1836. The vineyard garden is situated towards the top right, the parterre of the Neues Palais to the extreme left. The axis from the Hippodrome through Charlottenhof to the circular rose garden is apparent in the lower left portion of the plan; across the informal lake lies what was to become the Roman Baths complex. These features are seen today on pp. 150–151.

The Hippodrome formed the western end of the axis at Charlottenhof. Continuing eastwards the visitor of the 1830s would have emerged out of the woodland into open space, approaching the palace of Charlottenhof through a quincunx of chestnuts. The palace itself looked over a small garden to the east. This was terminated by an exedra and flanked on one side by a pergola; on the other side was a grass slope and pool, and beyond these extensive views across meadows to the New Palace. Fountains and rills enlivened the scene, a white and blue canopy or *velarium* provided shade over the exedra seat. A circular rose garden with pergola completed the eastern end of the axis where an informal lake offered views across to the Roman Baths.

The Roman Baths consisted in a complex of buildings, completed 1834–40. On the south side between the complex and a lake-side pavilion lay the flower garden with its fountain pool, carpet bedding and vine-clad pergola. To the north lay three pools for goldfish and marsh-turtles. To the west lay orchards, in which the trees were linked by vines and gourds; there were beds of corn, broccoli and artichokes and rows of mulberry trees and fig trees. Not all of this extraordinary planting has been preserved, but today's visitor may still enjoy the major part of this wonderful layout after extensive and careful restoration. Seen together, the formal and informal gardens of Potsdam and along the Havel form one of the finest extensive designed landscapes in the world.

Wrest Park

152–153 The grounds of Chatsworth in Derbyshire, Wrest Park in Bedfordshire and Cliveden in Buckinghamshire all suggest in their own way how features of earlier Baroque gardens were developed within new formal layouts of the early to mid nineteenth century. In the case of Chatsworth that process has continued to the present day under the Duke and Duchess of Devonshire.

Two sketch plans of the grounds at Wrest Park in 1828 and 1829 indicate how much of the geometry of the early eighteenth-century gardens survived the landscape improvements of 'Capability' Brown; his modifications of the 1750s to 1770s were largely confined to the serpentine water around the perimeter. When the 2nd Earl de Grey inherited the property in 1833, he had already acknowledged the gardens as 'the largest and most complete in their way in England, essentially in the French style of Louis XIV'.

Today we might question this stylistic label, since there had always been much that was distinctly English about Wrest. But the respect for the traditions of the past was significant and helped shape the Earl's plans. His attitude to the old house was less nostalgic; it was of 'no architectural value and bad construction'. In 1834, the year following demolition, work began on the new French-style house over four hundred yards to the north of the canal. In the resulting space, the Earl, who had been appointed the first president of the Institute of British Architects that year, created a matching 'French' garden. The parterre of broderie, grass and gravel designed around the forms of scroll and tulip was a heavier version of the French originals. It gave way to an area of lawn, intersected by paths and embellished with statues, quite unlike any models of the French Baroque. The Earl admitted in his *History of Wrest House* (1846) that the 'pattern of the French garden is certainly rather out of the common course, but at all events it is original and novel'. On the cross axis to the west he located an orangery. It was filled with Seville orange trees bought from the sale of the effects of King Louis Philippe of France.

Photographs taken for *Country Life* in 1904 express the beauty of this garden after seventy years of growth. By then, the massive trees provided a balance to the rather distended proportions of the garden between house and canal. Today, with the loss of the trees, the parterre is open to the sky and the clean lines of box, grass and gravel offer a pleasing but simplified version of the original. In time, under the present careful restoration, the glories of Earl de Grey's design will return.

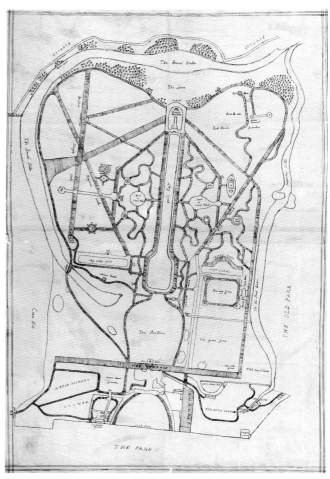

Sketch plan of Wrest Park in 1829, showing the survival of the early-eighteenth-century canal, pavilion, bowling green and bosquet within 'Capability' Brown's serpentine 'Broad Water'.

Bird's-eye view of the location for Earl de Grey's new house and 'French' garden immediately in front of it at Wrest Park, *c.* 1834.

Engraving of Cliveden from the south by Luke Sullivan, 1759, developed from a painting by an unknown artist. This view illustrates the simple geometry of Lord Orkney's 'quaker' parterre of 1723/4. The long terrace with its circular termination formed the platform for Barry and Fleming's elaborate parterre of the early 1850s.

Cliveden

156–157

The evolution of the garden at Cliveden in Buckinghamshire is as rich and complex as that at Chatsworth and Wrest. Here are some of the grandest and loveliest of grounds offering pleasant views of the hazy blue Thames valley below. Some two hundred years ago, Lord Orkney, after acquiring Cliveden in 1696, commissioned elaborate parterres from Le Nôtre's nephew and successor at Versailles, Claude Desgots. The designs of 1713 were, however, abandoned in 1723/4 in favour of what Orkney himself called a 'quaker' parterre: an enormous plain grass terrace bordered by gravel paths and rows of elm trees. The rectangle was terminated by a raised circle of lawn on which, it is said, Lord Orkney used to parade his horses – a kind of open-air manège. When Luke Sullivan produced his engraving of Cliveden in 1759, this simple formal arrangement was still in place to set off William Winde's magnificent architectural complex of the 1660s–70s, embellished with wings by Thomas Archer of 1706.

The structure of this grass parterre seems to have outlived the destruction of Winde's house by a fire in 1795, the rebuilding by William Burn and the subsequent fire of 1849; a proposal by Count d'Orsay in the 1830s to create formal parterre beds around a central fountain came to nothing. By this time, however, the simple manicured lawn had become a 'huge field of grass and wild flowers'. It was then that Charles Barry and John Fleming were asked to produce designs for a new parterre to match Barry's Italianate house of 1850–51.

The layout of large interlocking wedge-shaped beds was quite unlike anything in the traditions of the French or Italian Baroque. The overall form, though not the type of planting, owed more to indigenous traditions of the late seventeenth and early eighteenth centuries – features of gardens illustrated by Kip and Knyff such as the parterre or wilderness at Southwick Park in Hampshire. The planting design itself reflected new tendencies in Victorian gardening. The edging was no longer in box but in clipped privet and spruce. Eight inches high and nine broad, this edging enclosed a flower border nine feet wide. Within this border was a strip of lawn of equal width and the interior triangles were filled with azaleas and rhododendrons. Room was left between these for summer flowers: hollyhocks and the newly developed gladioli.

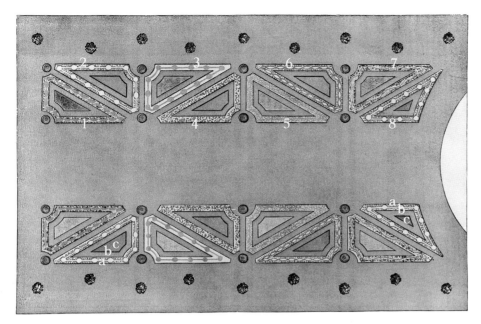

Plan of the spring planting at Cliveden, adapted from John Fleming's original colour plate for *The Journal of Horticulture and Cottage Gardener*, 29 July 1862. The planting of spring bulbs, which had been in 'mixtures' in 1862, was revised for 1863 on the basis of 'massing'. The following key elucidates the disposition of plants for 1863: **a** indicates the outer bed for spring flowers; **b** the strip of lawn and **c** the bed for rhododendrons, hollyhocks and gladioli.

No. 1. bed, blue Myosotis and La Candeur Tulip.
2. Anemone and yellow Jonquil.
3. Limnanthes Douglassii and Tournesol Tulip.
4. Silene pendula, pink, and Rex Rubrorum Tulip.
5. Silene pendula, white.
6. blue Myosotis, Queen Victoria Tulip.
7. mixed Anemone and Narcissus poeticus.
8. yellow Alyssum saxatile and yellow Rose Tulip.

Fleming's major contribution to planting design lay, however, with the reinstatement of spring bulbs. He contested that anemones, tulips and hyacinths used with the great range of pansies could produce as bright a palette as the summer bedding of tender exotics. He experimented in the borders around the parterre at Cliveden. In 1862 he found that 'mixing' detracted from the 'grand effect' of the design and relied thereafter on 'massing'. His plan of 1862/3 shows blue forget-me-nots, yellow jonquils and pink *Silene pendula* contrasting with a range of tulips.

We must visualize these in spring against the oranges and reds of azalea and rhododendron. To complete the dazzling display, the circles in the chamfered corners of the parterre were filled with bands of crocuses, snow-in-summer (*Cerastium tomentosum*), forget-me-nots, wallflowers and honesty. Hawthorns and lilacs enclosed the formal layout making a visit in April or May of the 1860s a spectacle of both colour and pattern. We may imagine the guests of the Duke and Duchess of Sutherland – Queen Victoria, Gladstone, Lord Acton or even Garibaldi – enjoying the displays from the terraces of the house. Later in 1896 William Waldorf Astor added the famous balustrade from the Villa Borghese in Rome.

Today's visitor to Cliveden finds the parterre as replanted by the National Trust in 1976. The structure has been maintained but the ebullient planting has been replaced by a simple but pleasing palette of grey *Santolina incana* and *Senecio* 'Sunshine'. These are referred to in the guide as 'the subtler colours of an Italian garden'. Yet the restricted hues and the massive forms of clipped box and yew belong within the traditions of nineteenth- to twentieth-century planting design – far from the *giardini dei semplici*. The bright colours of the Victorian parterre are as hard to find today as the brilliant beds of Renaissance Italy.

Shrubland Park

154–155 Brent Elliott writes of Shrubland Park in Suffolk as 'the High Victorian period's most important model of the complete architectural garden', adding that 'the series of well-defined descending stages between the architectural platform and the parkland became the ideal of graded transition between art and nature'. Informal areas lay alongside formal areas and the transition from the geometric to the wild was graduated.

View of the 'Panel Garden' at Shrubland Park from
E. Adveno Brooke's *The Gardens of England*, (1858).
It survives intact (compare colour plate on p.155)
though the planting has altered.

The terraced gardens were created by Charles Barry from 1848–52 for Sir
William and Lady Middleton. They were based on an earlier layout of c. 1830–32
by J. P. Gandy-Deering. Among the many formal gardens along the nearly mile-
long main terrace were the following: the fountain garden filled with roses and
half-hardy plants arranged in six colours; and the 'French' garden with laurel
wall, statues and boxwork lined in silver sand. This so-called 'green terrace'
formed a cross walk to the axis from the house. The central axial feature, which
emulated the splendour of the Villa Garzoni at Collodi, was composed of a series
of dramatic steps with ornamented and balustraded terrace platforms. The steps
led down to the 'panel garden' consisting in a slightly sunken parterre framed by a
loggia and overlooking the wooded countryside of Suffolk. It is this feature that
survives most completely in the Shrubland of today.

Visitors in the 1850s and 1860s recalled their vivid impressions of the
terraced steps and panel garden. The painting by E. Adveno Brooke of 1858 helps
us to visualize what they saw: the vases full of cascading nasturtiums and scarlet
pelargoniums, the cypress trees rising out of the box in unison with the vertical
thrust of the fountain below. In the *Gardeners' Chronicle* of 1867 we read the

following: 'Near the base of the steps a unique and pleasing effect is produced by a curious bed, formed of lines of Yew, about 18 inches high, and as much through, interwreathed in a singular manner, and enclosing scrolls of turf, silver-sand, and flowers. But the most striking feature consists of a large double-headed serpent, laying lazily across the back of each bed, formed of variegated Box, twisted over, among, in, and through the Yew'. A writer in the *Cottage Gardener* of 1857 added some further detail on the planting: 'These beds are filled with Geraniums on the shading system. The principle seems to be to begin with a white Geranium at the outside, as *Hendersonii*, called here *White Nosegay*; then a light pink or rose, and deepening the colour until scarlet was reached at the centre'.

To either side of the loggia the large panel parterres themselves were fan-shaped. They were edged with box. The centre bed was filled with yellow calceolarias and flanked by geraniums in hues graduating to bright rose. Scrolls to either side of the fan were filled with lilac and purple verbenas. These colour effects were championed at Shrubland; Donald Beaton, the head gardener until 1851, was a publicist of the bedding system. His successor, a Mr Davidson, planted geraniums in the thousands and Lady Middleton pioneered long ribbon beds of gently graduated hues like 'Berlin wool'. All this was anathema to William Robinson, who was brought in by James Saumarez in 1883 to reorganize the garden. He commented on how there had been 'strict orders that the walls were not to have a flower or a creeper of any kind upon them'. Yet he commended the stepped terracing in *The English Flower Garden*; it was all left intact and Robinson turned his attention to other parts of the grounds.

Thus today's visitor to Shrubland may still enjoy the breathtaking vistas from the top and bottom of the stairway. Only now the architectural fabric is softened by the effects of growth and by the clambering plants that deck the balustrades – what Robinson had striven for a hundred years before. The parterre of the panel garden remains essentially as designed, though the scrolls have vanished and the planting of *Santolina* and *Pelargonium* is much simplified.

Yet, through Brooke's art it is still easy to visualize the garden described by Donald Beaton in the 1850s. We may imagine the women in crinolines (those dresses whose lightweight steel-ribbed petticoats seemed to match the advances in greenhouse technology), carrying dainty parasols and accompanied by men in their dark coats and top hats. We may imagine the hundreds of visitors flocking to Shrubland on Fridays; the garden was open to all who wrote to Sir William for admission. We may imagine 'the gay, the giddy, and the more thoughtless' lost in the labyrinth, while 'the sedate, the grave, and the aged' waited for them in the tent at the centre (to which direct access was permitted). Or we may imagine Lady Middleton on a private day in her 'serviceable' cotton dress cleaning the dirty plates of the daguerreotypes she made to record the 'beauties and Italian character of the place'.

Weldam and Twickel

158–160 Two of the finest products of garden design in the last quarter of the nineteenth century are to be found in Holland; yet they are both offspring of the collaborative work of a French designer, Edouard André. Weldam and Twickel are tucked away in discreet locations in the eastern provinces close to the border of Germany. In pleasant pastoral landscapes, these small but exquisite gardens are worth the detour between the grand gardens of the north.

Florence Hopper has written that Weldam in Overijssel represents within the Dutch provinces the 'finest example of a late-19th-century reconstruction of a 17th-century layout'. The gardens were designed by the firm of Edouard André,

One of the plans for the layout at Weldam by Edouard André, 1886. The design incorporates several forms of parterre derived from Dézallier d'Argenville's *La Théorie . . .* (1709): To the lower right, the *parterre de compartiment* relates to plate 3B of *La Théorie . . .* (the same design was used at Nordkirchen; see p.210); in the centre of the *parterre de broderie* is the version of a *parterre à l'angloise* from plate 6B.

The beech *berceau* at Weldam.

The topiary of Twickel.

a landscape architect based in Paris. Created for the Count and Countess Bentinck, the design of 1886 was implemented by the Dutch manager of the site, H. A. C. Poortman. One of the original plans shows the rectangular site enclosed by canals in a manner typical of Dutch gardens of the seventeenth century. Yet the embellishments reflect an eclectic approach to historical restoration. The parterres, for example, were distinctly French and derived in part from A. J. Dézallier d'Argenville's *La Théorie et la pratique du jardinage*. On the other hand, the peacock's tail motif was characteristic of the late nineteenth century and occurs to this day in a similar form at the neighbouring site of Twickel.

Today's visitor to Weldam, approaching along a modest shady lane, will be struck by the feeling of a venerable site matching the delightful moated mansion of the seventeenth century. Yet this house too, for all its origins in the rebuilding of the 1640s, was romanticized in the late nineteenth century by the addition of twin Dutch-Renaissance towers; the architect was the Englishman W. Samuel Weatherly. The elaborate *parterres de compartiment* that originally flanked the approach have sadly been replaced by lawn and bright bedding plants. However, the rectangular *parterre de broderie* survives to one side of the house. With its massive boxwork it belongs to the tradition of historical revivals in the manner of Vaux-le-Vicomte. Giant pyramids of box, yew and *Chamaecyparis lawsoniana* punctuate the space and further enhance the sense of masses over lines. Along the full length of the parterre runs a spectacular beech *berceau*. It is some 450 feet long. This leads the visitor to the maze. It is composed of the American *Arbor-vitae* or *Thuya occidentalis*. The patient or 'giddy' visitor is rewarded at the centre with a view from a raised platform of the house set against some large scrolls of yew that replaced the peacock's tail in 1900. There are several vistas out beyond the garden along the main axes, and in the opposite direction, the *parterre de broderie* framed by the beech *berceau*.

Even more than Weldam, the nearby garden of Twickel seems to epitomize the traditional image of 'Dutch taste' – the moated house, the small rectilinear compartments and above all the fantastical topiary. Yet Twickel is the product of a late-nineteenth-century romantic vision of the past. As at Weldam, André was responsible for the initial design (1886) and Poortman for the implementation; in 1907 Poortman chose one of the three proposals of 1886 and changed it to his own design. The formal gardens are set within lush landscaped grounds planted up by the German landscape architect C. E. A. Petzold in 1885.

In front of the orangery is a small, slightly sunken parterre in the form of a peacock's tail – a motif that seems to suit the Art Nouveau sculpture bordering the surrounding shrubberies of purple rhododendron. After the late frosts of spring, exotic shrubs are set out in tubs overlooking the parterre: *Erythrina crista-galli* with waxen scarlet flowers, the sulphur yellow bottle-brush racemes of *Albizia lophantha* and the purple-red tubular blooms of *Cestrum elegans* amongst olives, oranges and giant agaves. From the circular fountain pool the feathers of the peacock's tail fan out in red and white begonias. The orangery garden is set off by an adjoining compartment of neat topiary and tubbed orange trees. The yew has been shaped after birds, spirals and crowns. Even on a day when raindrops fall gently into the moat, Twickel is a delightful place – serene and orderly in the midst of magnificent trees and lush meadows.

Taking a few further steps, the visitor comes into a flower garden designed by Baroness van Heeckeren van Wassenaar around 1928 in a cottage-garden style. Imperceptibly, the formal has given way to the informal. This sympathetic union of the two styles was to become a hallmark of gardens in the first few decades of the twentieth century.

The winter contours of Achille Duchêne's water parterre at
Blenheim, final result of the uneasy partnership between
Duchêne and the Duke of Marlborough.

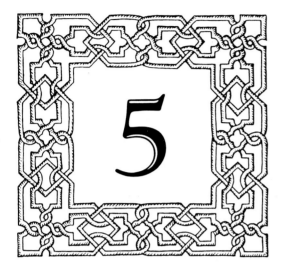

The Past in the Present

Knot and Parterre Reinvented

I T IS CLEAR that the idea of the formal as opposed to the informal meant something to garden theorists long before the twentieth century. However, with the publication of Reginald Blomfield's *The Formal Garden in England* in 1892 and H. Inigo Triggs's *Formal Gardens in England and Scotland* in 1902 the term 'formal' gained a new place in everyday English. At the same time, it acquired fresh ideological connotations. If today we have a sense of incompatibility between a garden of clipped box and yew and a garden of shrubberies and meadows, this is due in part to the fierce debate between rival theorists at the turn of the century.

There is some irony in this, since even as an exponent of the 'formal garden', Blomfield admitted: 'The Formal System of Gardening has suffered from a question-begging name . . . The formal treatment of gardens ought, perhaps, to be called the architectural treatment of gardens, for it consists in the extension of the principles of design which govern the house to the grounds which surround it'. With the success of his own propaganda, the term 'formal garden', replacing the mid-Victorian 'geometric garden', has remained ascendant to this day.

It was in the 1890s that some architects and horticulturists took up ideological positions behind opposing barricades. The point of contention: who was competent to make gardens? Blomfield considered that architects like himself should be responsible for the design while horticulturists should merely aid in the implementation. He argued that the architectural tradition, which produced houses and gardens of 'well-ordered harmony', had been undermined from the middle of the eighteenth century, adding: 'The question at issue is a very simple one. Is the garden to be considered in relation to the house, and as an integral part of a design which depends for its success on the combined effect of house and garden; or is the house to be ignored in dealing with the garden?' In response, the horticulturists William Robinson and H. E. Milner proposed that the garden should be a 'reflex of nature in her fairest moods'; it should 'express by its breadth of treatment most unmistakably that nature has triumphed over art', a viewpoint that harks back to the theorists of the landscape garden in the eighteenth century.

In practice, however, much of the hostility was produced out of shared disdain for the practices of Victorian formal planting. As Clive Aslet has pointed out, the ideas of both Blomfield and Robinson 'were in some measure a reaction against the showy Italianate parterres that had been unrolled like carpets in front of many great Victorian country houses by Paxton and William Andrews Nesfield'. Robinson contested, probably in the light of his experience of Shrubland, that: '*It is only where the plants of a garden are rigidly set out in geometrical design as in carpet-gardening and bedding-out that the term "formal" is rightly applied*'. Blomfield agreed that 'such dismal fiascoes in the Italian style as the Crystal Palace Gardens' were tasteless, but chose to appropriate the term 'formal' for the intimate walled spaces of gazebo and topiary in the 'old English garden'. That such layouts as Montacute were not entirely *old*, having been redesigned in the 1840s and 1890s, did not prevent their being cited as models.

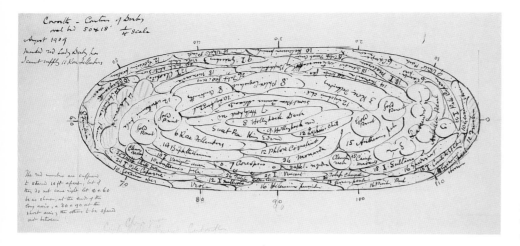

A planting plan for Coworth Park, Sunningdale, Berkshire by Gertrude Jekyll, 1909. This elongated oval 'island bed', designed for the Countess of Derby, represents a synthesis of formal and informal planting traditions: a geometric plan-form; some residual symmetry in the otherwise relaxed disposition of plants; a hierarchical profile up to hollyhocks at the centre; and a reconciliation between the bold effects of 'massing' and the myriad hues of 'mixing' or 'mingling'. It may be compared to the Hartwell planting plans of 1799 (see page 92).

In practice, moreover, there was some common ground. Contradicting his own narrow definition, Robinson acknowledged that 'Formality is often essential in the plan of a flower garden near a house'. Blomfield's home at Rye was situated on a cliff where formal gardening was out of the question. And in his design for Mellerstain (from 1909), Blomfield showed how the architectural garden could merge gradually into the blue of the horizon.

David Ottewill and Clive Aslet have both argued that what resulted from the cross-fertilization of ideas in the Edwardian era was the 'ideal resolution' – 'the combination of formal layout with exuberant informal planting'. In the gardens created by the partnership of Gertrude Jekyll and Edwin Lutyens this fusion of the structural and the decorative reached new heights, notably at Le Bois des Moutiers, Normandy, (from 1898) or Hestercombe, Somerset (1904–9). What Avray Tipping once called the 'successful inter-marriage of formal and natural gardening' can also be found in the 'Italian' gardens of Harold Peto, notably Iford Manor (from 1899), in Lord Aberconway's Bodnant (1874; and 1904–14), or indeed in the highly individualistic approach that Claude Monet worked out at Giverny (from 1890). Beatrix Farrand's Dumbarton Oaks (from 1922) offered a similar resolution across the Atlantic: snug formal terraces and flowing informal lawns; architect's plan and gardener's planting.

Lawrence Johnston's design for Hidcote, Gloucestershire, (from 1907), representative of a new type of garden subdivided into compartments or 'garden rooms' in different styles, was strict yet relaxed. Such compartments suited Jekyll's novel idea of gardens in a restricted palette – the 'red borders' at Hidcote or the 'white garden' at Sissinghurst, in Kent, (from 1930), for example. Thus, as Clive Aslet has emphasized, 'The real importance of Blomfield's book was its influence on the compartmental garden'.

The rejection of Victorian bedding schemes did not mean the end of the traditions of parterre design. At Blickling, in Norfolk, Lady Lothian demonstrated as early as the 1870s that she could fill the parterre with herbaceous plants rather than annuals; Norah Lindsay then remodelled the planting in 1932 in a simplified layout more appropriate to perennials. In the parterre of the Great Plat at Hestercombe, Lutyens and Jekyll provided an equally harmonious composition, suggestive of the past yet daringly modern. Through a sophisticated approach to colour and chromatic progression, moreover, Gertrude Jekyll succeeded in reconciling the bold effects of 'massing' with the myriad hues of 'mixing'. This was to reach its zenith in the herbaceous border.

The first image that comes to mind of Claude Monet's garden at **Giverny** is of water-lilies and weeping willows. Yet the earlier garden that Monet made was as remarkable for its tight rectilinear structure as for its cottage-garden-style planting. This flower garden – the 'Clos Normand' – was developed around 1890 in close axial relationship to the house. The grid of paths and beds was given further geometrical support by the use of a framework for climbing plants; here the order inherent in nature was expressed through art.

Edwardian innovation

During the Edwardian era, a number of garden designers achieved what has been called an 'ideal resolution' to the conflict, perhaps more theoretical than actual, between architect and horticulturist: the combination of formal layout with exuberant planting. Avray Tipping referred to it as the 'successful inter-marriage of formal and natural gardening'.

THE partnership of Gertrude Jekyll and Edwin Lutyens produced designs that were distinguished by an imaginative fusion of structural and decorative elements – in the planting at Hestercombe in Somerset or at **Le Bois des Moutiers** in Normandy (*below right*). Harold Peto's 'Italian' garden at **Iford Manor** in Wiltshire (*top right*) and Lord Aberconway's **Bodnant** in North Wales (*above*) suggested an equally successful blending of the architectonic and organic, a harmony between the architect's plan and the plantsman's craft. At **Hestercombe** (*opposite*), Lutyens and Jekyll did more than merely clothe the walls, steps and pergolas in verdure (*opposite, top left and right*). In the Great Plat (*opposite, below*) they provided a modern re-interpretation of historic traditions of parterre design – the *parterre de pièces coupées pour des fleurs* and the *parterre à l'angloise*. The edging to the flower beds was no longer box; the luxuriant leaves of *Bergenia cordifolia* enclosed roses, delphiniums and lilies. The patterns were no longer defined by gravel and grass but by stone and lawn. Between the piers of the pergola, the countryside was apparent. Today, the beautifully restored Hestercombe bears witness to Avray Tipping's original assessment – 'that an architect can be in unison with nature, that a formal garden can form part of a landscape'.

Hidcote and Blickling Hall

From 1907 Lawrence Johnston developed at Hidcote a new style of compartmental garden that combined formal hedges and topiary with herbaceous borders and luxuriant planting. In 1932 Norah Lindsay, who had worked at Hidcote, demonstrated at Blickling Hall how herbaceous plants could be used to advantage within a formal parterre.

Two contrasting views illustrate the new approaches to planting. The White Garden at Hidcote (*above*) shows the restricted palette of blush-white roses against the greens of topiary and *Acanthus*. In the east garden at Blickling Hall (*right*), using the structure established in the 1870s, Norah Lindsay reorganized the planting into four large quarters of flowers edged by roses and catmint; those squares close to the house were planted in dominant blues, pinks, mauves and whites, while those beyond were in warmer yellows and oranges. Today, in the height of late summer, feathery blooms of *Macleaya cordata*, golden rod and *Phalaris arundinacea* 'Picta' soften the textures. The oriental planes stand out in a lighter green against the woodland behind.

180

Château de la Roche-Courbon

The novelist Julien Viaud, otherwise known as Pierre Loti, once referred to the neglected site of La Roche-Courbon as 'the Sleeping Beauty's castle'. By the 1920s Loti's friend, the industrialist Paul Chénereau, had been persuaded to 'restore' the newly acquired estate. Achille Duchêne's younger contemporary Ferdinand Duprat oversaw the recreation of the gardens betwen 1925 and 1935. The seventeenth-century layout was all but lost. However, inspired by Hackaert's painting of around 1660, Duprat designed a splendid formal garden centred on a T-shaped canal.

DUPRAT's layout, more representative of his times than of the French Baroque garden, emphasizes plain geometry over ornate decoration. The traditional *parterre de broderie* has been replaced by simple plats of grass and evergreen cones (*left and opposite*). The 'jardin de fleurs' is confined to a small area on the south side of the château; to the north side are orchards and a 'potager' (*opposite*). The bosquet, being pushed back to the perimeter, is subordinate to the canal that dominates the site. It leads to a magnificent water stair as the termination of the central axis (*above*); a tangential axis to the north west is framed between poplars (*left*).

USA: Longwood and Gunston

From the 1910s Pierre S. du Pont, drawing on a wide range of European models for inspiration, employed new artistic means and the most advanced technology of water and lights at Longwood.

THE Main Fountain Garden at **Longwood** (*below left*), completed in the 1930s, was modelled on formal gardens as diverse as Villa d'Este and Vaux-le-Vicomte. The Upper Canal overflow, for example, is a distant echo of Cardinal d'Este's Alley of One Hundred Fountains at Tivoli. The magnificent fountains were at one time choreographed from a console of 300 switches and levers; during the 1980s lights, music and water were synchronized by computer. Although fireworks were used informally in garden parties in the 1920s, it was not until 1980 that grand formal displays began, using low-rising French effects. Adjoining the Main Fountain Garden are the Topiary Garden (*above*) and the Rose Garden with its attractive pavilion (*top left*). In May the lilac blossoms of the *Paulownia* form a delicate backdrop.

BY contrast, the small re-created garden at **Gunston Hall** looked back to Colonial traditions. Of William Mason's layout *c.* 1755 little survived and the present garden is an imaginative vision of the past. The view (*opposite*) from the pavilion at Gunston Hall over boxwork epitomizes Colonial Revival.

Mellerstain

Reginald Blomfield's original design for Mellerstain, recorded in Adrian Berrington's bird's-eye view of 1910 (see p.205), was modified after 1911 to offer a pleasing transition from the geometric to the wild: the lower terrace was removed, elements in the upper terraces were altered and, most important of all, an informal outline was adopted for the lake that terminates the vista.

THIS graduation is eased by the planting that softens the austerity of the formal terraces as they were first conceived; the topmost terrace is modified by topiary and the retaining walls are clothed in climbers or edged by herbaceous borders (*above*). The parterre terrace is dominated by grass, boxwork and flowers rather than by gravel (*left*). The eye is guided through a sequence of lawns to the lake ensconsed in woods.

Nordkirchen, Courances and Blenheim

At Courances in France, Nordkirchen in Germany and Blenheim in England, Achille Duchêne re-interpreted the traditions of *parterre de broderie*, *parterre de compartiment*, *parterre à l'angloise* and *parterre d'eau*.

At **Courances** (*below*), laid out before 1914 and again after 1948, the massive but elegant box broderie gives way to a simple basin enveloped in grass and trees; gravel is reduced to the minimum. Duchêne's north parterre at **Nordkirchen** (*above*), first conceived in 1906–14 and now recently restored, is loosely modelled on the work of Dézallier d'Argenville. The box patterns are infilled with white and red gravels that reflect light against the dark trees around. In the water parterre at **Blenheim**, created between 1925 and 1930 (*right*), Duchêne took inspiration from the design for the first *parterre d'eau* at Versailles.

Villandry

Designed by a Spaniard, Dr Joachim Carvallo, in the first two decades of the twentieth century, the garden of Villandry is a highly individual vision of the French Renaissance garden. In the absence of original planting at Chenonceaux, Fontainebleau or Anet, Villandry has come to act as a convincing substitute. Yet both the structure of the layout and the planting design itself are far from the traditions of the sixteenth century. The Renaissance gardener used herbs of different greens and a variety of flowers. At Villandry, massive box compartments filled with pansies and forget-me-nots in spring and dahlias in summer betray the style of the twentieth century – an inspired work of art beyond accurate restoration.

THE *potager* or vegetable garden is based on the work of Du Cerceau, but presents a more elaborate and fanciful version of sixteenth-century horticulture (*above*). The château of Villandry stands in one corner of its setting of knots, arbours and canal (*opposite*).

THREE contrasting views of the beautiful planting patterns at Villandry. The *potager* (*above and previous page*) is planted out in spring and summer displays: 90,000 vegetables a year with 30,000 flowers to decorate the borders. On the higher level is the Garden of Love (*right and below*). The foreground close to the château is devoted to four quarters symbolizing the moods of love. In the background, square compartments give way to diagonal lines that match the sloping ramps to the high terrace behind. These are laid out in the figures of the cross – for Malta, Languedoc and the Basque country. In the spring pinks and white tulips poke up out of blue forget-me-nots; in the summer red and yellow dwarf dahlias offer a bold palette.

Vizcaya

Between 1912 and 1922 James Deering's Vizcaya was created in the mangrove swamps and 'hammock' jungle of Biscayne Bay, Miami. Paul Chalfin was responsible for the overall direction, Diego Suarez for the initial planning. Although Italian inspiration was pronounced – from Villa Gamberaia and Caprarola to Villa Gori – the designers had absorbed wider European influences through their Beaux-Arts training; the parterres, for example, were more suggestive of France. Moreover, both the light and the vegetation, within and beyond the garden, made Vizcaya distinct from European models. Today the formal garden survives in splendid condition but without the informal tropical gardens to the south.

F ROM the south façade the garden extends along the three diverging vistas of a *patte d'oie*. The central one (*opposite top*) culminates in the casino and is framed between live oaks; those in front are trimmed architecturally while those above are allowed to grow rampantly. The middle ground is composed of an island in a central pool on which *Podocarpus* sentinels define the axis. The foreground consists in broderie and topiary on the cross axis. The two outer vistas are dominated by *parterres de broderie* (*left*). The patterns are traced not in box but in *Jasminum simplicifolium*, which tolerates both heat and salt spray; the texture is admirable though the lines are more organic than their European counterparts.

A LONGSIDE the main garden are a number of smaller spaces, notably the *giardino segreto* (*right*). The immediate inspiration was Villa Gamberaia. Yet the planting of *Plumbago*, mimicking the bands of frosted rustication, is a reminder of the tropical latitude. Through an opening in the wall of this secret garden access is provided to the light and space of the east terrace. Sea walls curve to form a harbour, terminated to the south by a trelliswork tea house (*opposite left*). The centre of the bay is dominated by Vizcaya's most celebrated architectural conceit – a breakwater in the form of a barge (*opposite right*). The barge's original design allowed for tropical plantings; these were lost in the hurricane of 1926 and never restored.

Nemours

The mansion of Nemours was built for Alfred I du Pont in 1909–10 in a Louis XVI style to reflect the family origins in France. This established a tone for the gardens which were laid out in the French manner along a dominant central axis. The scale is, however, drastically compressed by the standards of André Le Nôtre.

THE gardens are eclectic in combining French and Italian features with other European influences; a version of Schönbrunn's Gloriette is as much at home as a rotunda in its English-style landscape setting. Equally the planting forms a blend of Old World and New World styles. The central allée (*above*) is composed, for example, of Japanese *Cryptomeria* (recalling Italian cypresses), red horse chestnuts (reminiscent of France) and the North American pin oak, *Quercus palustris*.

A view from the Colonnade (*above*) looks back past the statue of 'Achievement' to the mansion framed by the trees of the triple allée.

A view from the circular Temple of Love (*above*) to the Sunken Gardens of 1928–32 and the Colonnade of 1926. The figure of Diana in the rotunda was cast by Jean Antoine Houdon in 1780. Two views (*left and below*) of the box parterre on the south side of the house illustrate this discrete area tucked away from the grandeur of the vista and enlivened by tulips in spring.

197

Dumbarton Oaks

First established in the 1920s to designs by Beatrix Farrand, the garden of Dumbarton Oaks has evolved over the years. Some formal areas such as the Pebble Garden or the Ellipse were created entirely anew around 1960, others such as the North Vista or the Box Terrace have been replanted after the repeated failure of box. Yet most of Farrand's original structure – both formal and informal – survives today.

THE Box Terrace (*above*), as first conceived, consisted in lawn within a plain box surround. Apart from the urn, the ornamentation was largely provided by climbers on the retaining wall above – *Wisteria, Pyracantha,* ivy, *Parthenocissus* and winter-flowering jasmine. Ruth Havey's later redesign introduced curved lines of ivy in place of straight lines of box and a base of coloured pebbles around the urn. The Pebble Garden (*left*) was created out of the old tennis court. Diverse pebbles from the beaches of Mexico ornament the spaces between stonework 'broderie'. To enhance the lustre of the pebbles, a thin film of water floats over the centre of the composition. The traditions of *parterre de broderie* and *parterre d'eau* have been unified in this beautiful composition.

Traditional Baroque broderie, however, was not entirely eclipsed by these new herbaceous parterres. The great French landscape designer Achille Duchêne, who had worked on the restoration of Vaux-le-Vicomte, continued the traditions of *parterre de compartiment, parterre à l'angloise, parterre d'eau* and *parterre de broderie* at Nordkirchen in Germany (1906–14), at Blenheim in England (1925–30) and at Courances in France (around 1914). Nevertheless, these interpretations of earlier forms showed a new concern for simple lines and masses. As Ernest de Ganay rightly discerned, the *parterre de broderie* was now made 'to conform to the strictest levelling of surfaces, while Le Nôtre liked to give them some relief, some "movement", by means of a variety of shrubs and topiary'.

Duchêne's younger contemporary Ferdinand Duprat revealed a similar liking for plain architectonic forms, when he 'restored' the gardens of the château de La Roche-Courbon from 1925. Baron Henri de Bastard's 'restoration' of Hautefort (from 1929) was full of boxwork shaved to perfection. We may see in this passion for simple geometry some parallels with the work of Cecil Pinsent (e.g. I Tatti from 1910) and Arthur Acton (e.g. La Pietra from 1904) in Italy – for all that the antecedents of their styles are entirely different. Claudia Lazzaro has written in the context of I Tatti: 'In the historicizing gardens of the first decades of the twentieth century, the Italian garden was similarly interpreted as architectonic and formal, primarily through the use of box, shaped into massive, precisely trimmed, and architectural patterns, hedges, and topiary.'

Erika Neubauer has correctly drawn attention to the integrity of such 'historicizing gardens' as styles in their own right. Nevertheless, the influence they exerted over the restoration of planting in what were originally Renaissance, Baroque or Colonial layouts – whether at Villa Gamberaia or Villandry, Weldam or Gunston Hall – has helped distort our view of the horticultural traditions of the past.

The scale and extravagance of layouts like Nordkirchen were matched by other grandiose projects: the alterations to the grounds of the Villa Pisani (now Nazionale) near Padua, for example. Although a labyrinth and coffee house dating back to the eighteenth century were preserved, the gardens were redesigned in 1911; the *parterre de broderie* was taken out to make way for a vast canal. In Britain, Port Lympne (1918–21), Tyringham (1926) and Ditchley Park (1933–36) represent a range of approaches to making grand formal gardens as late as the 1930s. At a house-warming ball in June 1937, the fountains of Ditchley, Oxfordshire, were floodlit and an orchestra played behind trelliswork covered in roses – recalling perhaps the screened orchestra gallery of the Villa Garzoni.

It was in North America, however, that the grand traditions of the Renaissance and Baroque continued to find a strong resonance. This was not merely a question of scale, style and lavishness as at Vizcaya (1914–22) or the appropriation of the past as at Nemours (1910–32). More importantly, the owners continued to use their gardens in ways that seem reminiscent of the courts of Europe, despite fundamental changes in social context, artistic means and garden technology.

The illuminations of the Clarence Mackay Estate at Harbour Hill for the visit of Edward Prince of Wales in 1919 required thousands of light bulbs, while servants outside provided hand-held lights for the 200 guests within. Pierre du Pont's garden at Longwood (1906 to 1930s), modelled on diverse European prototypes from Villa Gori to Villa Gamberaia and from Villa d'Este to Vaux-le-Vicomte, used new technology to emulate the traditional court festivities of Louis XIV: the garden fêtes, the displays of fireworks and fountains, the extravaganzas of garden theatre. Beneath Longwood's stage were 11 pumps recirculating 2,000 gallons of water per minute through 750 nozzles and

The garden of Hatfield House, made between 1607 and 1612 for Robert Cecil by Mountain Jennings, Salomon de Caus and John Tradescant the Elder, has been revitalized over many generations up to the present day. The Marchioness of Salisbury's East Parterre, replanted in the 1970s on the basis of an earlier layout, draws inspiration from the herbaceous parterres of Gertrude Jekyll and Norah Lindsay. In summer, old-fashioned roses, sweet peas, foxgloves, carnations and lilies create cascades and spikes of white, pinks, reds and mauves. Beyond on the terrace below is the dark geometry of the maze laid out in 1840 before the visit of the young Queen Victoria.

Illuminations in the Clarence Mackay Estate at Harbour Hill, 1919, famous for the thousands of light bulbs.

illuminated by over 600 lights. Nowadays the hydraulics of the Main Fountain Garden have been computerized to synchronize displays of water, lights, fireworks and music. With good reason, Colvin Randall has referred to Longwood as the 'electric Versailles'.

Contemporary with these new creations were the 'restorations' of Colonial gardens in the 1920s and 1930s, notably Williamsburg. In a recent publication devoted to developments in garden archaeology, *Earth Patterns*, the historical accuracy of Arthur Shurcliff's work at Williamsburg has been questioned: the archaeology was minimal and the research indicating that the Colonial gardens were 'simple, functional, and even somewhat bare' was ignored; Shurcliff was said to have had 'boxwood on the brain'. The gardens were thus 'more a creation of his depression-era vision of America's colonial landscape than . . . an accurate re-creation of town gardens in Virginia's colonial capital'. It is perhaps ironic that in the intervening years, some of this pioneering 'restoration', though seen as stylistically anachronistic or aberrant, has come to be regarded as worthy of conservation. A recent evaluation of the 1936–37 (and 1960–66) 'restoration' of the Great Garden at Herrenhausen has drawn attention to this.

The projects of Het Loo or Audley End and the restoration of Thomas Jefferson's garden at Monticello in Virginia demonstrate the advances that have been made since the 1930s in the quest for authenticity. In such cases, the fidelity to original planting stands out as both fitting and beautiful. Yet ultimately, there are limits to the 'authentic'. At Het Loo, giant copper beeches in the upper garden and a maple on the bowling green were retained, despite anachronism, as emblems of sentiment; materials were not always reproduced as the original.

The Italian Water Garden at Longwood, photograph taken in the early 1930s (see Villa Gamberaia, p.216).

At Monticello, moreover, questions have arisen that go beyond the physical reality. The garden archaeologist William Kelso has written, for example, of Jefferson's surprising tolerance for the 'unsightly': 'Excavations also leave little doubt that the walk to the garden led directly through the littered kitchen yard directly across another very visible eyesore: Mulberry Row, with its log servants' houses, craft buildings, and utilitarian outbuildings'. That Jefferson failed to see these features as 'eyesores' indicates the differences between past and present perception; they were, Kelso argues, too commonplace to be noticed. Thus, knowing how to restore a flower bed may be complex but possible; knowing how to represent the wider truth remains a matter of debate.

Monique Mosser has rightly underlined the difficulties inherent in conserving these ephemeral aspects – physical and metaphysical – in her article entitled: 'The Impossible Quest for the Past: Thoughts on the Restoration of Gardens'. Original meaning is lost with original functions. Flowers will always fade and even trees grow old. Gardens change or are changed continuously after the image of the ideal. Repose can only come with age. Yet, for all that the authentic is elusive, the quest is surely worthwhile. It leads to two diverging paths: along one the wonderful *plate-bandes* of Het Loo or the pin-cushion beds of Klein-Glienicke Park; along the other the inspired reinventions of knot and topiary at Villandry or Hatfield House. Both ways have their charms and challenges.

Longwood, open-air theatre in June 1916, when Bessie Cazenove du Pont and John Darby were performing.

Above right: pantomime at the estate of Benjamin Stern at Roslyn, New York, from *The Garden Magazine*, August 1919.

Right: new pastimes and new perspectives on the formal garden – an autogiro in flight over the Stotesbury Estate of Whitemarsh Hall, 29 September 1930.

Mellerstain

186–187 One of Reginald Blomfield's most important garden commissions was Mellerstain in Berwickshire. He recalled in his *Memoirs* of 1932: 'Lord and Lady
Binning were enthusiastic on the matter of garden design, and with their help I
laid out an important garden here with terraces, a cryptoporticus, parterres and
water-pieces, and my scheme was to have been carried on to an immense grass
hemicycle overlooking the lake at the foot of the hill, in the best manner of Le
Nôtre, but we had to abandon this; indeed it would have required the resources of
Louis XIV to carry out the whole of my design'.

The original vision was captured in a superb bird's-eye perspective of 1910
by Adrian Berrington. The parterre, steps, loggias, bastions and concave
amphitheatre scooped out in lawn are quite unlike the work of the French master
– in everything but scale. As planned and as executed, Mellerstain has a
somewhat Italian resonance. Yet with its expansive lawns it belongs firmly
within the traditions of British garden design, sharing some kinship to Cliveden.
In the modified scheme after 1911 Blomfield removed the lower terrace, altered
elements in the upper terraces, and, most importantly, adopted an informal
outline for the lake as the culmination of the vista. As David Ottewill has
pointed out, Blomfield's treatment of the lake 'shows how much less doctrinaire
he had become in the twenty years since writing his book'. Indeed, Blomfield
went out of his way to return the water feature to its original informality; for it
would appear that William Adam, architect of the first house, had created a
'Dutch Canal' out of the River Eden around 1725. The new lake was made to
look 'natural'.

Thus, for the visitor today the prospect from the upper floors of the
battlemented house offers a pleasing transition from the geometric to the wild.
The graduation is eased by the planting, which softens the austerity of the formal
terraces as they were first conceived; the topmost terrace is modified by the
topiary and the retaining walls are clothed in climbers. The parterre terrace is
dominated by grass, boxwork and flowers rather than by gravel. The eye is guided
through a sequence of lawns to the lake ensconced in woods. In the far distance
are the misty Cheviot hills.

Hestercombe

178 It was the use of planting to soften the angularity of architectural composition
that led to some of the finest garden design in the Edwardian period. As Clive
Aslet has written: 'The harmony between formal planning and informal planting
in a Lutyens-Jekyll or Harold Peto garden represents an ideal synthesis, in which
the country-house garden was possibly more successful than the country house'.
There is no better example of this 'ideal synthesis' than Hestercombe in
Somerset. Its restoration in the 1970s has ensured its survival as a supreme
achievement of the partnership between architect Edwin Lutyens and garden
designer Gertrude Jekyll. The commission came from the Hon. E. W. B.
Portman, the eldest son of the 2nd Viscount Portman; the garden was laid out
between 1904 and 1909.

The Great Plat forms the centrepiece of the design. It is a parterre of lawn
and flower beds. Following the traditions of seventeenth-century gardens like
Pitmedden, the pattern of these beds may be enjoyed not so much from the
vantage of the house but more from raised terraces around all four sides; on the
south terrace a pergola acts as a transparent structure between the garden and the
countryside beyond. If the influences on this parterre can be codified, then the
primary one is the *parterre de pièces coupées pour des fleurs* and the secondary

Adrian Berrington, bird's-eye view of Reginald
Blomfield's proposed scheme for Mellerstain, 1910.
Blomfield recalled in 1932 that the completion of his
layout 'in the best manner of Le Nôtre' would have
required the 'resources of Louis XIV'; after 1911 it
was duly modified. It is interesting to see Blomfield
using here a large grass hemicycle, recalling the
vertugadin of Chantilly, for example. The proposal
was otherwise quite unlike the work of the great
French master (see pp. 186–7).

MELLERSTAIN
Col. Lord Binning C.B.
BIRDS EYE VIEW
OF NEW GARDENS from HOUSE to CANAL
DISTANCE FROM HOUSE TO CANAL 1170 FEET. CANAL 1800 FEET X 400 FEET.
Reginald Blomfield A.R.A. Architect.
invenit 1910.

one is the *parterre à l'angloise*. Yet the flower compartments are set out in paving and lawn not in gravel. They are quite unlike the raised stone beds or box-edged beds of the Renaissance and Baroque. The informal edging is provided by thick bands of *Bergenia cordifolia*. Enveloped by their luxuriant leaves, pink China roses, blue delphiniums and white lilies form a voluptuous bouquet. Ornamental grasses soften the textures. The composition derives its elegance from the diagonal lines traced on grass in stone from the quadrant steps that lead down to the corners of the parterre.

The surrounding rough-stone walls have recessed mortar joints in which flowers take root – the *Erigeron* or fleabane has made itself at home. The pergola of alternated round and square piers is of the same rough stone softened by climbing roses and clematis. Along the east and west terraces rills of Moorish inspiration were filled with irises, forget-me-nots, arum lilies, water plantain and arrowhead. Yet in the stone edging Gertrude Jekyll acknowledged another influence: at even intervals it turns, after 'the manner of the gathered ribbon strapwork of ancient needlework'.

A certain rustic quality and the fusion of planting with stonework makes Hestercombe quite unlike the formal gardens of the preceding centuries. Furthermore, the visitor perceives a pleasing union between the garden and landscape through the pergola's interstices, the piers made organic through verdure. To Avray Tipping, the gardens at Hestercombe 'proved that an architect can be in unison with nature, that a formal garden can form part of a landscape'.

The rill at Hestercombe: Gertrude Jekyll compared the design for the stone pattern to 'gathered ribbon strapwork of ancient needlework'.

Blickling Hall

180–181 The gardens at Blickling Hall in Norfolk provide an elegant example of how formal traditions could be reinterpreted over two centuries to produce a design of consummate beauty. The flower parterre to the east front of the Jacobean house was redesigned by Norah Lindsay in 1932. It replaced an earlier parterre by Lady Lothian within an architectural setting by Matthew Digby Wyatt and Markham Nesfield. This had in turn superseded the proposal made by Nesfield c. 1872 for a French-style *parterre de broderie*; Lady Lothian preferred herbaceous beds. What was thus a formal flower garden of many generations took up an axial relationship to a 'wood walk' terminated by a temple dating back to the eighteenth century.

Blickling Hall was built between 1616 and 1626 for Sir Henry Hobart to a design by Robert Lyminge; alterations followed from 1765 and again in 1864. A map of 1729 by James Corbridge indicates that by this time the parterre to the east consisted in a simple lawn leading to a symmetrical wilderness on either side of the central axis from the house. It was laid out with crossed, diagonal paths. Soon after, probably in the 1730s, the wilderness was furnished with a temple on a raised bastion to form an eyecatcher to the central wood walk. During the 1760s the straight paths of the wilderness were made serpentine, but a century later, whether on the basis of the Corbridge map or of surviving elements, it proved possible to resurrect the old formality.

The wilderness of 1861–64 was a larger version of the original, and the orthogonal and diagonal walks were planted with limes, oaks, beeches and Turkey oaks backed by a sea of laurel and rhododendrons. In 1870/2 Wyatt and Nesfield provided a new sense of enclosure by setting the parterre below a buttressed brick wall with flights of steps leading up to the main wood walk. This was to assume an increasingly sombre aspect as conifers grew up to frame the temple. The sculpture, fountain, and Lady Lothian's elaborate flower parterre followed after 1872 and the design was completed by 1877.

Lady Lothian's rejection of broderie and bedding reflected new tastes. For she was a pioneer in the use of herbaceous plants within the parterre; until this time they had been kept in borders. Unlike the bright bedding plants, the herbaceous flowers were noted by commentators from the 1870s onwards for their restrained colours in 'this new, or shall we not say, revived old style of planting'. This did not prevent Lady Lothian's design from being a jumble in which unity, as Christopher Hussey pointed out in 1930, was 'lost in a multiplicity of dotted beds'. No doubt this criticism helped promote Norah Lindsay's elegant redesign when the 11th Marquis of Lothian moved to Blickling in 1932.

Norah Lindsay's reputation at this time was based partly on her work with Lawrence Johnston at Hidcote. At Blickling she reduced the multitude of small beds to four large squares, but retained the yew pillars and 'grand pianos' of Lady Lothian's scheme. The beds were in carefully graduated colours. These ranged from the dominant blues, pinks, mauves and whites close to the house to the warmer yellows and oranges on the far side. All were surrounded by a symmetrical arrangement of red and pink or red roses edged by catmint and punctuated by the yew sentinels at the corners.

Today's visitor may enjoy this masterful design in any season. In the spring, the pattern of the four squares is clearly etched in freshly hoed earth. Shoots and tufts of green give promise of the summer, at a time when the branches of ancient, gnarled oriental planes still look gaunt. There are daffodils everywhere and bluebells along one of the wood walks. The eye is attracted up the central vista to the azaleas that Norah Lindsay planted in 1934 in place of the conifers.

In the height of the late summer season the visitor will gaze over the feathery fronds of golden rod and *Phalaris arundinacea* 'Picta' and the creamy bells of the yucca rising above the red rose beds. In the background the oriental planes are now a light green to the darker woods behind. In autumn, when the beds are bare again, the visitor may still enjoy the colours of the woods, the garden ornaments and the great yew hedges. When the winds feel chillier it is easy to imagine the household in the 1930s under the 11th Marquis of Lothian. On some weekends, the guests required all thirty-six fires; a pall of smoke gathered over the house. In the South Drawing Room, there were gatherings at Round Table 'moots' – Lord Halifax, Lionel Curtis and the Astors from Cliveden amongst diplomats and politicians – while the younger generation were on shooting sprees in the grounds, or in cut-flower fights and bath-salt battles in the house.

Country Life photograph of the flower parterre at Blickling Hall in 1930, showing Lady Lothian's planting scheme before Norah Lindsay's alterations of 1932. Its present appearance is shown in colour on p. 181.

View from the north of Achille Duchêne's parterre at Nordkirchen, recently restored as part of a long-term management plan.

Nordkirchen

188 Nordkirchen, near Münster in north Germany, was considered the 'Versailles of Westphalia' in the eighteenth century. The architect Johann Conrad Schlaun was commissioned by Ferdinand von Plettenberg in 1725 to create an elaborate layout of parterres and bosquet. Completed largely by 1733, the formal gardens fell victim in the 1830s to landscape improvement by Maximilian Friedrich Weyhe. When, however, Herzog von Arenberg took over possession of the property in 1903 he engaged Achille Duchêne to resurrect the splendour of the formal setting.

Between 1906 and 1914, a magnificent parterre was laid out to the north side of the palace. From 1918 to 1950 a period of decay set in. Thus, like some of its Baroque forerunners, the heyday of Duchêne's design was remarkably short-lived. Recently, however, under the management of the Land Nordrhein-Westfalen, the parterre has been restored as part of a long-term management plan. The restoration of parts of the Schlaun layout remains a possibility for the future, but the parterre alone is worth the travel across the lovely undulating countryside of Westphalia lying so close to the industrial centres of the Ruhr.

Today's visitor to Nordkirchen, approaching on foot from the north, sees the staggered brick façades of the palace across a broad sheet of water. The parterre lies between this lake and the mansion, as though on an island; access is along causeways to the west and east of the palace. The palace itself sits on its own moated island. Enclosed by massive squadrons of horse chestnut – shady promenades on sultry summer days – the parterre and its sculpture act as light against dark. For, as in the traditions of the Baroque, the predominant base colour is white – here, pristine white marble chips. The traditional highlighting of black in the interstices of the broderie, however, is missing. The palmettes or shells in the four corners of the square *parterre de compartiment* are filled out in red in a manner reminiscent of Dézallier d'Argenville. The two flanking *parterres à l'angloise* offer the green relief of grass. Unlike the parterres of the Baroque,

Opposite: Herzog von Arenberg's open-air ballroom, drawn by Dupré after a design by Duchêne for the park at Nordkirchen; and (below) bird's-eye view of Duchêne's masterplan for the neo-Baroque revitalization of Nordkirchen, completed in part between 1906 and 1914. The *parterre de compartiment* may be compared to Dézallier d'Argenville's original (overleaf); Duchêne used grass instead of water at the centre of his composition.

however, in which the *plate-bandes* provided a bright palette of mixed flowers, this is a design exclusively in green, white and red. Even the narrow borders of flowers in the grass parterres are composed of red begonias and white *Nicotiana*.

The pattern for the *parterre de compartiment* is derived from a plan illustrated by A. J. Dézallier d'Argenville in his *La Théorie et la pratique du jardinage* – the same as that used for Weldam. Here, however, the palmettes are reversed in direction and the interiors of grass are omitted. The centre of the whole composition is devoted to sculpture rather than to the original pool and fountain. The elaborate topiary and the *plate-bandes* are missing and vertical emphasis is provided by statues of extraordinary diversity, and by yew balls and standard privets. The grass parterres pick up the rhythm in yew pyramids and the same little trees of privet; quaint strips of white marble chips and bands of white *Nicotiana* and red begonias are incised in the grass. Duchêne's was an inventive interpretation rather than a faithful restoration of garden art in the age of Louis XIV.

In the Musée des Arts Décoratifs in Paris, there is a superb drawing by Dupré of Herzog von Arenberg's open-air ballroom after Duchêne's design. Based on the Colonnade of the 1680s at Versailles (and thereby, heir to a tradition extending back to Colonna), this feature evokes the attempt to create something of the festive ambience of the royal courts as well as an imitation of the physical setting. It is notable, however, that the architecture of the colonnade is softened by planting – in a manner that betrays the twentieth century and that is quite alien to the original as conceived by Jules Hardouin-Mansart.

Thus the Herzog von Arenberg demonstrated extravagant taste on the eve of the First World War. Today, it is perhaps fitting that the palace of Nordkirchen is full of students of finance. Outside, the grounds are a tranquil place, but on some days the gravel walks are enlivened by wedding parties, adding their own black and white pattern to the beautifully restored parterre of white, green and red. It seems that Nordkirchen, like many historic gardens, has become the ideal setting for the wedding photographer.

Dézallier d'Argenville's *parterre de compartiment*, plate 3B of *La Théorie et la pratique du jardinage* (1709; this edition 1723).

View of one of the flanking *parterres à l'angloise* at Nordkirchen.

View from the water parterre terrace at Blenheim over the lower terrace; the *modello* for Bernini's River Gods fountain in the Piazza Navona in Rome is at its centre.

Blenheim

The water parterre at Blenheim is one of Achille Duchêne's most felicitous creations. When contrasted with Nordkirchen and Courances, it shows the versatility of his skills as a designer. Yet, commissioned by the 9th Duke of Marlborough in 1925, its conception and construction were far from easy; they were troubled by antagonism between client and architect. Duchêne took inspiration directly from the first *parterre d'eau* at Versailles which was created from 1671–74. The Duke, however, had his own ideas. He told Duchêne to work less in the spirit of Le Nôtre and more in the style of Bernini. He rejected Duchêne's proposal for fountains and running water. The architect was instructed: 'Limpidity of water is pleasing and possesses a romance. You have got this effect in the basins and in the large area of water contained by the Lake. Be careful not to destroy this major emotion which Nature has granted you for the sake of what may possibly be a vulgar display of waterworks which can be seen at any exhibition or public park'. He told Duchêne to sleep on it, 'for it is only by thought, constant thought and mature reflection that artists have left their great works for the enjoyment of posterity'.

Both seem to have got their way. On the second terrace below the water parterre, a *modello* for Bernini's river-gods fountain in the Piazza Navona in Rome was given pride of place amidst sphinxes bearing the features of the 9th Duke's second Duchess (following a practice that goes back at least to the sphinxes modelled after Louis xiv's mistress). The water parterre remained, however, close to the spirit of Le Nôtre and Le Brun. The original consisted in a circular central basin connected to four subsidiary basins in the form of a cartouche; two smaller side basins finished the composition.

The water parterre at Blenheim is based on the same disposition of elements, although four instead of two basins take up the gaps between the tributary cartouches. The cartouches, in turn, consist in two levels rather than the one designed at Versailles, thus producing the effect of a very slight cascade. The five

189

fountains broadly replicate the Versailles prototype as it was executed, though not the many jets originally envisaged by Le Brun. A major difference between the two concepts lay in the planting and sculptural embellishments. Israel Silvestre's view of 1682 suggests the much stronger vertical accent of the originals which came not only from the sculptural figures but also from the topiary set out in vases amidst the broderie. In contrast, Duchêne's composition is restrained yet bold, the statuary being confined to the outer corners only. The box broderie is elegantly laced into the spaces between the pools, but the planting is essentially flat. When the fountains play this is a joyful design. But when the fountains fall silent this is a most restful composition on misty autumn mornings or snowy winter days; here the Duke's limpid emotions are reflected.

Courances

189 Reworking an axial layout of the seventeenth and eighteenth centuries, Achille Duchêne helped produce one of the world's most pleasing formal gardens – Courances. The Marquise de Ganay employed Duchêne in the period just before the outbreak of war in 1914; he was to return the gardens to the French style lost after 1872 in the Picturesque landscaping under the Baron de Haber. A third campaign of work was instituted from 1948 after the gardens had been ravaged by the war; this followed Duchêne's death in 1947 and was a rehabilitation of the earlier designs but adapted to the times. Kenneth Woodbridge has written of Courances: 'The result is a restrained version of the French grand manner . . . The *parterre de broderie* adjoining the château is of modest size, sufficient to mediate between the house and the park without being dominant. In the same way the simplicity of the carefully proportioned basin beyond introduces the vista, and joins art to nature by the trees and sky reflected in its surface'.

Courances differs from the gardens of Le Nôtre in several important respects. At Vaux-le-Vicomte, Versailles and Chantilly there are considerable changes in level with terracing, steps, ramps and cascades. Courances is essentially on flat terrain. The surprises for the visitor arise primarily through the artful concealment of planting, not through what is hidden in descending or ascending from one architectural level to the next. Moreover, grass forms the unifying surface at Courances unlike the gravel or sand walks and the stone steps of Le Nôtre's gardens. Statuary and sculpture are reduced to passing incidents from their dominant place in the iconography of Versailles. The purity and simplicity of the vocabulary in the main vista and subsidiary walks – variations on the theme of fine sward and lofty trees, of reflecting basins and effervescent cascades, of light and shade playing over white swans gliding on water dark as pitch – makes Courances seem reticent yet relaxed, perfect in fresh spring green or faded autumn rust.

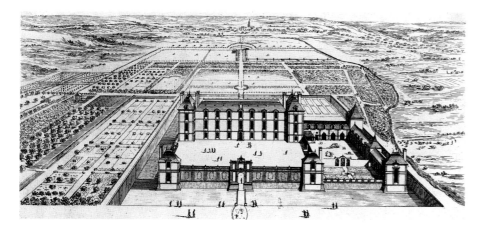

Seventeenth-century engraving of Courances; and a view of one of the allées at Courances today.

Villandry

View of one of the terraces at Hautefort in Aquitaine, re-created after 1929 by the baron de Bastard and his wife in evocation of sixteenth- to seventeenth-century planting.

If Nordkirchen, Blenheim, Courances and La Roche-Courbon represent attempts at reinterpreting the traditions of the Baroque, Villandry near Tours is the most inventive revival of the French Renaissance garden. In the absence of original sixteenth-century planting, whether at Chenonceaux, Fontainebleau or Anet, gardens of the twentieth century such as Hautefort and Villandry have come to act as illusory but convincing substitutes. So entirely satisfying are both the composition and planting at Villandry that even the connoisseur struggles hard not to believe in its authenticity. Arriving on foot, the visitor is at first unaware of gardens hidden behind the château and tucked in snugly between a wooded hillside to the east, orchards to the south and the village to the west. Ascending the high terrace that runs along the east side of the garden, however, the visitor is transported suddenly to a vision of perfect order and harmony. 190–193

Villandry was the creation of a Spaniard, Dr Joachim Carvallo, and his American wife, who took over a site largely converted into an English-style park. Planning began after 1906 and continued through the period of the First World War. Despite the absence of original plans, Dr Carvallo developed the conception of a 'restoration' of the sixteenth-century garden around the terraces, basins and canals laid down by 1762. In part, this wish to restore was motivated by philosophical and political concerns – to reverse the effects of social progress, in which, as he put it, 'men and their belongings slid imperceptibly towards the stables, while the animals, without the least difficulty, could come into the drawing room'.

The development of the plan came in two phases. The first, prior to 1914, involved the creation of a box parterre to the south of the château in place of the nineteenth-century garden of lawns and flower beds. The figures cut out in box were meant to symbolize the different moods of love – *l'amour volage* (horns and fans), *l'amour tendre* (hearts and masks), *l'amour tragique* (dagger blades), *l'amour passioné* or *folie* (broken and dancing hearts). Kenneth Woodbridge has pointed out that this has 'no evident precedents in French tradition, except for the tendency of the sixteenth-century mentality to express itself in emblematic form'; he argued that since the figures had been reduced to abstract forms, they were no longer recognizable as emblems and had become instead 'symbolist'.

The use of box, especially in such monumental forms is, moreover, entirely alien to the sixteenth century; it will be recalled that herbs of different greens were used in all French gardens until Claude Mollet introduced box to Anet after 1582 and to Saint-Germain-en-Laye around 1595. In the Renaissance compartments, a variety of flowers counterbalanced the unity and symmetry of the composition. At Villandry, the perfect symmetry is reinforced by the bedding plants. Yet, for all the historical latitude, the box parterre is a marvel. The compartments of love give way to a diagonal composition based on the symbol of the cross – for Malta, Languedoc and the Basque country. The lines reflect the ramps of the eighteenth-century terrace above which enclose the whole parterre. In spring, pink and white tulips rise in the midst of forget-me-nots like cotton grass in the mist.

The second phase involved the celebrated *potager* or vegetable garden. This was constructed on the lower levels to the west between 1914 and 1918. It consists of nine squares laid out after illustrations from Jacques Androuet du Cerceau's *Les Plus excellents bastiments de France* (1576 and 1579). The contrasts of colour and texture achieved in the compositions of vegetables within small box-edged beds are one of the perennial triumphs of gardening. Two plantings a year are required, in March and June, and the ceaseless toil of six gardeners.

The effects of planting in the *potager* transcend the modesty of sixteenth-century prototypes. They form part of the illusion Dr Carvallo created out of his romantic but socially regressive vision of the past. The garden of Villandry is a decorative *tour de force*, primarily a spectacle to gaze upon. For despite the symbolism of the parterre, Dr Carvallo's creation lacks the complex meaning of the Renaissance original – once informed by iconography and mythology, once animated as settings for fêtes and entertainments.

Unlike the French Renaissance garden, which was composed typically of square and rectangular compartments, the units at Villandry are not quite regular due to the trapezoidal shape of the site. By skilful adjustment of lines and the use of diagonal as well as crossed paths, Dr Carvallo succeeded in making the garden appear entirely regular. Kenneth Woodbridge has written in reviewing the complex influences on the composition as a whole: 'The principle at Villandry is the one used by Le Nôtre, balance about a controlling axis where, given the space, the design could theoretically expand indefinitely from the centre. The renaissance ideal was symmetry and closure. Villandry is not the model of a sixteenth-century garden; but this does not detract from the magnitude of Dr Carvallo's achievement'. Monique Mosser has called Villandry an 'inspired work of art' created by 'marrying "post-Troubadour" Renaissance and *fin de siècle* symbolism'.

Vizcaya

194–195 Gardens such as Nemours in Delaware and Vizcaya in Florida are often described as being a recreation of French or Italian gardens in an American setting. Yet this simplifies the complex stylistic influences and undervalues the distinctness of their form and meaning as gardens, indeed as unique products of New World conditions – American society, American landscape and American climate.

Clive Aslet has written about the estate of Vizcaya as the epitome of all that was distinct in the American country house of the twentieth century: in the interior, the organ, the bowling alley and the splendid technology – from central heating (even in Florida's climate) to private telephone system; in the outlying areas, the dairy, farm and estate village; and in its creation, the 'heroic determination to overcome all natural and manmade obstacles'. The latter applies especially to the making of the formal gardens in the mangrove swamps and 'hammock' jungle of Biscayne Bay, Miami, where salt spray and occasional hurricanes leave their corrosive and destructive imprint. No wonder its creator, Paul Chalfin, exclaimed: 'Is this a dream made real, or a reality greater than a dream?'.

Chalfin was commissioned by James Deering to realize this dream in the years between 1912 and 1922. From 1910 Chafin had already been advising on purchases of art; from 1910 to 1912 he accompanied Deering on a visit to Europe. Deering's fortune had come from the family business in farm equipment. Suffering from ill health, he decided to return to America to purchase 130 acres of land to the south of what was then a relatively small settlement in the midst of jungle – Miami. That autumn Chalfin co-opted the talents of architect F. Burrall Hoffman; by 1914 they had the additional support of a Colombian designer Diego Suarez, who had been working for Arthur Acton on his 'restoration' of the gardens at Villa La Pietra in Florence. Suarez later attributed much of his understanding of landscape to Acton, whom he called a 'disciple' of Henri Duchêne (the father of Achille Duchêne): 'He gave me my teaching in classical Italian garden design, and he taught me Duchêne's ideals'.

In January 1915 Suarez made his first visit to the site from the office in New York. He realized then that his plans were faulty: 'I had made a terrible mistake

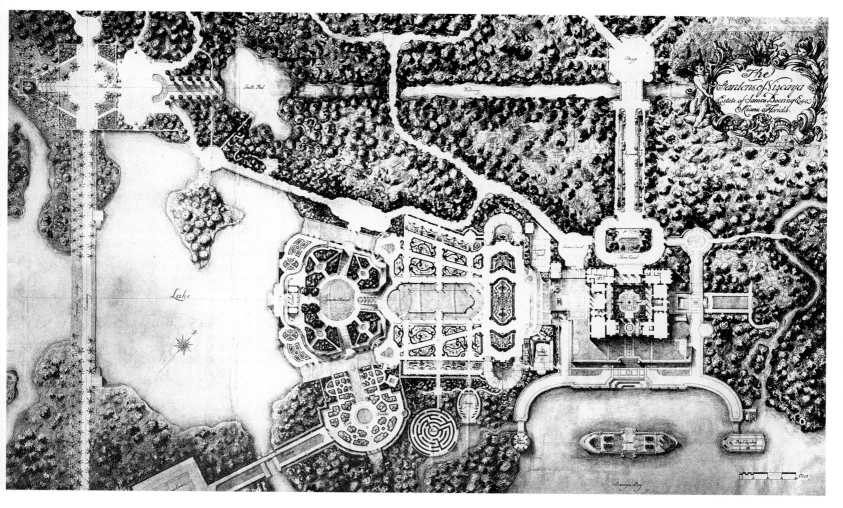

Site plan of the garden of Villa Vizcaya at Miami, Florida, from *The Architectural Review*, July 1917. The main axis of the formal garden is apparent as it extends left from the villa towards the mount and casino; directly below lie the 'Rose Garden' (or more appropriately 'Fountain Garden' since roses never prospered), the circular maze, the theatre and the *giardino segreto*.

. . . It was exactly noon and I looked straight ahead where the gardens would be, and *I couldn't see a thing*. I was blinded by light, for out there at the far end was a lake. It was like a mirror'. This produced the impulse towards the second plan in which a protective hill was envisaged to the south surmounted by a casino. How much Suarez subsequently influenced the design of the garden is a matter of debate. By 1917 he had left the project, but even as early as 1915 Chalfin seems to have adopted an increasingly assertive role. By 1916 the house was largely complete, but with shortages of materials and labour during the First World War, the construction of the gardens continued until 1922. Despite the mosquitoes and a plague of land crabs, despite the need to raise the level of the land for the house by up to twelve feet above mean tide level, the project was finally accomplished in the midst of Deering's preserved 'jungle effect'.

A plan published in the *Architectural Review* in 1917 indicates the broad lines of the formal garden. What is striking for a layout supposedly modelled on Italian forerunners is how the plan seems entirely alien to the principles of the Italian Renaissance. Indeed, if there is one plan-form that Vizcaya resembles, it is surely that of the Karlsaue in Kassel; its Baroque principles Chalfin and Suarez may have absorbed, along with other European models, through their Beaux-Arts training. The diverging sightlines – the *patte d'oie* – certainly belong within the traditions of Baroque city planning, notably the Piazza del Popolo in Rome, and within the traditions of seventeenth- to eighteenth-century garden design. The dominance of the *parterre de broderie* at Vizcaya, moreover, suggests French prototypes of the seventeenth century. The gardens represent, therefore, an eclectic mix; and in this mix, the native vegetation plays an important role. For all this, Italian inspiration is evident in much of the detailing of the design, especially around the casino. And since the four different façades of the villa are derivative of various Italian architectural styles – from the Villa Rezzonico on

215

the Brenta River to the Villa Gamberaia at Settignano or the Villa Farnesina in Rome – the effect of the whole against the dark foliage of live oaks remains resonant of Italy.

From the terrace in front of the south facade, the visitor gazes over a parterre to a casino framed between clipped trees; it sits on the mount raised by Suarez as the termination of the central axis. *Parterres de broderie* extend along the two subsidiary vistas of the patte d'oie. These diverging allées are separated from the central axis by the trimmed rows of live oaks (*Quercus virginiana*) and by a large central pool. Before, however, reaching any one of these three enticing walks, the visitor descends a series of steps and passes through a parterre on the cross-axis. This was originally designed as one broad *parterre de compartiment*. Today the most complex broderie is confined to the centre and flanked by two parterres of lawn and broderie (whose plan-form in three segments is reminiscent of the north parterre at Versailles or Plate 4A, Fig. 1 of Dézallier d'Argenville). These are enclosed by semi-circular pools and gazebos covered with the creeping fig, *Ficus pumila*. Across the whole parterre, the surface of gravel has been reduced in area by large circles and rectangles of lawn. The merits of the *parterre à l'angloise* have thus been appropriated in this version of a *parterre de compartiment*.

Closer inspection of the *parterre de broderie* along the two diverging vistas proves that this is not boxwork; the embroidery is traced out in a type of native jasmine, *Jasminum simplicifolium*. This shrub tolerates the tropical sun; the texture of the broderie is admirable. While the original patterns have been maintained, the spaces are filled with annuals rather than the coloured sand and gravel originally envisaged.

If the visitor returns to the central axis, an Italian flavour replaces the French. For the island in the central pool recalls the models of the lower terrace at Villa Lante and the Isolotto of the Boboli Gardens in Florence. At Vizcaya, however, elaborate stonework and terracotta pots are translated into a plain treatment of grass; two rows of *Podocarpus macrophylla*, trimmed as sentinels, help define the island's place within the vista. The pool leads in turn to the water stair, forming an architectural approach to the casino on top of the mount. With high retaining walls to either side, the setting is reminiscent of the casino at the Villa Farnese, Caprarola. Yet the cascade itself shares no kinship with the Farnese water chain; it is derived instead from the water stair at the Villa Corsini in Rome. Moreover, Suarez acknowledged that the detailing of the grottoes, which are lodged within the retaining walls, owed something to Gamberaia and the Boboli Gardens as well as to Caprarola. The intertwining branches and dark foliage of the live oaks above recall the ilex groves of many an Italian garden.

During those last four years after the project was complete, James Deering found the walks in the garden increasingly difficult. Guests were received in the patio. But for those who escaped on to the parterre, the ascent to the casino promised more than merely nostalgia for Italy. There was the possibility of rest and refreshment within the delightful eighteenth-century French-style rooms. There was the view over an informal lake to extensive tropical gardens and to an avenue of two hundred and sixty-five royal palms on the causeway to the boathouse; at eighteen feet high, these had been brought all the way from Cuba on oxcart and schooner. And there were the curved steps leading down to the Venetian gondola landing quay beneath the casino, against which clear tropical waters must have lapped gently.

Today, the lake has become a muddy inlet, hemmed in by the grounds of a hospital that was built after the land was sold off in 1945. Thus, to the south of Vizcaya the important relationship of the formal to the informal has been lost. The visitor turns back instead to gaze from the casino at the lovely south façade of the villa. It is time to find the other hidden delights of the formal garden and to

View of the water parterre at Villa Gamberaia, Florence. Through this replanted layout of *c.* 1900, the vision of the Italian garden was re-interpreted in North America and Europe – from Longwood to Ambleville near Paris.

The sunken secret garden at Villa Gamberaia, the model for the *giardino segreto* at Villa Vizcaya, Florida.

The central feature of the Labyrinth at Villa Pisani, Stra. Still extant in the early twentieth century, the essentially circular form of the labyrinth at Villa Pisani may have inspired the maze at Villa Vizcaya, Florida. It survives from the original design by Girolamo Frigimelica of the early eighteenth century.

return to the great east façade looking out over Biscayne Bay where pelicans and egrets fish.

Apart from a 'rose garden' to the east of the mount (which sustains the circular rosary style), there are three smaller gardens in the formal tradition: a maze, a garden theatre and a *giardino segreto*. The maze is of the circular type like that at the Villa Pisani at Stra. Until destroyed by the hurricane of 1926, Australian pine (*Casuarina equisetifolia*) formed the hedgework. After unsuccessful trials with hibiscus, the coco plum (*Chrysobalanus icaco*) was found to withstand the salt spray. The theatre, like that at Longwood, seems to have been inspired by the one at the Villa Gori in Siena. Suarez himself recalled also the influence of the theatre at the Villa La Pietra. As for the walled *giardino segreto*, the Villa Gamberaia was the immediate inspiration. But, if its decorative stonework recalled Italy, the embellishment with orchids reminded Deering's guests of their tropical latitude. Victims of the salt, they have now been replaced by *Plumbago auriculata*, which, being arranged in stepped planters, seems to mimic the bands of frosted rustication.

Through an opening in the north wall of the secret garden, the visitor is able to pass into the light and space of the east terrace. Sea walls curve to form a harbour, terminated to the south by a trelliswork tea-house and to the north by a mooring. Here Deering's yachts were once anchored. The centre of the bay is dominated by Vizcaya's most celebrated architectural conceit – a breakwater in the form of a barge. It encloses the harbour just as the keys of Florida enclose natural lagoons. In response to the challenge created by the presence of mounds of rubbish after dredging, Suarez developed an idea previously voiced by Chalfin: a stone ship – 'the proudest architectural creation of my life, inspired by the Isola Bella on Lake Maggiore', as Suarez recalled. Surrounded by a balustrade and decorated with sculpture, the original design allowed for tropical plantings; these were lost in the hurricane of 1926 and never restored. As Rebecca Davidson has written: 'Vizcaya's design here shows the clearest expression of that interplay between art and nature first formulated as an ideal in the Italian Renaissance garden. The house and gardens are both protected from their natural surroundings and extended into them by the stone breakwater. Architecture and landscape form an integral composition, and the boundaries of each disappear'.

Nemours

In the lovely Brandywine Valley to the northwest of Wilmington, Delaware, lies 196–197 a clutch of historic sites: Longwood, Winterthur and Nemours. The mansion of Nemours was built for Alfred I du Pont in 1909–10 by the firm of Carrère and Hastings. It was reminiscent of the style of the Louis XVI period. The architecture, reflecting the family origins in France, thereby established a tone for the gardens. The dominant central axis was meant to summon up an image of the French formal style. Yet from the outset, the layout differed markedly from the prototype – in form, scale and planting. The construction of a colonnade in 1926 further curtailed an already foreshortened vista and added the new associations of Schönbrunn's Gloriette. Moreover, when Alfred Victor du Pont made additions to his father's original design in the years between 1928 and 1932, this was to provide an architectural transition into the informality of an English-style landscape garden.

Nemours has thus evolved over the years into a garden of many influences and many souvenirs. Here are marble sphinxes, modelled after Louise de la Vallière, who, as Louis XIV's mistress, helped instigate the downfall of Nicolas Fouquet at Vaux-le-Vicomte; these were transported from Jean-Baptiste Colbert's château of Sceaux. Here are gates constructed in 1588 and brought from Wimbledon Manor. And here are gates made for Catherine the Great and brought from the old St Petersburg. Yet in spring the dogwoods remind the visitor that Europe is far away.

Nemours's attractive little mansion is rendered in pink stucco with Indiana limestone trim. To the west side stretches the main axis without the mediation of a parterre, which is tucked away instead on the south side. A modest configuration in box, the parterre is filled with tulips in the spring and provides a discrete area away from the grandeur of the vista.

The land to the west dips and then rises to the colonnade which, standing out white against a backdrop of woodland, dominates the main axis. The vista is framed from the mansion by stepped planting to either side: *Cryptomeria japonica*, whose conical habit recalls the cypresses of Italy; compact pink-flowering horse chestnut, evocative of France; and the noble pin oaks (*Quercus palustris*) of North America towering above and behind. The Japanese cryptomeria have recently been replanted and have yet to regain their intended shape. Within this allée large vases mark the progressive fall of steps set in lawn. The gentle descent leads to a large reflecting pool and to a so-called 'maze garden' on the rise to the colonnade.

The pattern of the 'maze' can best be appreciated when seen from the air or from atop the colonnade; it suggests a *parterre de compartiment* in the style of Dézallier d'Argenville. Yet this pattern is expressed not as a low parterre but as a relief in taller hedgework; from this comes the somewhat misleading notion of a maze. The outer hedges are the tallest and composed of Canadian hemlock (*Tsuga canadensis*); the inner ones are of Helleri holly, set off by the contrasting green of grass. Tulips enliven the design in spring. The centre of the composition is dominated by the figures of 'Achievement' by Henri Crenier. They were originally in gold leaf, now just painted gold. Rising out of a bowl like a Renaissance fountain, they are surely intended to recall the figure of Oceanus in the Isolotto of the Boboli Gardens. The copies of the tritons or mermen from the Boboli Gardens to either side of 'Achievement' reinforce the allusion; the bases are carved with the face of Neptune. The four seasons around the reflecting pool – classical mythology with Art Nouveau style – take up the traditional supporting roles in the cosmology.

Before the construction of the colonnade – a severely reduced version of Schönbrunn's celebrated Gloriette – the vista led to a second reflecting pool; the garden must have felt more expansive. This pool was replaced by the so-called

The Isolotto in the Boboli Gardens in Florence with the Fountain of Oceanus at its centre, the inspiration for 'Achievement' at Nemours, shown on p.197.

View from the mansion of Nemours down the central axis to the west towards the 'maze garden' and the colonnade; photograph taken *c.* 1926–28.

'sunken gardens' – a cascade, steps and retaining walls built in travertine marble. From the terrace beneath the colonnade, the vista to the west is over undulating lawns and a serpentine lake to a circular temple as the termination of the axis. While the formal relationship is maintained by the position of the temple and supporting lines of planting, regularity in the landscape has all but dissolved. The rotunda houses the statue of Diana the Huntress, cast by Jean Antoine Houdon in 1780. Looking back to the east, the visitor can enjoy once more the view over clipped hedges to the mansion framed by the trees of the triple allée.

View from the Box Walk at Dumbarton Oaks down into the Hornbeam Ellipse.

Dumbarton Oaks

The gardens of Dumbarton Oaks in Georgetown, Washington D.C., are closely 198–199 associated with the name of Beatrix Farrand; they are usually cited as the masterpiece of 'America's Gertrude Jekyll'. It is often assumed that what we see today was created entirely by Farrand working hand-in-hand with the owners, Robert and more especially Mildred Bliss, during the 1920s and 1930s. This is only part of the story. Many of the most memorable features of the formal layout – the Pebble Garden or the Ellipse for example – only received their final embellishments some forty years after the initial design and following Farrand's death; other features – notably the North Vista – have lost their first plantings; and others again – notably the Rose Garden – represent a modified version of Farrand's true conception. Moreover, with the loss of some twenty-eight acres of the original garden along the stream to the north (now Rock Creek Park), the relationship of the formal to informal has changed beyond bounds.

Dumbarton Oaks has thus evolved continuously. Despite alterations of form and function, it remains an exceedingly satisfying alliance of art and nature: still the creation of Beatrix Farrand, but equally the work of colleagues and disciples. In spring, after the sudden burst of magnolias, the visitor may enjoy the views over terraces to pink puffs of cherry blossom against silver-branched beeches and

DUMBARTON · OAKS · GEORGETOWN · D·C·

woodland tinged lime green. In the heat of summer evenings, when the fire-flies glow and the cicadas chirp, the Arbor Terrace is scented with tuberose. And on clear autumn mornings, when the grass and fallen leaves are moist with dew, the visitor may still enjoy persisting herbaceous borders and the berries of crab apple and *Ampelopsis*.

A topographical watercolour of 1935 by Ernest Clegg illustrates the structure of the garden Beatrix Farrand helped create between 1922 and 1933 – 'the best and most deeply-felt work of a fifty-year practice', as she later recalled. Most of what we know of Dumbarton Oaks today is present in outline if not in detail: the configuration of interlocking terraces that lead into a long Box Walk and the Ellipse; the North Vista placed axially to the north façade of the house; the silver maple allée and vegetable gardens to the eastern boundary; the informal gardens towards the lower slopes of the hillside. Of the original planting, however, much has changed over time. This is due, above all, to the failure of box in the severity of Washington's summer and winter. It seems ironic that the plant Claude Mollet had used at Anet around 1582 for its resistance to the 'extremes of heat and cold' should have proved a victim to the vicissitudes of frost and sunshine.

The North Vista was entirely enclosed by box hedging. It was narrowed by insets to a straight walk or 'tunnel' leading down to the Forsythia Dell. This was an elegantly simple layout of three sets of shallow brick steps set into lawn as at Nemours. Two cedars emphasized the symmetry. With the demise of the box,

Topographical view in watercolour by Ernest Clegg, 1935. The North Vista is apparent below the house; the Box Walk and Box Ellipse (later the Hornbeam Ellipse) run parallel to it from the Box Terrace and Rose Garden (top to centre left); along the side of the Box Walk is the tennis court which later became the Pebble Garden. Part of the lower informal landscape along the stream was later severed from the garden and incorporated into Rock Creek Park.

220

Farrand reproduced the effect through stone walls, on which carefully pruned wisterias were trained; when flowering in May they transform the North Vista. The Box Terrace with central urn also witnessed a successful replanting in ivy around ornate pebblework. This was by Farrand's colleague Ruth Havey and shows a characteristically more elaborate approach.

The loss of box edging in the Rose Garden has resulted in less felicitous alterations. In her *Plant Book* of 1941, prepared as a record for Dumbarton Oaks, Farrand recalled the importance of the winter season when Robert and Mildred Bliss were usually in residence. She wrote that 'the thought behind the planting of the Rose Garden has been given quite as much to the evergreen and enduring outlines and form as to the Roses, which, at their season, give added charm to this level. The Roses in the Rose Garden are really only secondary to the general design of the garden and its form and mass'. At first the box edging was replaced by candytuft, but then subsequently by bluestone. Two photographs of 1927 and 1964 show how delightful the original must have looked – suggestive of an old English parterre. The influence of Gertrude Jekyll is apparent in the careful gradation of colours. Farrand wrote: 'In choosing the colors for the Roses in general, the pink and salmon color-sorts have been selected for the south third, together with a few of the very deep red ones, such as Etoile de Hollande and Ami Quinard. The centre third of the garden was planted more particularly with salmon-colored and yellowish pink Roses, while the northern third was given over entirely to yellow or predominantly yellow and orange sorts'. Preserving the original effects and the stocks of old roses remains a challenging task.

Nowhere is the replacement of the box more dramatic than in the Ellipse. This was originally a space of extreme simplicity and quietness: a central fountain pool, wreathed in ivy, surrounded by lawn and box and overhung with silver maples. The new design by Alden Hopkins, at the time of Farrand's death in 1959, achieved a grander, more architectonic quality through the use of pleached hornbeams – rather French in character. The central pool was converted into a dominant architectural focus, yet a greater sense of space resulted from the glimpses out between the sinewy hornbeam stems. For all these changes, the space retains the tranquillity Farrand always intended.

The Pebble Garden illustrates still further the progression towards the more elaborate decorative style that replaced Farrand's original designs. For the water

The Rose Garden in 1927 showing the dominant role of boxwork; and (above) the Rose Garden today, the box edging replaced with bluestone.

parterre was completed in 1961, being converted from the old tennis court. This is a compelling reinterpretation of traditional parterre forms. Diverse pebbles from the beaches of Mexico are used between curving patterns in stone; this is like the coloured materials between box broderie. To enhance the lustre of the pebbles, a thin film of water floats over the centre of the composition. *Parterre de broderie* and *parterre d'eau* have become unified.

Hatfield House

200   If one had to choose a single garden to exemplify formal planting traditions over five centuries, it would surely be Hatfield House in Hertfordshire. As Roy Strong has written: 'Robert Cecil's Hatfield, planted between 1607 and 1612, is the most fully documented of all Jacobean gardens'. What the visitor sees today, however, is primarily the creation of the Marchioness of Salisbury over the past two decades, her layouts deftly matched to medieval and Renaissance brick façades and to Victorian parterre, maze and gazebos. Through inspired planting, she has succeeded in crafting a series of gardens that look as though they survive from the time of Robert Cecil and his gardeners Mountain Jennings, Salomon de Caus and John Tradescant the Elder.

Cecil's splendid mansion was built under Robert Lyminge's direction to replace the Old Palace of c. 1480–97, most of which was demolished in 1608. The fortunate preservation of the west wing of this Palace, the Banqueting Hall, has left a backdrop for the Knot Garden. This was created in 1980–81 as part of the more extensive West Gardens which include the Privy Garden, the Scented Garden and the Wilderness.

The patterns of the four quarters may be enjoyed from the raised walks. Here are 'open knots' of gravel and 'closed knots' of flowers, but the circles and squares are traced in box rather than the herbs of the original Jacobean models. Here are phillyreas clipped into balls – the *Phillyrea latifolia* of Gerard as well as the Victorian *P. decora*. And here are columbines, *Aquilegia* 'Red Spurless' and 'Cottage Double Pink', as well as the North American aster, *Aster tradescantii*, introduced in 1633 and named after the son of Cecil's plantsman. In spring this is a delightful mosaic of orange crown imperial, pink and white tulip 'Lac van Rijn', white hyacinth and yellow jonquils. They follow the chaste pink blossoms of the sweet almond tree.

The walk from the Knot Garden along the east side of the Privy Garden takes the visitor beneath pleached limes that may date back to the eighteenth century. In the shadow of a wall, shade-loving flowers light up the squally days of early spring – anemones, primroses and hellebores. In summer, the limes cast welcome shade. The Privy Garden was originally designed c. 1900 by Lady Gwendolen Cecil, the youngest daughter of the 3rd Marquess, but has been replanted in recent years with new forms of old-fashioned roses, flowering not once but perpetually throughout the summer season.

Perhaps the consummate achievement in planting design, however, is the parterre of the East Gardens. In the 1970s, making use of the sixteen square plots inherited from the Victorian scheme and from the replanting under the 5th Marquess, Lady Salisbury created an herbaceous parterre, framed by walks of mop-headed evergreen oaks. It draws inspiration from the traditions of Gertrude Jekyll and Norah Lindsay. It lies beneath the windows of the east façade. The simple beds are edged with box and filled with a profusion of flowers and shrubs. In the summer, old-fashioned roses, sweet peas, foxgloves, carnations, lavender and lilies create cascades and spikes of white, pinks, reds and mauves. Beyond, on the terrace below, is the dark geometry of the maze laid out in 1840; and further still, the 'New Pond' with its irregular shoreline.

In spring, the Lent Lily *Narcissus pseudonarcissus* carpets the ground around the New Pond. A few bulbs, brought from a copse at Cranborne in Dorset by Lady Gwendolen Cecil, have given rise to hundreds and thousands of wild daffodils. Here the imagination may roam over generations past. In the hollow where the New Pond now lies, we might think of Mountain Jennings laying out the formal diamond-shaped 'Dell' in the cold of January 1612. At the centre of his 'water parterre' he designed a pavalion to float like a miniature Chenonceaux; it was flanked by sea-monster fountains. We might think of the Dutchman Simon Sturtevant the previous summer furnishing a rock fountain with the figure of Neptune. Or we might think of Buckett painting Neptune in polychrome for the visit of James I. We might think of Marie de Médicis' gardeners coming all the way from Paris to plant her gift of five hundred fruit trees in the winter of 1611. Or we might think of Tradescant receiving one of those double anemones from the botanist L'Ecluse that were to grace the Duke of Sermoneta's garden near Cisterna.

Some two hundred years later the 2nd Marquess of Salisbury revived the Jacobean terraces in time for the visit of the young Queen Victoria in 1846. We may see the parterre and maze being planted out over the seasons of 1840 and 1841. They replaced the open parkland where Lady Emily Mary Hill, wife of the 1st Marquess, had hunted the hounds till nearly eighty, half-blind and strapped to her horse. During the spring and summer of 1873, we may see the head gardener Mr Bennett organizing the planting of calceolarias and pelargoniums in the Privy Garden or checking the progress of the carpet bedding in the East Garden. Or we may see the 3rd Marquess, Prime Minster three times, peddling his tricycle along the asphalt beneath the pleached limes. We may see guests playing croquet on the lawn just as their forerunners had played bowls. Or we may see Lady Gwendolen lifting the sod to place the first generation of Lent Lilies around the New Pond, where giant plane trees remained the only witness to all that had passed before.

Some three generations later, Lady Salisbury received a present from Count Charles de Noailles. It was some plants of *Anemone coronaria* sub species *grassensis*, the species that gives rise to the doubles anemones. He had found them in the South of France. Thus, today's visitor to Hatfield will do well to look out for Tradescant's velvet anemones. Jacobean knots, water parterre and sea monsters may have vanished with the lives of those who once animated the garden, but in this one flower there is a glimpse of the Renaissance garden.

*　　*　　*

In the future as in the past, garden designers will take inspiration from their predecessors in the formal tradition. Lady Salisbury's work at Hatfield House is matched by recent creations that are both modern in expression and historical in allusion – from Sutton Place in Surrey to the Manoir d'Eyrignac in the Dordogne. The future for the historic garden itself is less certain. For some, the way forward lies with increasing attention to physical authenticity, whether through research into materials and methods, or through garden archaeology and the re-creation of *plate-bandes* or carpet bedding. For others, the museum of garden history offers the best model: Geoffrey Jellicoe's Moody Gardens in Galveston, Texas, for example. For some, it is more a matter of fidelity to the garden as a text, the palimpsest that has been worked on by generation after generation. And for others, it is the challenge of revitalizing the activities and functions that once gave meaning to the original. Whatever truth there diverse ways embody, one thing is certain: the past must continue to fire the imagination of the owner and visitor alike as it has done for five centuries.

Manoir d'Eyrignac, Aquitaine, a modern garden that evokes the formality of the past.

Gazetteer of Major Formal Gardens

100 gardens representing the formal tradition over five centuries

---

The gazetteer contains a selection of sites referred to in the main text. It provides supplementary information on the history of these sites and indicates what features survive from the original layouts. Information on opening is based on 1991 times or on times given in other recent publications. Place-names have been left in their original languages. Where the garden has been described at length in the text, the entry is left brief. Gardens illustrated are distinguished by an asterisk.

Anet (château d'), Anet, Centre. Original design by Philibert de l'Orme from c. 1546 to 1552 for Henri II's mistress Diane de Poitiers. The architectural fragments that survive from the garden of this period include the following: charming terraces linking the gatehouse to pavilions, approached up oval steps based on Bramante's Belvedere Court in Rome and surmounted by a chimney in the form of a sarcophagus; a marble fountain (relocated in grounds); small portion of brick and stone mosaic paving from the original gallery. Grounds completely redesigned by Le Nôtre or more probably Claude Desgots 1681–88, then later as an informal park.
Owner: M. de Yturbe, tel: 37 41 90 07. Garden largely visible (but not accessible) during visits to château. Open from All Saints to 1 April inclusive, Sat 2pm to 5pm, Sun and holidays 10am to 11.30am and 2pm to 5pm; from 1 April to 1 November inclusive, daily 2.30pm to 6.30pm, Sun and holidays 10am to 11.30am and 2.30pm to 6.30pm. Closed Tuesday.

*Audley End, Saffron Walden, Essex. Original design of 1825–33 (probably by William Sawrey Gilpin and owner, 3rd Baron Braybrooke) for geometric flower garden before east façade of house restored with great care in recent years. To north-west of house lies the remains of its informal predecessor, the Elysian Garden of the 1780s. In the house, paintings by William Tompkins of 1788 show the regular configuration of the flower beds that decorated the Elysian Garden (comparable to the Hartwell Plans of 1799). To the immediate west of the Elysian Garden lies the formal Rose Garden, laid out with otter pool in 1868.
Owner: English Heritage, tel: 0799 22399. Open from Good Friday or April 1 (whichever is earlier) to September 30, Tues to Sun (except Bank Hols) 1pm to 6pm; park and garden open from 12 noon.

*Augustusburg, Brühl, Nordrhein-Westfalen. Of the original layout of 1728 by Dominique Girard for Kurfürst and Fürstbischof Clemens August, only the parterre zone survives largely intact. Restored in the 1930s and again after the Second World War, it represents a modified version of the original *parterre de broderie mêlée de massifs de gazon*: the *plate-bandes* contain modern flowers; and the original ornamentation of figures or vases, having been lost, were at first replaced by yew pyramids. These were later removed, since topiary was absent in Girard's design – as at Nymphenburg and Nordkirchen.
Owner: Land Nordrhein-Westfalen, tel: 022 32 42471. Open daily from dawn to dusk.

Bacon's Castle, Surry County, Virginia. Bacon's Castle dates from 1665 and the garden would appear to have been laid out c. 1680 by Arthur Allen II. Through recent extensive excavations, the garden has been unearthed and it now represents, albeit as a reconstruction, the earliest surviving example of garden design in the New World. The style is simple and functional: a rectangle some 362′ by 192′ divided by paths into eight principal rectilinear plots. The whole was bounded on the north side by a wall and on the other three sides by a hedge or ditch that has left no trace in the ground; there were some signs of additional garden structures, possibly ornamental seats. Largely used as a kitchen garden, as evidence of planting rows and bell jars indicates. The archaeologist, Nicholas Luccketti, writes that the material and cultural conditions prevented more elaborate gardening: 'Rampant disease, dreadfully short life spans, and hostile inhabitants created a harsh disrupted world where normal behaviour patterns were distorted'.
Owner: Association for the Preservation of Virginia Antiquities, tel: 804 357 5976 or 804 866 8483. Open Tues to Fri and Sunday 12 noon to 4pm and Sat 10am to 4pm.

*Beeckesteyn, Velsen-Zuid, Noord-Holland. Original design of c. 1766–72 by Johann Georg Michael (1738–1800), in which irregular landscape garden was added to essentially regular layout of first half of eighteenth century. The new style suggests Michael's acquaintance with English models from Batty Langley to Stowe, but many formal or axial elements were retained as Michael's plan of 1772 indicates. 'Restoration' of the 1950s reinstated only the broad outlines of this plan and added some modern features. 'Beeckestijn' is an alternative spelling.
Owner: Gemeente Velsen, tel: 02550-61444. Open daily.

*Biltmore, Asheville, North Carolina. Frederick Law Olmsted was engaged in 1888 to provide landscaping to George Vanderbilt's 255-room château and vast estate. In a wider informal setting, Olmsted created a series of formal areas including the following: a lawn, ramps and avenue (the Esplanade and Vista) stretching up to the figure of Diana; the walled garden with elaborate pergola; and a terrace known as the Italian Garden. The first design for this terrace (1892) indicated a series of parterres between pools, but in the plan of 1894 this was simplified to the three large pools that dominate the garden today. These recall the fish ponds of Villa d'Este, but the planting of lotus and water-lilies give them a very different character. Although designated for tennis, the terrace lawn was used for croquet by 1905; Olmsted envisaged a separate bowling garden in his plans of 1892 and 1894.
Owner: Biltmore Estate, tel: 704 255 1776. Open daily 9am to 5pm (except Thanksgiving, Christmas and New Year's Day).

*Blenheim Palace, Woodstock, Oxfordshire. Achille Duchêne's design from 1925 to 1930 for the two water terraces on the west side of the palace overlooking 'Capability' Brown's lake. Also of interest is the Italian Garden before the east façade (1900s). Designed by Duchêne, the box broderie is more characteristically French; the parterre is embellished with roses and orange trees. The Mermaid Fountain at the centre is by the American sculptor Waldo Story who had worked previously at Cliveden (Shell Fountain 1897).
Owner: His Grace the Duke of Marlborough, tel: 0993 811325. Formal gardens open from March to October, 11am to 6pm.

*Blickling Hall, Aylsham, Norfolk. Norah Lindsay's replanting from 1932 of earlier east parterre by Lady Lothian in formal setting by Matthew Digby Wyatt and Markham Nesfield (1871–77). Axial relationship of this garden to temple of 1730s and to flanking wildernesses that date back to the early eighteenth century. These were replanted in formal configuration in the 1860s and are presently in course of restoration. South front of Blickling Hall set off by magnificent yew hedges.
Owner: The National Trust, tel: Aylsham 733084. Open from March 30 to October 27, Tues, Wed, Fri, Sat, Sun and Bank Hol Mon, 12 noon to 5pm. (house from 1pm).

*Boboli (Giardino di), Firenze. Orginally designed by Tribolo for Cosimo de' Medici and his wife Eleonora of Toledo from 1549, but embellished by a range of other artists including Baccio Bandinelli, Vasari, Ammannati, Buontalenti and Giambologna until 1590. The lunette by Giusto Utens of 1599 records this first phase. A second phase was instituted in the 1630s. It brought the transformation of the planted amphitheatre into a stone one and the extension of the garden to the west along the long cypress avenue or Viottolone to the oval pool and island or Isolotto, embellished by the Oceanus Fountain and orange trees. The enhanced architectonic quality and the expansion in scale represented the influence of new Baroque garden planning.

Owner: Italian State. Open daily from 9am to sunset. Closed on public holidays.

*Bodnant Garden, Tal-y-Cafn, Gwynedd, Wales. Although the gardens were begun by Henry Pochin after 1874, the formal terraces were largely the work of his daughter Laura and grandson Henry, later the second Lord Aberconway. In the period between 1901 and 1953 through patronage of plant collectors from George Forrest to Kingdon Ward, Lord Aberconway also helped embellish the woodland garden known as the Dell. Especially interesting in the formal gardens is the Canal Terrace with the following features: the Pin Mill at one end, reconstructed in 1939 from a derelict building in Gloucestershire (c. 1730); and the garden theatre at the other end, constructed out of yew hedges in the manner of Italian prototypes (Marlia, Rizzardi etc.) and furnished with a seat after William Kent.

Owner: The National Trust, tel: 0492 650460. Open March 16 to October 31, daily 10am to 5pm.

Bowood House, Calne, Wiltshire. Within the wider setting of 'Capability' Brown's landscape grounds (including cascade by Charles Hamilton of Painshill), there is a superb formal terrace garden redeveloped by George Kennedy in the early 1850s. This was first called 'French' and only later 'Italian'. It was depicted by E. Adveno Brooke in 1856 with individual beds devoted to separate species (e.g. red pelargoniums) in the style known as 'massing'; the columnar trees were suggestive of the cypresses of Italy. It is well preserved today.

Owner: The Earl and Countess of Shelburne, tel: 0249 812102. Open March to November, daily including Bank Hols, 11am to 6pm.

Bramham Park, Wetherby, West Yorkshire. Initial layout c. 1670–1710, possibly by the owner Robert Benson (d.1731) and his gardener Robert Fleming. Alterations made in 1720s may have been to designs by John Wood the Elder, who produced a plan of the finished garden c. 1725–28. Bramham belongs within the tradition of woodland or forest gardens, stretching back to Cassiobury in the seventeenth century. Like the contemporary St Paul's Walden Bury or Chiswick House, the 'parterre' was reduced to a minimum, and trees came close to the house which was completed in 1710 (restored 1906–15 after fire of 1828). Parterre now replaced with rose garden and only the head of former cascade leading southwards remains. The many woodland walks laid out in asymmetrical configuration have been preserved and replanting took place after the storm of 1962. Tall beech hedges are notable. A range of garden build-ings or ornaments survive, some from the period of George Lane Fox (d.1773).

Owner: Mr and Mrs George Lane Fox, tel: 0937 844265. House and Grounds open from June 16 to September 1 – Suns, Tues, Weds and Thurs also Bank Hol Mon 1.15pm to 5.30pm. Gardens only open on some holidays in spring.

*Brécy (château de), Saint-Gabriel-Brécy, Basse-Normandie. François Mansart, one of the creators of the French Classical style of architecture, may have been associated with this small but sophisticated layout of five terraces rising and broadening away from the house. Certainly, the decorative style of the stonework corresponds to the contemporary *Livre d'architecture* (1631) by Alexandre Francini. The curved steps between the second and third terraces, guarded by two-headed lions, are noteworthy as a reinterpretation of the form displayed at the Vatican Belvedere and later at Anet. The box broderie of the first terrace is a modern planting based on André Mollet's *Le Jardin de plaisir* (1651).

Owner: Mme Yolande de Lacretelle, tel: 31 80 11 48. Open daily (except Wed) from 10 am to 12 noon and from 3pm to 6pm; closed from 5 January to 28 February.

*Buonaccorsi (Giardino), Potenza Picena, Le Marche. Of great importance is the survival on the upper terrace of Renaissance-style flower beds in diamond, lozenge and star shapes. These are depicted in an anonymous painting of the mid-eighteenth century. The terraces immediately below the upper terrace have also remained largely as portrayed and contain notable sculptural figures.

Owner: Società Agripicena, tel: 0733 688189. Open daily from 8am to 12 noon.

*Canon (château de), Canon, Basse-Normandie. This essentially woodland garden was created by Elie de Beaumont between 1768 and 1783 taking advantage of an earlier geometric layout of 1727. The central axis to the west of the house consists in a grass parterre with busts and a rectangular water basin enclosed by pleached limes, and an avenue stretching into the distance. The main cross axis is terminated by the crimson Kiosque Chinois and the Temple de la Pleureuse respectively; subsidiary walks lead to other varied garden structures. The kitchen garden or Chartreuses is especially remarkable with its 13 walled enclosures.

Owner: famille de Mézerac tel: 31 20 05 07 or 31 20 02 72. Open from Easter to 30 June, Sat, Sun and public hols 2pm to 7pm; and from 1 July to 30 September, daily (except Tues), afternoons from 2pm.

*Caserta (Palazzo Reale), near Napoli, Campania. Original design as presented by Luigi Vanvitelli in 1756 much modified by his son Carlo during construction from 1777 to 1783. To the celebrated formal 'river road' an informal English garden was added by John Graefer after 1786. Many later alterations around palace and 'river road'.

Owner: Italian State, Open daily 9am to 1 hour before sunset except Mon and public hols.

Castle Bromwich Hall Gardens, near Birmingham, West Midlands. The gardens of Castle Bromwich Hall are of interest as an example of a formal layout of the late seventeenth and early eighteenth century revitalized in the nineteenth century. The original layout goes back to the time of Sir John Bridgeman I (1631–1710). He and his wife consulted the architect William Winde, who appears to have provided designs for parterres c. 1698 and who wrote with instructions on planting. An alternative parterre design of 1701 is attributed to George London, and Charles Hatton provided a detailed account of planting a wilderness in 1699. The gardens were then extended westwards by Bridgeman's son. A Holly Walk terminated by an Orangery and a Music Room, a wilderness and kitchen gardens were in existence by the 1730s. An engraving of 1726 by Henry Beighton suggests that the main parterre to the west of the house was of *gazon coupé*; recent archaeology, however, indicates that a simpler design may have been implemented.

Although 'Capability' Brown was subsequently employed in landscaping the park from 1766, the walls and terraces survived. After a period of absence, the family returned to Castle Bromwich Hall in 1820 and the gardens were brought back to life again. A further phase of formal gardening began in the mid-nineteenth century; a flower parterre in the form of four Maltese Crosses, unearthed in excavation, corresponds approximately to a photograph of 1868.

At present the lower terraces are in process of restoration to the period c.1740 (CBHG Trust launched 1985); the upper terraces around the house are under separate ownership.

Owner: CBHG Trust, tel: 021 749 4100.

Open from April 2 to September 30, Mon to Thur 1.30pm to 4.30pm (closed Friday), and Sat, Sun and Bank Hol Mon 2pm to 6pm.

*Chantilly (château de), Chantilly, Picardie. First created by Le Nôtre from 1662/3 for Louis II de Bourbon, a great military figure known as 'Le Grand Condé'. He was assisted by his brother-in-law and nephew, Pierre and Claude Desgots, the hydraulic engineer Jacques de Manse and the architect Daniel Gittard. The central axis of the layout passes to the east of the château. Taking advantage of a change in level, the approach forms a dramatic slope up to the palace, from where the gardens are first visible. The axis continues through two identical water parterres (1666) across a gigantic canal (on the cross axis) to a grass theatre, originally a formal *vertugadin*. This canal was built between 1671–2 and 1681. To the west lay the Parterre de l'Orangerie with orangery of 1683–86 designed by Hardouin-Mansart, forming part of elaborate gardens stretching some half a mile to the west; all this was later replaced by English gardens. The woodland zone to the south east was developed into a geometric bosquet garden in the mid-eighteenth century; here was the spiral course for the game of 'goose' and the pinwheel labyrinth. The formal Ile d'Amour and Ile des Jeux were redesigned in the triangle between the orangery and water parterres in 1765. Little of all this remains today, but the informal Hameau garden of 1774/5 survives to the east of the water parterres as a charming complement to the grand formal layout.

Owner: Institut de France, tel: 44 57 03 62 or 44 57 08 00. Open from 1 April to 30 October, daily except Tues, 10am to 6pm (10.30am to 5pm in off season).

*Charlottenhof, Potsdam, Berlin. Created by Peter Joseph Lenné from 1826 and largely in the 1830s as an adjunct to the extensive formal and informal grounds at Potsdam, stretching between Sanssouci and the Neues Palais. The influence of ancient Rome is apparent, whether in the Hippodrome Garden, the garden around the villa of Charlottenhof itself or the area known as the Roman Baths. Restored in recent years.

Owner: Staatliche Schlösser und Gärten, Potsdam-Sanssouci, tel: 970281. Open daily from 6am to dusk.

*Chastleton House, Chastleton, Oxfordshire. Formal garden of concentric rose beds, box topiary and yew hedges dating back to the early seventeenth century but probably replanted around 1828.

Owner: The National Trust, but not yet open to the public.

*Chatsworth, near Bakewell, Derbyshire. From the original formal layout of 1685–c. 1703 for the 1st Duke of Devonshire by George London and others, the following features were incorporated into the later landscaping: Grillet's cascade (c. 1696; rebuilt c. 1702) and Archer's pavilion (1703) to the east; and Cibber's Seahorse Fountain (1690s) and the long Canal Pond (1702–3) to the south. The elaborate parterres and bosquets depicted by Kip and Knyff in 1699 were, however, replaced by informal lawns when 'Capability' Brown worked for the 4th Duke c. 1755–64. A painting by William Marlow shows the cascade and canal terrace in the midst of the new landscape park.
Around these formal features, the grounds have been restructured continuously from the early nineteenth century to the present day. To the east lies: Wyatville's Broad Walk of the 1820s, replanted with golden and fastigiate yews around 1900; the formal Rose Garden alongside the 1st Duke's greenhouse of c. 1697–99, which replaced the 'French Garden' of the nineteenth century; the cascade partially reconstructed c. 1833 and topped by an aqueduct modelled by Paxton on that at Wilhelmshöhe. To the south east lies: the Ring Pond (1690s) integrated into the formal Serpentine Beech Hedge of 1953; and the Maze of 1962 planted on the site of Paxton's Great Conservatory (1836–40 and demolished 1920). To the south lies: the Seahorse Fountain framed by pleached limes planted in 1952; and the Canal Pond with Paxton's Emperor Fountain of 1843–4. And to the west lies: the private formal garden, first laid out by Wyatville c. 1830 and replanted as a parterre in 1963.

Owner: Chatsworth House Trust, tel: 0246

582204. *Open from March 24 to November 3, daily 11am to 4.30pm.*

*Chenonceaux (château de), near Tours, Centre. Of the original layout at the time of Diane de Poitiers and Catherine de Médicis (1550s to 1570s) only the architectural outlines and the setting remain; the planted structure is of a later date and style.

Owner: famille Menier, tel: 47 23 90 07. Open every day in conjunction with visits to the château, from 16 March to 15 September, 9am to 7pm; for remainder of the year from 9am to dusk.

*Chiswick House, Chiswick, London. Grounds of mixed formal and informal styles established during the following main periods: from 1710s to 1740s under Lord Burlington (1695–1753) and William Kent (1684–1748); from 1770s–80s under the 5th Duke of Devonshire and Samuel Lapidge (c. 1740–1806); and from 1810s under the 6th Duke and Lewis Kennedy (1789–c. 1840); with restoration c. 1950 and again from the late 1980s (still in progress).

Owner: English Heritage, tel: 081 995 0508. Open daily from dawn to dusk.

Circus (No 4, Circus), Bath, Avon. Reconstruction from late 1980s of a town garden of c. 1760 on the basis of archaeological excavation. Essentially symmetrical formal layout with straight flower borders and circular and elliptical arrangement of flower beds. Small scale of around 100 feet × 40 feet.

Owner: Bath Museums Service & Bath Archaeological Trust, tel: 0225 461111, ext. 2760. Open from beginning of May until end of October, Mon to Fri, 9am to 4.30pm. Closed weekends and Bank Hol.

*Cleves (Tiergarten with Amphitheatre Garden), near Kleve, Nordrhein-Westfalen. Johan Maurits van Nassau-Siegen's Amphitheatre formed part of an extensive landscape on an escarpment at Cleves overlooking the Rhine plain. After returning from the Dutch colonies in Brazil and having become the elector's stadholder at Cleves in 1647, he created a series of artificial viewing mounts, many furnished with trophies symbolizing peace. The Amphitheatre of c. 1660 consisted in an exedra overlooking three pools and a long canal. It seems that an optical device was installed in the window of the exedra to exaggerate the perspective, down past the figures of Minerva in a pool and Mars on a column, to the canal and a hill on the horizon. Minerva and Mars were meant here to personify peace after war. A further dimension was added by the *Fontana Miranda*, an exhibition wall for displaying the wonders of nature and art – water tricks, trophies of hunting and (apparently) four monkey-puzzle trees brought from their native Chile. In the nineteenth century, the Amphitheatre was transformed into a landscape park by the royal gardener, Maximilian Friedrich Weyhe. Under recent restoration a semblance of the original has been reconstructed around the figure of Minerva, a temple and obelisk (1850s).

Owner: Stadtverwaltung Kleve, tel: 02821/8 42 67. Open daily at all times.

*Cliveden, near Maidenhead, Buckinghamshire. Formal gardens from diverse periods. Under Lord Orkney (resident 1696–1739) the grass parterre was established to the south of the house in 1723–4 and this formed the basis for the Victorian parterre of 1851–53 (partially restored 1976). From 1720s and 1730s there are also two garden buildings by Giacomo Leoni and the remains of a yew walk and a grass amphitheatre, later used for plays, concerts and pantomimes. Charles Bridgeman and Alexander Pope are associated with this work. Notable from the period of William Waldorf Astor (resident 1893–1906) are: the Shell Fountain (Fountain of Love) by sculptor Waldo Story at the northern end of the approach avenue; and the Long Garden with its topiary and eighteenth-century Venetian statues.

Owner: The National Trust, tel: 0628 605069. Open from Good Friday to end of October, daily 11am to 6pm or sunset if earlier; from November to December, daily 11am to 4pm. Closed January and February.

*Courances (château de), Courances, Ile-de-France. Site of seventeenth century formal garden, modified in the eighteenth century (the planes along the canals date from 1782 and the rectangular basin replaced a circular one) and swept away by baron de Haber after 1872. Imaginative 'restoration' by Achille Duchêne in the years before the 1914 war; further reconstruction after damage in Second World War.

Owner: M. Jean-Louis de Ganay, tel: 1 64 98 41 18 or 1 45 50 34 24. Open from 31 March to 1 November, Sat, Sun and public hols, 2pm to 6.30pm.

Crowfield Plantation Gardens, near Charleston, South Carolina. Remains of formal garden first laid out for William Middleton c. 1730s and described by Eliza Lucas Pinckney in the early 1740s. According to her account it contained a large rectangular fishpond with a mount at its centre, surmounted by a temple; the garden was terminated by enclosing canals. Grass and flower parterres, a bowling green surrounded by catalpas and 'a thicket of young tall live oaks' were also featured in the description. Vestiges of another mount and the water basins apparent today although only foundations of house survive.

For current status of ownership and conservation, consult Historic Charleston Foundation.

*Drummond Castle Gardens, Muthill, Perthshire (Tayside). Originally laid out about 1630, the terrace garden was reconstructed in the 1820s and 1830s by Lewis Kennedy and his son George, who completed the work in 1838–42. The pattern of beds around a sundial was in the form of a St Andrew's cross. The planting was of rhododendrons and heathers. In an undated painting by Jacob Thompson, however, a flower border seems to be filled with hollyhocks, pelargoniums and stocks, punctuated by conical evergreens – not unlike a French *plate-bande*. Commentators in the period saw the garden as combining

Italian, French and Dutch styles. Today the planting consists in a splendid display of roses and miscellaneous forms of clipped trees.

Owner: The Grimsthorpe and Drummond Castle Trust Ltd. Open from May to August, daily 2pm to 6pm; in September, Wed and Sun 2pm to 6pm.

*Dumbarton Oaks, Georgetown, Washington D.C.** Formal and informal grounds by Beatrix Jones Farrand (1872–1959) for Robert and Mildred Bliss. Established in 1920s and 30s, but developed subsequently by Ruth Havey and Alden Hopkins amongst others.

Owner: Trustees for Harvard University, tel: 202 342 3290. Open from April to October, daily 2pm to 5pm.

*Eremitage (Hofgarten), near Bayreuth, Bayern.** Garden developed by the Markgräfin Wilhelmine, sister of Frederick the Great, around the old palace (Altes Schloss) of 1715–18 and other garden features. The new palace (Neues Schloss), built in 1749–53, resembled the orangery-style of Frederick's Sanssouci, but the centre of the curved structure was dominated by a large water parterre of fanciful sculpture and fountains. With potted plants arranged in tiers it also recalled the orangery gardens of Holland. The outside walls of Joseph Saint-Pierre's building were encrusted with a mosaic of blue, red and yellow glass and glittering crystals and the enclosure was completed by berceaux decked with plants. Today, 'das Neue Schloss' is restored after bomb damage in 1945 but without the trelliswork and original planting. 'Das alte Schloss' survived the bombing. Although it had been altered by Wilhelmine, it retained the original illusion of being a hewn rather than built structure; the rock-encrusted entrance leads into a grotto full of Renaissance-style water tricks. A range of other spectacular garden features are disposed around the grounds in both formal and a somewhat irregular manner that seems to anticipate the English landscape style: the recently restored cascade of the earlier period; Joseph Saint-Pierre's magnificent Lower Grotto (before 1745); and the Ruined Theatre of 1743.

Owner: Bayerische Verwaltung der staatlichen Schlösser, Gärten und Seen, tel: 0921 92561. Open daily.

*Eyrignac (manoir d'Eyrignac), near Salignac, Aquitaine.** A modern formal garden of lawn and clipped trees and shrubs, essentially in shades of green. Created by the owners over the past thirty years on the basis of an earlier layout that had been lost under later plantings. Amongst the notable features are the following: on the axis from the eighteenth-century house a charming parterre of box, set on lawn, framed by a border of flowers in shades of white, yellow, and blue and leading into a stepped walk between clipped yews; an Allée des Charmes on the cross axis, consisting in a symmetrical, repeated pattern of hornbeam buttresses against yew cylinders; and the Allée des Vases, also on the cross axis, formed by indented yew hedging, in the recesses of which sit vases with yew topiary.

Owner: P. Sermadiras de Pouzols de Lile,

tel: 53 28 80 10. Open from 1 July to 30 September, daily 2pm to 6.30pm.*

*Giverny (Fondation Claude Monet), near Evreux, Haute-Normandie.** Gardens of mixed formality and informality created by the artist from around 1890 to his death in 1926 and faithfully restored from 1976. The area close to the house, the so-called Clos Normand (in memory of 'pastures'), combined the order of a botanic garden with the profusion of a cottage garden. The water-lily pond, beyond a railway line (now a road), suggested the English romantic style with oriental influences.

Owner: Institut de France, Académie des beaux-arts, tel: 32 51 28 21, Open from 1 April to 31 October, daily (except Mon) 10am to 6pm (house closed between 12 noon and 2pm).

*Gross-Sedlitz (Barockpark), Heidenau near Dresden.** Of the gardens associated with the court of August der Starke (der Zwinger, der Grosse Garten and Pillnitz) Gross-Sedlitz was one of the most magnificent and survives partially to this day. The original structure of these gardens was strongly determined by August's love of festivity and games. Gross-Sedlitz seems to have received its first design from Johann Christoph Knöffel in 1719, but after the king took possession of the garden in 1723, the work was continued by a Frenchman, Zacharias Longuelune with Matthes Daniel Pöppelmann responsible for the architectural elements. Notable here is Pöppelmann's splendid series of curving steps, known as 'Stille Musik' after the tritons playing music along the balustrade. Italian influences were dominant in these steps and cascades, with French models evident in the fountains. Yet, as Dieter Hennebo points out, this wider inspiration does not detract from the distinctness of Gross-Sedlitz as 'amongst the most individualistic creations in the realm of German garden art'.

Owner: Verwaltung der Schlösser und Gärten des Freistaates Sachsen, tel: Heidenau 79212. Open daily from dawn to dusk.

*Gunston Hall, Lorton, Virginia.** Home of George Mason (1725–92), friend of Washington and Jefferson and political thinker (through his help in drafting the Virginia Declaration of Rights, he provided inspiration to later charters of human rights). The house was designed from 1755 with the help of William Buckland and the original garden probably dates from this time. As at Mount Vernon, formal gardens to the south of the house overlooked a naturalistic landscape falling to the River Potomac. Here was a deer park. Very little contemporary evidence survives of the original layout and the best written account – by Mason's son John as late as 1834 – gives few details of style or planting. Only in the description of the four diverging rows of cherry trees on the north front is it possible to visualize something of the original. The restoration of the formal garden around a massive central box allée (grown impressively out of scale) was by the Garden Club of Virginia on the basis of a conjectural appraisal,

without archaeology. It reflects an imaginative vision of the past.

Owner: Commonwealth of Virginia and The National Society of The Colonial Dames of America, tel: 703 550 9220. Open daily (except Christmas) from 9.30am to 5pm.

*Hampton Court Palace, Hampton Court, London.** Gardens of enormous complexity. Although the layout achieved a zenith under William and Mary, the gardens date back originally to the time of Henry VIII. Under Charles II the Great Canal and the later *patte d'oie* was established to the east of the palace; this survives today, although substantially replanted. On the east side of the new Wren block, the Great Parterre was designed by Daniel Marot from 1689 in the form of a hemisphere enclosed by limes. The inner sections were implemented in broderie and the outer ones in grass; 304 clipped yews and 24 clipped silver hollies lined the paths. Today some of those yews have survived as giant mushroom-shaped trees. Although the limes have been replanted recently, the parterre remains essentially in a later style. The Privy Garden to the south of the Wren Block was redesigned in 1690–91 with *gazon coupé*. Although yews and hollies remain, the planting is generally more recent. Of the Wilderness to the north only the Maze has survived, replanted and in somewhat shabby condition, in the midst of later plantings. The knot garden adjoining the Privy Garden was redesigned by Ernest Law in the 1920s. Thus little remains today of the original layouts of Henry VIII or William and Mary, or indeed of the work of Marot, Wren, Talman and George London with Henry Wise.

Owner: Historic Royal Palaces, tel: 081 977 8441. Open daily until dusk or 9pm at the latest.

*Hatfield House, Hatfield, Hertfordshire.** Gardens first created for Robert Cecil 1608–12. These formal gardens were swept away during the eighteenth century when Lady Salisbury, wife of the 1st Marquess, enjoyed hunting in parkland that surrounded the house. The terraced gardens were then re-created by her son the 2nd Marquess from the 1840s and these have been embellished and enriched by further formal gardens up to the present day.

Owner: The Marquess and Marchioness of Salisbury, tel: 0707 262823. West Gardens open daily except Good Friday, 11am to 6pm and East Gardens open only on Mon (except Bank Hol Mon), 2pm to 5pm.

*Hautefort (château de), Hautefort, Aquitaine.** The gardens were created after 1929 when the baron de Bastard and his wife bought the estate and initiated a programme of 'restoration'. On the terraces to the south and east, beneath the dominating château, they laid out parterres decorated by bedding plants – begonias, verbenas and pelargoniums – and topiary in box, yew and thuja. Along the northern side of the esplanade to the west lies an immense tunnel of thuja. This 'restoration' is an imaginative interpretation of earlier traditions of planting, massive in the geometry of its patterns. The gardens have continued to flourish despite a fire in the château in 1968 and the subsequent architectural restoration.

Owner: Mme Durosoy, tel: 53 50 51 23.
Open in conjunction with visits to château, from Palm Sunday to All Saints, daily 9am to 12noon and 2pm to 7pm (Sun afternoon off season, 2pm to 6pm and closed from 25 December to 25 January).

∗**Herrenhausen (Grosser Garten), Hannover, Niedersachsen.** A first, very modest design dates back to 1665–6 under Johann Friedrich von Brunswick-Lüneberg. A second phase came around 1673 under the court architect, Hieronymo Sartorio, and the gardener, Henri Perronet; the Haute Cascade and grotto survive from this period. The final form, however, emerged under Kurfürst Ernst August (later Elector) and more especially his wife Sophie, who brought her gardener to Hanover from Osnabrück in 1682; this was the Frenchman, Martin Charbonnier. At first he was involved in improvements to the existing layout, adding the garden theatre in 1689–93, but after a visit to Holland, he returned in 1696 to enlarge the garden before Sophie died in 1714. This Nouveau Jardin extended the area to the south by over double the previous dimension. Charbonnier created thereby a large zone of diagonal walks and circular spaces for basins and fountains. The hedged quarters were full of fruit trees in regimented ranks. The boundaries were articulated by the canal or Graft (with a hemispherical bulge at the end of the main axis) and by two pavilions at the corners. The influences suggest Dutch gardens like Honselaarsdijk and French models such as Charleval, but brought together in what Dieter Hennebo has called a 'synthesis' of French and Dutch styles. The garden today as restored in 1936–7 and 1960–66, retains much of the original structure and many built features but only aspects of the original planting: the inner *parterre à l'angloise* in cutwork patterns are replaced by broderie, for example; the quarters of the bosquet contain woodland trees instead of fruit trees.

Owner: Städtische Verwaltung der Herrenhäuser Gärten, tel: 0511 168–75 76 or 73 76. Open daily, 8am to sunset.

∗**Hestercombe, near Taunton, Somerset.** Laid out for the Hon. E. W. B. Portman between 1904 and 1909 by Edwin Lutyens and Getrude Jekyll. Restored by Somerset County Council after 1973. In addition to the central Great Plat, there are other formal gardens: an Orangery and adjoining Dutch Garden, a Rose Garden, and the Grey Walk to the north of the parterre.

Owner: Somerset County Council, tel: 0823 87222 or 337222. Open year-round daily, Mon to Fri, 9am to 5pm; and from 1 May to 30 September, Sat and Sun, 2pm to 5pm.

∗**Het Loo (Rijksmuseum), Apeldoorn, Gelderland.** On 20 June 1984 the palace and gardens of Het Loo were opened to the public after a seven-year restoration programme. This returned the grounds to the original formality of the William and Mary period, reversing the process of informal landscaping that had taken place in the eighteenth and nineteenth centuries. They now represent the most authentic example of Baroque planting design. Aspects of the restoration that depart from the original include the following: the parterres of the Upper Garden are only partially restored to accommodate mature trees from the landscape style; the colonnades were reconstructed in artificial stone for financial reasons; most of the sculptures are in synthetic resin and the ornamental features in artificial stone. Also, interestingly, many of the rooms in the palace have been left with later furnishings. The overall impact is, however, remarkable for its fidelity to the original design.

Owner: Netherlands State, tel: 055 212244.
Open daily from April to October, Tues to Sun, 10am to 5pm.

∗**Hidcote Manor Garden, near Mickleton, Gloucestershire.** Created by Major Lawrence Johnston after 1907. Johnston was an American who, having spent his earlier years in France, became a British citizen. Hidcote developed traditions of formal planning into a new type of compartmentalized garden – 'garden rooms' enclosed by hedges – in which the planting effects seemed as casual and haphazard as a cottage garden, yet were carefully ordered. The Red Borders and the White Garden reflect new, calculated effects of colour composition. Hidcote's formal 'garden rooms' include the following: the Old Garden to the south of the house, dominated by a cedar of Lebanon that Johnston inherited and embellished with luxuriant herbaceous borders; the White Garden full of topiary birds and blush-white roses; the Red Borders leading into the Stilt Garden of pleached hornbeam; and the Fuchsia Garden enclosed by a 'tapestry' hedge of green and variegated holly, yew, box and copper beech and filled with a profusion of fuchsias in box-edged beds. Larger formal areas of simple planting are: the Long Walk, a wide grass path on dipping and rising ground, framed by hornbeam hedges; and the Theatre Lawn, enclosed by a yew hedge and focused on an old beech tree at centre-stage. These formal 'garden rooms' are interspersed with informal areas.

Owner: The National Trust, tel: 0386 438333. Open from April to end of October, daily (except Tues and Fri) 11am to 8pm.

Hortus Palatinus (Schlossgarten), Heidelberg, Baden-Württemberg. Salomon de Caus's uncompleted project for Friedrich V's Hortus Palatinus (1614–19 and publicized in De Caus's *Hortus Palatinus* of 1620) was one of the most distinguished manifestations of wider European influences absorbed into German garden design. The terracing suggested Italian models, yet the compartments were without axial dominance. The diverse parterres reflected varied traditions: old-fashioned knots (which were still flourishing in England), discrete flower beds (occurring from Italy to the Low Countries and later known as *parterres de pièces coupées*) and the new broderie of French inspiration. The water parterre was similar to the one planned later by Isaac de Caus for Wilton. The hydraulics and grotto embodied the traditions of Italy and France; it was Salomon who had helped bring those traditions to England. The iconography was complex. Symbols of nature were interwoven with symbols of authority. Friedrich V was equated with mythological or symbolic figures – Hercules and Apollo, Vertumnus and the river gods of the Rhine, Neckar and Main. As Reinhard Zimmermann writes: 'The Hortus Palatinus is at once a symbol of the order of the state, an image of the territory of the Palatinate, and the successor to the ancient Roman practice of controlling Nature'. Of this significant layout, only the following features survive: the structure of the terracing; ruins of most of the stone buildings; and architectural and sculptural elements rebuilt in recent years such as the portal of the large grotto and some ornamented water basins.

Owner: Land Baden-Württemberg. Open at all times.

∗**Iford Manor Gardens, Bradford-on-Avon, Wiltshire.** Sixteenth- to seventeenth-century manor house (remodelled c. 1725–30) purchased by Harold Ainsworth Peto (1854–1933) in 1899. The gardens were created in the first three decades of the twentieth century, taking advantage of some earlier features and plantings, and have been restored since 1965. Three main terraces dominate the site, but their architectural structure is softened by informal planting and by the surrounding landscape. Notable is the main terrace lined with a varied arrangement of columns and antique sculpture and terminated by an eighteenth-century octagonal summer house; from this terrace there are views of hilly countryside through a colonnade and over an oval lily pond. The terraces, artefacts and evergreen plantings – cypress, juniper and phillyrea – recall Italian gardens, but the relaxed disposition of trees, shrubs and climbers is typical of the Edwardian English garden – what Avray Tipping called 'the successful inter-marriage of formal and natural gardening'.

Owner: Mrs Cartwright-Hignett, tel: 02216 3146 or 2840. Open from May to September, Tues, Wed, Thur, Sat and Sun (also Summer Bank Hol) 2pm to 5pm. In April and October, Sun and Easter Mon.

I Tatti (Villa), Settignano, Toscana. This entirely green formal garden set in informal grounds was designed by Cecil Pinsent for Bernard Berenson from 1910. The formal terraces below the villa are ornamented with pebble paving, steps and geometric patterns in clipped box; only on the top terrace are flowers permitted. The central axis is articulated by pyramids in box either side of the pebble-mosaic walk. This highly disciplined evergreen planting characterizes the 'neo-Renaissance' gardens of the early twentieth century.

Owner: Harvard University (Center for Italian Renaissance Studies). Open only on written application or as part of garden tours.

∗**Klein-Glienicke Park, Berlin.** Informal plea-

sure ground first established by Peter Joseph Lenné from 1816, but furnished subsequently with formal elements, both built and planted. Especially notable are the circular flower beds. Under recent restoration the garden is being returned to its condition c. 1840. By then it had been embellished with architectural features to designs by Ludwig Persius and Karl Friedrich Schinkel.
Owner: Schlossverwaltung Schloss Glienicke, tel: 030 8 053041 Open daily from sunrise to sunset.

La Pietra (Villa), Firenze, Toscana. Arthur Acton created the garden from 1904 around the villa dating back to the fifteenth century. Like I Tatti this is primarily an evergreen garden, the hedges enclosing 'garden rooms'. Notable features include: a garden room centred on a fountain and decorated with a colonnade and statuary; a green theatre with Venetian figures by Francesco Bonazza.
Owner: La Pietra Corporation, tel: 055 287838. Open from April to June, by arrangement with Agriturist, Piazza San Firenze 3, Firenze 50100.

•**La Roche-Courbon (château de), Saint-Porchaire, Poitou-Charentes.** Ferdinand Duprat's imaginative re-creation of the formal garden from 1925 to 1935 on the basis of a seventeenth-century painting by Hackaert.
Owner: Société du domaine de la Roche-Courbon, M. and Mme Jacques Badois, tel: 46 95 60 10. Open daily, 9am to 12 noon and 2pm to 6.30pm (5.30 in winter).

•**Le Bois des Moutiers, Varengeville-sur-Mer, Haute-Normandie.** To the house designed by Edwin Lutyens in 1898, a garden was added around the turn of the century with the help of Gertrude Jekyll. Notable features include: the straight approach to the circular forecourt, softened by herbaceous borders and climbers; and a formal rose garden filled with white flowers in box-edged beds. This geometric layout fuses with the surrounding woodland gardens full of rhododendrons.
Owner: famille Mallet, tel: 35 85 10 02. Open from 15 March to 15 November daily, 10am to 12 noon and 2pm to 6pm.

•**Levens Hall, Kendal, Cumbria.** Formal topiary garden orginally laid out from 1689 under the direction of Guillaume Beaumont, but replanned and replanted in the early nineteenth century and box-edged beds now furnished with modern bedding plants. A plan of c. 1730 by Skyring records the earlier layout.
Owner: Mr C. H. Bagot, tel: 05395 60321. Open from Easter Sunday to September 30, daily (except Fri and Sat), 11am to 5pm.

•**Longwood Gardens, Kennett Square, Pennsylvania.** After several tours to Europe, Pierre S. du Pont created the gardens of Longwood, emulating Italian and French prototypes but using modern technology to create spectacular effects of water and lighting. The garden theatre was constructed in 1913–14 and modelled on what he had seen at the Villa Gori in Siena (the original is enclosed by ilex hedges and has wings composed of cypress). By 1915 fountains were in operation on the stage, and these were improved with lighting after 1926.

The Italian Water Garden was laid out between 1925 and 1927 after the example of the water parterre at Villa Gamberaia (itself only redesigned around 1900). Its simplified planting of clipped ivy and grass, and its excessive fountains are far from Gamberaia. The Main Fountain Garden is an eclectic mix, in which there are echoes of the fountains of Villa d'Este and the terraces of Vaux-le-Vicomte. This was completed in the 1930s with an instant backdrop of 500 mature trees, some transplanted at 70 feet. The traditions of garden festivities and fireworks continue today with computerized effects of music, water and lights.
Owner: Longwood Gardens, Inc., tel: 215 388 6741. Open daily, 9am to 6pm (from November to March until 5pm).

Melbourne Hall, Melbourne, Derbyshire. The formal garden of Thomas Coke was first established around 1704 to 1722 on an earlier layout depicted in plan of 1630. London and Wise were consulted, but William Cooke of Warcot seems to have been responsible for the implementation of work in 1704. A plan of 1722 by J. Kirkland illustrates the completed design. Essentially the structure of the layout has survived intact along with water basins, sculpture by Van Nost and an elaborate iron arbour by Robert Bakewell (1706) terminating the main vista. The original planting, however, has been affected by growth and decay and by alterations in the mid-nineteenth century. Fine iron baskets by Devigne are notable near the house in the style that became fashionable in the early nineteenth century. Despite altered planting, a remarkable garden.
Owner: Lord Ralph Kerr, tel: 0332 862502. Open from April to September, Wed, Sat, Sun and Bank Hol Mon 2pm to 6pm.

•**Mellerstain, Gordon, Berwickshire (Borders Region).** Reginald Blomfield's grandiose garden design, created for Lord Binning from 1909 and modified after 1911.
Owner: The Earl of Haddington, tel: 057 381 225. Open at Easter and then from May 1 to September 30, daily (except Sat) 12.30pm to 5pm.

Middleton Place, near Charleston, South Carolina. Home of Henry Middleton from 1741, the original house was destroyed in 1865 during the Civil War and in an earthquake of 1886; only the flanking wing to the south survived. The gardens endured but have been altered over the two subsequent centuries. Notable is the relationship of the formal garden of terraces and pools to the natural landscape beyond. On the main axis, the series of descending grass ramps overlooking the twin 'butterfly lakes' recall the fashion for natural terracing, first made popular through publications by Dézallier d'Argenville and John James (1709 and 1712). These were characteristic of English gardens of the 1720s and 1730s (e.g. Castle Hill, South Molton, Devon) and later of American gardens (e.g. Carter's Grove, James River, Virginia). Most of the planting at Middleton Place altered, although camellias survive from the originals.

Damage was caused by the recent hurricane.
Owner: Middleton Place Foundation, tel: 803 556 6020. Open daily 9am to 5pm.

Montacute House, Yeovil, Somerset. Around the house dating back to late sixteenth century are a series of beautiful formal gardens, largely redesigned in the nineteenth century. The north garden was laid out in the 1840s; the central fountain basin was added in 1894 by R. S. Balfour. Roy Strong writes further that the forecourt with its handsome pavilions and balustraded walls, 'centres on a late nineteenth-century fountain surrounded by flower-beds in the Jekyll vein that can give no notion of the real appearance of a forecourt of an Elizabethan great house'.
Owner: The National Trust, tel: 0935 823289. Open daily (except Tues) 11.30am to 5.30pm or dusk, if earlier.

Monticello, Charlottesville, Virginia. Thomas Jefferson's garden of mixed informality and formality. Created from the 1770s to 1810s, the garden was restored by the Garden Club of Virginia in 1939–41 and has been undergoing further authentic restoration since the late 1970s on the basis of extensive archaeology and archival research. Although Monticello was modelled on certain features of the English landscape style, the design reveals both an underlying geometry as well as regular elements of planting (e.g. elliptical flower beds, symmetrically disposed). As the archaeologist William M. Kelso writes: 'Elsewhere symmetry was obviously the goal; consider the bounds of the rectangular leveled lawns, the rigorous symmetry of the vegetable garden platform, the straight row of houses on the straight Mulberry Row, and the gridiron of trees and vineyard on the south slope'. A notable geometric feature of planting was the pinwheel wilderness of broom which appears on a plan of the 1790s (compare the pinwheel labyrinth of Dézallier d'Argenville 1709, the Rococo labyrinth of Chantilly and the flower garden in the plan of Beeckesteyn).
Owner: Thomas Jefferson Memorial Foundation Inc., tel: 804 295 8181. Open from March 1 to October 31, daily 8am to 5pm and from November 1 to February 28/29, daily (except Christmas) 9am to 4.30pm.

•**Mount Edgcumbe, near Plymouth, Cornwall.** Within the wider setting of a beautiful eighteenth-century landscape park are located the formal 'French' and 'Italian' gardens. Dating back to the first decade of the nineteenth century, they represent a very early example of formal revival. Davis Jacques writes that the French garden 'had beds of flowers, a central fountain, high clipped hedges of ilex and bays, and surrounding trellis-work' while in the Italian garden 'balustraded steps were made to an upper level above a small grotto'. Replanting of the French and Italian gardens began in 1987–88 after several years of research by the Garden History Society.
Owner: City of Plymouth and Cornwall County Council, tel: 0752 822236. Open daily, from sunrise to sunset.
•**Mount Vernon, near Washington, Virginia.**

Home of George Washington from 1754 until 1799. A garden of mixed regularity and irregularity, attached originally to an informal deer park on the banks of the Potomac River. The bowling green on the west side represents a feature of seventeenth- and early-eighteenth-century English gardens retained throughout the pleasure grounds of Maryland and Virginia until the later eighteenth century (e.g. at Mount Clare, Baltimore or Mount Airy, Richmond County). Mount Vernon gardens restored from the 1930s.
Owner: Mount Vernon Ladies' Association, tel: 703 780 2000. Open daily, 9am to 5pm (4pm from November 1 to February 28/9).

*Nemours, Wilmington, Delaware. Formal gardens and informal grounds designed during 1910s to 1930s.
Owner: Alfred I. du Pont Institute of The Nemours Foundation, tel: 302 651 6912. Open for tours from May 1 to November 30, Tues-Sat 9am, 11am, 1pm and 3pm; Sun 11am 1pm and 3pm.

*Nordkirchen (Schlosspark), Nordkirchen, Nordrhein—Westfalen. Recently restored north garden of Achille Duchêne's design (1906–14) within wider formal setting of earlier layout by J. C. Schlaun (from 1725), now decayed but awaiting restoration.
Owner: Land Nordrhein-Westfalen, tel: 02596-1001. Open daily from sunrise to sunset.

*Nymphenburg (Schlosspark), München, Bayern. The origins of the palace and gardens of Nymphenburg date back to the middle years of the seventeenth century. From 1701 the Kurfürst Max Emanuel had the grounds developed, first by Charles Carbonet (canal begun 1701) and then by Dominique Girard and Joseph Effner (from 1715). A plan attributed to Girard c. 1715–20 shows the elaborate parterres and bosquets. That *parterres à l'angloise* framed by low flower borders held a dominant position on the central axis indicates the ascendancy of grass and flowers over broderie and topiary in the Régence and Rococo styles. To the side of the parterres were a series of small bosquets containing courts for skittles and 'Passspiel', a green theatre and a maze. Joseph Effner added a cascade at the far western end of the canal in 1717 and his pavilions (1716–21) formed focal points in the extensive woodland zone to either side of the canal. To the north of one, the so-called Pagodenburg, was a pall-mall court. During the eighteenth century other features were added to the Baroque layout, notably the Amalienburg of 1734–39 and a menagerie of 1781. Between 1804 and 1823, however, F. L. von Sckell transformed the grounds into an informal landscape park, yet retaining the central axis of the canal.
Owner: Bayerische Verwaltung der staatlichen Schlösser, Gärten und Seen, tel: 089 17908-0. Open daily from sunrise to sunset.

*Orto Botanico, Padova, Veneto. Founded in 1545, the botanic garden is primarily of interest in this context for the stone-edged flower beds laid out in various patterns.

Claudia Lazzaro writes: 'The configuration of the entire garden, a great circle in which four large squares are inscribed, remains as it was originally planned. Although the designs within each square were replaced with simpler geometric patterns in the eighteenth century, each unit is a bed of earth planted with specimens, as was the practice in the sixteenth century. Even in its altered state, the garden at Padua suggests more precisely than almost any other extant garden the appearance of compartments of simples in the Renaissance'.
Owner: Università degli Studi di Padova, tel: 049 656614. Open in summer, daily 9am to 5pm, in winter 9am to 1pm and on public hols in summer 10am to 1pm.

*Packwood House, Hockley Heath, Warwickshire. Formal garden dating back to the early seventeenth century but with yew topiary supposedly representing the Sermon on the Mount from the Victorian period.
Owner: The National Trust, tel: 0564 782024. Open from April 1 to September 30, Wed–Sun and Bank Hol Mon 2pm to 6pm; October, Wed–Sun 12.30pm to 4pm.

Pitmedden Garden, Udny, Aberdeenshire (Grampian). Original garden of Sir Alexander Seton dates back to 1664–75. In the restoration since 1956, the parterres were based on those shown in a view of Holyroodhouse, Edinburgh, a generation earlier (1647). The use of bright modern bedding plants in the box-edged beds is striking but inauthentic.
Owner: The National Trust for Scotland, tel: 06513 2352. Open daily 9.30am to sunset.

*Powis Castle, Welshpool, Powys. The original terraced garden has been attributed to William Winde, who had been involved with similar constructions at Cliveden (from 1684–88 he was rebuilding the first Marquess of Powis's London house, while in 1697 he was engaged with 'the D of Powis to the Read [red] Castel'). However, the name of a Frenchman, 'Adrian Duval, native of Rouen', also appears in accounts; payments in 1713 and 1717 confirm a continued involvement stretching back to his arrival in England in 1703. By 1705 John Bridgeman could write: 'I din'd this week at Powis Castle the water-works and fountains that are finished there are much beyond anything I ever saw whose streams play near twenty yards in height the Cascade has too falls of water which concludes in a noble Bason'. The top of that cascade is probably depicted in the foreground of the engraving by Samuel and Nathaniel Buck (1742), but the whole seems to have been removed by 1771 along with parterres and topiary on the low ground. A plan of that date by T. F. Pritchard shows only the basins intact. These were not even cleared away under the landscaping of William Emes in the 1770s. Remarkably, he left the terraces (embellished with statues from Van Nost's workshop, and with aviary and greenhouse) untouched. Despite neglect, Richard Colt Hoare was able to recognize in 1806 that Powis still had the potential to become 'a Villa D'Este in miniature'. One hundred years later that vision was realized

through the restoration work of Violet, wife of the fourth Earl of Powis. From 1911 she began a replanting campaign continued by the National Trust after 1952. With the original yew pyramids and balls grown into vast amorphous shapes and with dramatic additions to the planting palette (e.g. the *Phormium tenax* of New Zealand), the effect today is a remarkable blend of old and new.
Owner: The National Trust, tel: 0938 554336. Open from March 28 to June 30, daily (except Mon and Tues), July 1 to August 31, daily (except Mon) and September 1 to November 3, daily (except Mon and Tues) 12 noon to sunset.

Rosendael (Park), Rozendaal, Gelderland. This site remains important evidence of how features from a formal layout were sometimes incorporated into a landscape park. The original formal garden was modernized by Jan van Arnhem after his marriage in 1667. It is well recorded in descriptions and illustrations around 1700. The heart of the design was to the south of the house and consisted in parterres and a series of water features on the central axis: channels, cascades and a shell grotto with trick fountains. Other features included a hunting pavilion for William III by Daniel Marot and a 'Queen's summer-house' (near a 'cascade with the antlers') which is thought to be by Marot; these were all removed from the garden after 1721 by Lubbert Torck. He had the grounds redesigned and Daniel Marot was responsible for a pavilion and possibly for the shell gallery (both now restored). In the landscape garden by J. D. Zocher Jr. of 1836–7 these elements were then preserved and survive to this day.
Owner: Stichting Geldersch Landschap, tel: 085 420944. Open from May to end of Oct, Tues to Sun 10am to 5pm; Sun 11am to 5pm.

*St Paul's Walden Bury, Whitwell, Hertfordshire. This woodland garden appears to date back to the 1730s but has been revitalized through additions and alterations in the twentieth century.
Owner: Simon Bowes Lyon, tel: 0438 871218 or 871229. Garden open only under National Gardens Scheme on certain days during spring and early summer.

Sanssouci (Lustgarten), Potsdam. Frederick the Great's vineyard garden built originally between 1744 and 1764. It formed part of an extensive park (Rehgarten or Deerpark) stretching west to the Neues Palais. Within this wider landscape were located features such as the Chinese Teahouse (1755) and Marble Colonnade (1754) and the resulting blend of regular and irregular areas is represented in a plan c. 1786. During the nineteenth century the park was redesigned by Peter Joseph Lenné with the major addition of the Park Charlottenhof to the south (from 1826). The vineyard terraces were restored in 1982–3 but without the parterre shown in the engraving by J. D. Schleuen c. 1760–70.
Owner: Stiftung Schlösser und Gärten, Potsdam-Sanssouci, tel: Potsdam 23819. Open daily from 6am until dusk.

*Schleissheim (Hofgarten), near München, Bayern.** Amongst the most significant Baroque layouts in Germany, Schleissheim dates back to the period of Kurfürst Max Emanuel and is primarily the work of Dominique Girard (1715–17), developing earlier ideas by Enrico Zuccalli. The gardens lie between the hunting lodge, Schloss Lustheim, (1684–89) and the main palace or Neues Schloss (implemented from 1701). The layout was repeatedly altered and replanted during the following centuries. The pall mall course on the central axis, for example, appears to have been converted into a long canal in the late eighteenth century. During the 1860s Carl von Effner revived the original layout and, following bomb damage in the Second World War, the grounds were restored, but without all the original parterres and bosquets.
Owner: Bayerische Verwaltung der staatlichen Schlösser, Gärten und Seen, tel: 089 3150212. Open daily from 8am to sunset.

*Schwetzingener Schlossgarten, Schwetzingen, Baden-Württemberg.** The formal garden from the 1750s to 1770s transformed around its outer edges into a landscape garden after 1777. The fountain of the 'water-spitting birds' in the trellised aviary near the bathhouse was brought from the garden of Lunéville in 1776; it dates from c. 1750. A plan of 1830 by Gartenbaudirektor Johann Michael Zeyher shows the final stage of informalization: the 1823/4 alteration of the formal basin into an irregular lake. Restored carefully from the 1970s.
Owner: Land Baden-Württemberg, tel: 06202 81481. Open daily 8 to sunset in summer and 9 to sunset off season.

*Shrubland Park, Barham, Suffolk.** Terraced gardens 1848–52 by Charles Barry, based on layout of c. 1830–32 by J. P. Gandy-Deering and modified by William Robinson in 1883.
Owner: Used now as a health clinic, tel: 0473 830404. Not generally open to public.

Sutton Place, near Guildford, Surrey. Geoffrey and Susan Jellicoe's design for Stanley J. Seegar from early 1980s around sixteenth-century house built by Sir Richard Weston. In response to the parkland setting from the time of 'Capability' Brown and the gardens of the early 1900s, Jellicoe created a garden which, in his own words, 'expresses the modern mind, was sympathetic to the ethos of the place, which comprehends the past, the present and the future'. On the east façade lies a water-lily pool with balustraded viewing platforms inspired by Giovanni Bellini's 'The Allegory of Souls'. Stepping stones over this pool lead to the Paradise Garden of mixed serpentine and straight walks. Iron arbours derived from Renaissance prototypes as re-created at Villandry, are clothed in roses, clematis and honeysuckle. Other notable features include: a formal Surrealist Garden, evocative of the work of Magritte; and a garden devoted to Ben Nicholson's wall carving – positioned to catch a reflection in a formal lily pond. Susan Jellicoe's planting draws inspiration from the past as in the border of the South Walk inspired by Gertrude Jekyll, yet is strikingly modern.
Owner: Edward Koch, Not open to the public.

Tanlay (château de), Tanlay, Bourgogne. Along with Wideville, Brécy and Balleroy, Tanlay represents a partial survival of the garden art created for a new financial elite in the first half of the seventeenth century. The architect Pierre le Muet was responsible for the design of château and gardens between 1643 and 1648. The owner was Michel Particelli d'Emery. Especially notable is the 526 m-long canal on a tangential axis to the charming château, lined with trees and terminated by an exceptional grotto or *nymphée* in rusticated style.
Owner: M. de la Chauvinière, tel: 86 75 70 61. Open from Easter to All Saints, daily (except Tues).

*Tudor House Museum Garden, Southampton, Hampshire.** A collection of garden features of the sixteenth century recreated in the early 1980s. The original plants and planting methods are especially noteworthy: a raised bed with lattice supports for growing carnations; a rose arbour; and topiary. The knot is based on a guilloche pattern found in the house and consists of box, lavender cotton, wall germander and winter savory. This is the closest representation today of an authentic Tudor knot, (although it deviates from the original in the use of box, which only became widespread in England in the Jacobean period following the French fashion of Claude Mollet at Anet).
Owner: Museum, tel: 0703 24216. Open daily (except Mon).

*Twickel (Kasteel), Delden, Overijssel.** The surrounding parkland at Twickel was redesigned by the German landscape gardener C. E. A. Petzold in 1885. The following year the Frenchman Edouard André supplied three alternative designs for the formal garden around the orangery and in 1907 H. A. C. Portman brought one of these to fruition through his own version of the design. The topiary of that period is notable. An informal flower garden of the 1920s was then added to the orangery garden.
Owner: Stichting Twickel, tel: 05407 61309. Open from mid May to mid October, Wed and Sat 1.30pm to 5pm.

*Vaux-le-Vicomte (château de), Maincy, Ile-de-France.** Originally the creation of André Le Nôtre for Nicolas Fouquet from 1650s. Substantially re-created in the late nineteenth century and early twentieth century by landscape architects Lainé and Achille Duchêne.
Owner: comte de Vogüé, tel: 1 60 66 97 09. Open year-round (except Christmas), from April 1 to October 31, 10am to 6pm and from November 1 to March 31, 11am to 5pm.

*Veitshöchheim (Hofgarten), near Würzburg, Bayern.** The garden, evolving out of a design undertaken for Fürstbischof Johann Philipp von Greiffenklau in 1702–3, was given its essential structure and embellishments from 1763 through the patronage of Fürstbischof Adam Friedrich von Seinsheim. Much alteration to planting from the nineteenth century and replacement of original sculpture by Ferdinand Tietz and others in early twentieth century. Restored in 1950s–60s without original parterres or bosquets.
Owner: Bayerische Verwaltung der staatlichen Schlösser, Gärten und Seen, tel: 0931 52743. Open daily from 7am to sunset.

*Versailles (château de), Versailles, Ile-de-France.** So complex and diverse are the elements that make up the design, meaning and evolution of the gardens at Versailles that no one history is sufficient. The iconography of Versailles at the time of Louis XIV has, for example, merited an entire study by Robert W. Berger. In order to understand the significance of the original layout and its hold over generations of garden makers thereafter, it is important to keep in mind the meaning of the sculpture and fountains still visible today from the original design of the 1660s to 1700. Some such as the Fountains of the Four Seasons are easy to interpret: Flora (Spring), Ceres (Summer), Bacchus (Autumn) and Saturn (Winter). Others require further explanation. As a dominant theme in the iconography, the symbolism of the Sun King as equated with the sun god Apollo is well known. This seems to have been formulated as a central artistic and political image from 1664–5. It manifests itself through many of the fountains and much of the sculpture that survive today: the sun represented as rising in the Bassin d' Apollon, for example. In the Bassin du Dragon, Louis XIV's supression of subversion is celebrated through a loose association with the image of the Dragon-Python slain by Apollo. Likewise, the Bassin de Latone on the central axis alludes indirectly to Apollo's victory and thereby the Sun King's authority. It depicts Latona (Leto) with her two children, Diana and Apollo, mobbed by Lycian peasants when fleeing the wrath of Hera; the peasants are metamorphosed into frogs after preventing Leto and children from drinking the water. This Ovidian scene is meant to refer to the erruption of the Fronde in 1648, in which the young Louis was forced to flee with his mother and brother. Later Louis crushed the rebellion just as the young Apollo slew the Python. Further support to the imagery was provided by sphinxes with putti which originally sat above the Bassin de Latone; they symbolized the power of kings and the faithfulness of subjects (the body of the sphinx was coverted into that of a dog, the traditional symbol of fidelity).

Less well known than this political imagery is the iconography of the Labyrinth, begun c. 1666 and essentially finished in 1673–4. Yet it too was imitated in gardens across Europe. The Labyrinth combined two themes: the maze of love and Aesop's fables. The latter were evoked in 39 fountains; the fountain animals were painted naturalistically and their voices were mimicked by water. At the entrance, for example, was the fable of the 'horned owl and the birds', in which the owl, having been mocked by all the birds for its

poor song and appearance, was forced to emerge only at night. The moral intended was as follows: that the man who wishes to go through the maze of love must attend to his dress and speech if he wishes to avoid the assaults of women, pouncing like birds upon the owl. The other fables were chosen to expand on this *moralité galante*. In 1775 the Labyrinth was replaced by the Bosquet de la Reine. Ironically, at about the same time at Schwetzingen in Germany, this same fable was depicted in the aviary near the Bathhouse and survives in splendid condition today.
Owner: French State, domaine national, tel: 1 30 84 74 00. Open year-round from 7 to sunset (fountain display every Sun from the beginning of May to the beginning of October; 'fêtes nocturnes' from July to September).

⋆**Villa Aldobrandini, Frascati, Lazio.** Villa and garden created by Giacomo della Porta and Carlo Maderno from 1598–1603 for nephew of Pope Clement VIII, Cardinal Aldobrandini. Hydraulic work by Giovanni Fontana and Orazio Olivieri. Most notable element to survive from this period is the nymphaeum or garden theatre with cascade. Hall of Apollo within nymphaeum restored in recent years.
Owner: Aldobrandini family. Open weekdays 9am to 1pm; tickets from Azienda di Soggiorno, Piazza Marconi 1, Frascati.

⋆**Villa Crivelli Sormani-Verri, Castellazzo near Milano, Lombardia.** Original layout by Jean Gianda for Arconati family, lavishly publicized in *Delizie della Villa di Castellazzo* in 1743. Interesting example of Rococo style translated by French designer to Italian context. It included a menagerie. Parts of original survive though no longer fully maintained.
Privately owned and not normally open to the public.

⋆**Villa d'Este, Tivoli, Lazio.** First laid out during the 1560s for Cardinal d'Este, governor of Tivoli from 1550, to a design of Pirro Ligorio. The provision of water through aqueducts permitted the development of the garden's outstanding fountains and water features and influenced the iconographical programme. In the iconography, several complex themes were interwoven, celebrating the relationship of art to nature, depicting the fertile region, its local geography, rivers and centres and linking the virtues and artistic patronage of the Cardinal to Hercules and the mythical Garden of the Hesperides. At Cardinal d'Este's death in 1572 the garden was still not completed and in later years it was subjected to alterations and neglect. In the seventeenth century, the labyrinths and pergolas of the lowest terrace were replaced by simpler plantings; statues and fountains were added and moved, the Water Organ embellished with new adornments. After a long period of disrepair, the villa was then purchased by Cardinal Gustav von Hohenlohe in the mid-nineteenth century and he instituted restoration, adding new elements. After bomb damage in the Second World War, further restoration took place, re-creating anew the

Fountain of the Cascade. The original intricacies of planting (flowers on the lowest level, fruit trees in the middle ground and woodland on the steep upper slopes) have been lost in the picturesque, overgrown vegetation. Recent problems of water purity have threatened the functioning of the fountains.
Owner: Italian State. Open year-round 9am to sunset (fountains from 10am to 1pm and from 2pm to closing). Closed Mon.

⋆**Villa Farnese, Caprarola, Lazio.** The main gardens attached to the palace were begun in 1557 to complement Vignola's redesign for the building, but only the north garden of the summer apartment was complete on Vignola's death in 1573. In 1584 Cardinal Farnese decided to create a casino garden and outdoor dining area, the Barchetto, separated from the main garden by woods. This was probably by Giacomo del Duca but was completed by Girolamo Rainaldi after 1620. The planting has been altered repeatedly until the present day.
Owner: Italian State. Open daily (except Mon) 9am to 4pm.

⋆**Villa Gamberaia, Settignano near Firenze, Toscana.** The history of Gamberaia remains obscure. Although originating in the early seventeenth century, it appears that its essential structure dates from around 1717 when the Capponi family acquired the property. A view by Zocchi of 1735–50 depicts most of the elements known today; the immature state of the vegetation would confirm the replanting after 1717. Of special interest is the unusual site-plan and the long bowling-green walk on the east side of the villa, bounded by a high retaining wall, which Judith A. Kinnard has likened to an idealized reinterpretation of an 'urban space'. Off that 'street', opposite the villa, lie the raised lemon garden and the lower grotto garden. The latter has been influential in subsequent garden design, notably in the walled *giardino segreto* at Vizcaya, Florida. But it is the water parterre to the south of the villa that has been most admired and copied in the twentieth century (from the well-known Italian Garden at Longwood to the little-known Ambleville to the north west of Paris). Originally a broderie parterre around an oval fishpond, this was converted into its present form by Princess Ghyka of Serbia and her American companion Miss Blood about the turn of the century. A photograph in Inigo Triggs's *The Art of Garden Design in Italy* (1906) emphasizes that their planting was dominated by herbaceous borders rather than the massive topiary and annuals of the present.
Owner: Marchi family. Open weekdays, summer 8am to 12 noon and 2pm to 6pm; winter 8am to 12 noon and 1pm to 5pm.

⋆**Villa Garzoni (now Villa Gardi), Collodi near Lucca, Toscana.** The garden, dominated by a splendid monumental stairway and cascade on a tangential axis to the villa, was laid out in the second half of the seventeenth century. A plan and survey of 1692 provide the best evidence of the original layout, which included a garden theatre and labyrinth. But as

early as Francesco Sbarra's poem of 1652 there was reference to a number of features including clipped cypress forming shapes in topiary: 'a tower, now a ship, now . . . the semblance of a pear, now that of an angel'. Of special interest are the parterres of the lower garden beneath the terraces. In the plan of 1692 there are two types. While the upper compartments were decorated with the Garzoni coat of arms, reflecting Renaissance emblematic traditions, the lower ones were in a freer Baroque style. Today, these have been transformed into wispy, isolated flourishes in box no longer connected by coloured gravels. The upper ones have been affected by nineteenth-century traditions of 'mosaiculture' and 'bedding-out' and by horticultural strangers to the seventeenth century – pampas grass for example. Combined with the fantastical modern topiary, the planting of Villa Garzoni has thus departed radically from the original. For a more authentic example of French influence in Italy, the visitor should turn to the *parterre de broderie* at the Villa Allegri at Cuzzano near Verona (open only by appointment).
Owner: Contessa Grazini Gardi. Open daily from May to October 8am to sunset; November to April 8am to 1pm and 2.30pm to 4.30pm.

⋆**Villa Lante, Bagnaia, Lazio.** First created for Cardinal Gambara after 1568 to design of Vignola but aided by the architect and hydraulics expert, Tommaso Ghinucci. Completed under Cardinal Montalto through Carlo Maderno between 1590 and the early years of the seventeenth century. Planting of the lowest terrace much altered over time. An illustration by Francesco Pannini of c. 1780 shows a new parterre, which was filled with various coloured materials characteristic of the period. By the early twentieth century box broderie was introduced with flowering plants between; these have now been removed and replaced with a uniform red background of inorganic material (terracotta powder).
Owner: Italian State. Open daily (except Mon), 9am to sunset.

Villa Marlia (Villa Reale), near Lucca, Toscana. Important garden laid out for the Orsetti family in the late seventeenth century. A garden theatre survives from this period. John Dixon Hunt has pointed out the range of other features that are 'shaped with the same theatrical effect', and Georgina Masson refers to one of these as the 'most magnificent garden room in Italy'.
Owner: Conte Pecci Blunt. Open daily (except Mon). Guided tours only. Summer 10am, 11am, 4pm, 5pm and 6pm; and in winter, 10am, 11am, 2pm, 3pm and 4pm. In August and September only on Tues, Thurs and Sat.

⋆**Villa Medici, Castello, Toscana.** Of Cosimo de' Medici's original layout, begun by Niccolò Tribolo after 1537, the following elements survive: the Fountain of Hercules and Antaeus (Tribolo from c. 1543) but without the figures themselves; the magnificent Grotto of the Animals and the garden of

orange trees; and the figure of Appennino by Bartolomeo Ammannati (1563–65) on the upper area of the bosco. The Fountain of the Labyrinth (Tribolo c. 1545) with its bronze figure of Florence by Giambologna (1572) was removed to Villa Petraia. The present planting in 16 large rectangles was reorganized in the eighteenth century; the removal of the wall between the main garden and the orange tree garden in the nineteenth century further added to the openness of today's layout.
Owner: Italian State. Open daily (except Mon) 9am to 6.30pm in summer and 9am to 4.30pm in winter.

•**Villa Pisani, Stra, Veneto.** The original layout was the work of Girolamo Frigimelica (1653–1732) for the brothers Alvise and Almorò Pisani. Alvise was ambassador to France between 1699 and 1704, where Louis XIV was godfather to his son. In 1735 he became Doge of Venice. In that year the villa was built to a design by Francesco Maria Preti (1701–74). It superseded Frigimelica's unrealized project of 1719 but his concept for the grounds and garden buildings remained intact. Of Frigimelica's layout, surviving features include today: parts of the axial structure, French in inspiration; the Labirinto or maze of essentially circular form, lodged within a five-sided area and overlooked by a central tower; the hexagonal Esedra flanked by Cedraie for the cultivation of citrus fruit; and the Coffee House, originally on a mound decorated by four stepped hedges, but now surrounded by a circular moat. These occupy the area of woodland to the east of the central axis; the zone to the west was divided into five distinct sections by vistas, but little of interest remains today. In the eighteenth century the main axis between the villa and elegant stables was occupied by *parterres de broderie*, but in 1911 after a century of neglect, this area was converted into a grandiose canal on which naval scale models were tested. This now dominates the setting. The initiative was taken in 1980 to set in motion some conservation measures. Apart from the maze, the original planting has largely vanished.
Owner: Italian State. Open daily (except Mon and public hols) 9am to 6pm.

Villa Rizzardi, Negrar, Veneto. A fascinating formal layout originally designed by Luigi Trezza from 1783. Especially remarkable is the garden theatre planned in 1796; the seats are turfed and ornamented with clipped box. In the surrounding hedge are statues in niches. Georgina Masson describes it as the 'largest and finest of its kind in Italy'.
Owner: Contessa Cristina Rizzardi, tel: 045 7210088. Open only by advance permission.

•**Villandry (château de), Villandry, Centre.** Imaginative and individualistic re-creation of a French Renaissance garden by the owner Joachim Carvallo in the years between 1906 and 1918. Beautifully maintained planting.
Owner: M. Robert Carvallo, tel: 47 50 02 09. Open year round, 8.30am to 8pm in summer and 9am to sunset in winter.

•**Vizcaya (Villa), Miami, Florida.** James Deering's villa and garden designed by Paul Chalfin, F. Burrall Hoffman Jr and Diego Suarez between 1912 and 1922. The formal garden of Italian and French influences is well preserved but the informal gardens are now lost.
Owner: The Metro-Dade County Park and Recreation Department, tel: 305 579 2767 or 2708. Open daily (except Christmas), 9am to 5pm.

•**Weikersheim (Schlossgarten), Weikersheim, Baden-Württemberg.** Attached to the palace which dates back to 1586 (redesigned from 1679 and in early eighteenth century) is the Baroque garden of 1708–25. The plan has been always been attributed to Daniel Matthieu, but this attribution has been challenged on account of his age and inexperience. Johann Christian Lüttich was responsible for the two-part orangery of 1719–23. In 1729–30 fountains were added in the centres of each of the four quarters of the parterre. (By 1802 when the parterres were redesigned, these had been removed). The unified sculptural programme of Johann Jakob Sommer and others is still the chief glory of Weikersheim; the restoration of original planting remains a project for the future.
Owner: Land Baden-Württemberg, tel: 07934 8364. Open daily 8am to sunset.

•**Weldam (Kasteel), Goor, Overijssel.** Design of 1886 by Edouard André implemented by H. A. C. Poortman. Survives in good condition with modifications to original planting.
Owner: Graaf zu Solms, tel: 05470 72647. Open year round, Mon to Sat 10am to 12 noon and 1pm to 4pm.

•**Westbury Court Garden, Westbury-on-Severn, Gloucestershire.** Original garden of 1696–1705 (additions from c. 1715) with Dutch-style canals and summerhouse. Restoration work of 1970s with imaginative re-creation or re-interpretation of planting. Excellent collection of period plants.
Owner: The National Trust, tel: 045276 461. Open from April to end of October, Wed to Sun and Bank Hol Mon, 11am to 6pm.

•**Wilhelmshöhe (Bergpark), Kassel, Hessen.** Original design for cascade and Octagon by Giovanni Francesco Guerniero after Landgraf Karl von Hessen-Kassel's visit to Italy in 1699–1700; it was inspired by Villa Aldobrandini and Villa Farnese. Only one third of the layout as illustrated in 1705 was completed. In a plan of c. 1780 by the court gardener Fuchs the cascade is featured as a small part of an immense formal/informal park. In the 1780s–90s the park was remodelled by H. C. Jussow on the principles of the English landscape style. As Hans-Christoph Dittscheid writes: 'Jussow created an heroic naturalistic landscape with wildly cleft rocks artificially piled up, the ruins of a Roman aqueduct, torrential waterfalls and a Devil's Bridge'. These survive today along with the artificial ruin, the neo-Gothic Löwenburg, of the same period and magnificent mature ornamental planting.
Owner: Land Hessen, Gartenverwaltung Wilhelmshöhe, tel: 0561 32280. Open daily from sunset to sunrise. Cascade and 'Wasserkünste' from end of May to end of September, Wed, Sun and public holidays, 2.30pm to 3.30pm.

Williamsburg (Colonial), Williamsburg, Virginia. Apart from the garden attached to the College of William and Mary, which was founded in 1693, there was little in the way of gardens at Williamsburg when Governor Alexander Spotswood arrived in 1710. The initial grid plan of the town had been established by Governor Francis Nicholson in 1700–04. Spotswood strengthened this structure, completing the vista of Palace Green to the south of the new Governor's Palace. Surprisingly little is known about the gardens Spotswood laid out around the Palace, although they are the most celebrated today. These were restored in the 1930s on the basis of a representation in the so-called Bodleian Plate of c. 1736–40 and with the support of some rudimentary archaeology. Recent advances in garden archaeology have helped to challenge the work of the past. The accuracy of the initial 'restoration' is now questioned and similar reservations apply to the re-creation of smaller house gardens with their attractive boxwood patterns. Contributors to the recent publication *Earth Patterns* have written for example: 'These vernacular gardens are the ones that the Colonial Williamsburg Foundation would like to portray more accurately. While there are several notable gardens whose stature as monuments to the Colonial Revival vision argue for their preservation, there are many more small and less visible gardens which are now recognized as too formal for the backyard work spaces where they have been planted. Already, as part of Colonial Williamsburg's new interpretation at the Bejamin Powell House, its garden has been greatly simplified, losing ground to Powell's lumber-yard and storage shed'.
Owner: Colonial Williamsburg Foundation, tel: 804 229 1000 ext. 2751. Open daily from 9am to 5pm and for longer hours in the spring and summer.

•**William Paca Garden (The), Annapolis, Maryland.** William Paca's garden of the 1760s as re-created in the 1970s after excavations in the late 1960s. A formal and informal layout, of which the walls, levels, path network, water features and pavilion were reconstructed from site evidence and the evidence of a contemporary painting. The main conjectural features are the parterres of the upper terraces, for which no evidence of planting survived; they were based on contemporary models. The steps may well have been ramps originally following the traditions of the period. Although an idealized portrait of planting and gardening, it represents a remarkable tribute to the horticulture of the past.
Owner: Historic Annapolis Incorporated, tel: 301 263 5553. Open daily, Mon to Sat 10am to 4pm and Sun, 1pm to 5pm.

Wilton House, Salisbury, Wiltshire. Of the remarkable formal gardens of the early seventeenth century with which Isaac de Caus is associated, little remains; there are a few sculptural pieces by Nicholas Stone that once embellished the fountains of the *parterre de*

broderie and the water parterre. Part of the grotto survives, although altered. During the eighteenth century the grounds were landscaped. However, in the 1820s Lady Pembroke and Richard Westmacott created a new formal terrace, known as the Italian garden. It contained cypresses and statuary. (The grotto is not normally open to the public).
Owner: The Earl of Pembroke. Open from April to mid October, Tues to Sat and Bank Hol Mon, 11am to 6pm and Sun 12.30pm to 6pm.
Woburn Abbey, Woburn, Bedfordshire. Remarkable grotto, built by Isaac de Caus for Lucy Harington before 1627, survives in good condition. As Sir Roy Strong writes: 'The grotto at Woburn alone remains to conjure up the marvels of those Salomon [de Caus] had made at Richmond and Heidelberg

and that Isaac was to make at Wilton'.
Owner: The Marquess of Tavistock and Trustees of the Bedford Estates, tel: 0525 290666. Open during main season from end of March to early November, weekdays 10am to 4.45pm and Sun 10am to 5.45pm. Off season Sat and Sun only, 10.30am to 3.45pm.
*Wrest Park, Silsoe, Bedfordshire. A garden of extraordinary diversity now in course of restoration. The original house and formal gardens depicted by Kip c. 1705 have disappeared; these gardens were created in the first phase under the 11th Earl of Kent and only the long canal survives. The Great Garden dates from 1706 to 1740 under the 12th Earl. Of this the following elements survive: the Archer pavilion of 1709–11; many of the woodland allées and enclosures with garden buildings and

ornaments; and the Bowling Green House of c. 1735 with its bowling lawn and hedgework and a grass amphitheatre across a formal water basin. The woodland garden was modified by 'Capability' Brown who created the serpentine waters around the boundary (1758–60). A commemorative column of 1760 records his work. A Chinese Pavilion, attributed to William Chambers, survives along the serpentine canal and appears to date from 1761. The existing house was built by the Earl de Grey from 1834–39 and the 'French Garden' and Orangery date from this period. Also of interest are the rustic Bath House and Cascade Bridge.
Owner: English Heritage, tel: 0525 60718. Open from Good Friday or April 1 (whichever is earlier) to September 30, weekends and Bank Hol only, 10am to 6pm.

Glossary of Planting Terms

Allée A formal hedged walk or ride within the bosquet or 'wilderness'.
Berceau A trelliswork arbour on which plants were trained.
Bosco and Boschetto Areas of ornamental woodland in the Italian garden.
Bosquet Areas of ornamental woodland in the French garden (called 'grove', 'wilderness' etc., in English).
Erbette The herbs that edged flower beds in the Italian garden.
Knots Developing in the fifteenth century, the knot consisted in a pattern of intersecting bands of different herbs (p. 6, motif from Didymus Mountain's *The Gardeners Labyrinth* (1571); and p. 15). During the early seventeenth century it was gradually replaced by box broderie. See p. 16 for distinction between 'open' and 'closed' knots.
Mixing, mingling and massing Terms used especially in the nineteenth century to distinguish systems of planting: 'mixing' or 'mingling' involved an assortment of different flowers in various colours, 'massing' was the use of a single type of flower in each bed.
Palissade (*palisade*) The clipped hedges of the bosquet, often in hornbeam. At Versailles after 1674 climbers (jasmine, honeysuckle, rose) were trained up wooden or iron trellis as can be seen in J.B. Martin's painting of La Salle des Antiques (p. 79).
Parterre The ornamental garden close to the palace or house, composed of low patterns in boxwork, grass or flowers. The main types are outlined below. (See Dézallier for *parterre d'orangerie* and *boulingrin* not discussed in this book).
Parterre à l'angloise Consisting primarily of grass, this parterre derives its name from England where 'naturalness' and ease of maintenance made it popular (p. 89). The simplest form was lawn and sand (p. 75); more usually it

was framed by flower borders, topiary and even broderie (pp. 77, 81, 94). When the grass was cut into scrolls and palmettes, it was known as *gazon coupé* (pp. 44, 88).
Parterre d'eau (*water parterre*) A parterre developing in the late Renaissance in which water and stone were the dominant elements. The form at Villa Lante (p. 27) was reinterpreted at Saint-Germain-en-Laye, and at the Hortus Palatinus and Wilton circular motifs occurred. At Versailles and Chantilly (p. 43) there were elaborate water parterres. And at Blenheim (p. 174) Achille Duchêne looked back to the first *parterre d'eau* of Le Brun and Le Nôtre at Versailles.
Parterre de broderie originally **compartiment en broderie** (*broderie*) Arabesque box patterns that resembled embroidery at the time of Henri IV and Louis XIII (c. 1600s). The early Baroque broderie of Claude Mollet and Jacques Boyceau was contained within an edging of box (p. 42); this tradition continued as late as Vaux-le-Vicomte (p. 75). By the time of André Mollet, however, flower borders had been introduced (though these too remain lined by box; see title page). André Le Nôtre developed such *plate-bandes*, brought a greater unity to flowing boxwork patterns and loosened the outlines of the composition. The interiors of his broderie were highlighted in black; contrasts of coloured materials increased in the early eighteenth century.
Parterre de broderie mêlée de massifs de gazon A variant on the *parterre de broderie*; ornamental bands of grass were introduced into the box embroidery. Although occurring as early as André Mollet, it never became a dominant type. It is encountered in Dézallier d'Argenville and in Dominique Girard's plans for Brühl (p. 64) and Schleissheim. The grass strips were typically outlined with red in contrast to the background of light sand. This

type should not be confused with the parterres of mixed broderie and grass – *broderie mêlée de gazon*, or *gazon mêlé de broderie* as at Schwetzingen (pp. 94 and 128).
Parterre de compartiment This parterre differed from the *parterre de broderie* in retaining symmetry along the top, bottom and sides of the composition (pp. 125, 162, 210). In addition to broderie, it might also have contained grass and flower borders as Dézallier d'Argenville shows (pp. 162, 210). See also the central parterres of Het Loo.
Parterre de pièces coupées pour des fleurs ('cut-work' parterre) A parterre divided into a symmetrical arrangement of flower beds in the shapes of square, rectangle, circle, triangle, heart, star or even organic forms such as leaves, fruit etc. (pp. 2, 13, 24, 37, 39, 47, 95). These beds were defined by narrow paths that allowed the gardener to tend the flowers. Raised beds edged in stone, wood or brick or low beds edged in herbs were typical of the Renaissance, while Baroque beds were edged in box (pp. 43, 75, 82). Shrubs and topiary often appeared in the flower beds. See also pp. 86, 90, 162, 164, 200, 207, 221 for later variations on these prototypes.
Patte d'oie (*goose's foot*) Three allées radiating from a central point.
Pianelle Special tiles or bricks that edged the flower beds of the Italian garden.
Plate-bande The flower border surrounding the parterre; it often contained shrubs and topiary.
Potager The vegetable or kitchen garden.
Semplici The 'simples' or herbs and flowers in the Italian garden.
Topiary Clipped evergreens, sometimes in elaborate forms, sometimes in simple cones or pyramids.
Vertugadin Formal concave or convex grass slope or 'amphitheatre'.

Bibliography

There are some useful articles for all chapters in Monique Mosser and George Teyssot eds., *The History of Garden Design: The Western Tradition from the Renaissance to the Present Day* (London, 1991). For individual chapters, see the following select bibliography:

Chapter 1: David R. Coffin, *The Villa in the Life of Renaissance Rome* (Princeton, 1979; paperback 1988) and D. R. Coffin ed., *The Italian Garden* (Washington, D.C., 1972); Claudia Lazzaro, *The Italian Renaissance Garden* (New Haven and London, 1990); John Dixon Hunt, *Garden and Grove: The Italian Renaissance Garden in the English Imagination, 1600–1750* (Princeton, 1986); Kenneth Woodbridge, *Princely Gardens: The Origins and Development of the French Formal Style* (London and New York, 1986); Wilfried Hansmann, *Gartenkunst der Renaissance und des Barock* (Cologne, 1983); Dieter Hennebo and Alfred Hoffmann, *Geschichte der Deutschen Gartenkunst*, 3 vols. of which vol. II is *Der Architektonische Garten: Renaissance und Barock* (Hamburg 1965; reprint Koenigstein 1981); Dieter Hennebo ed., *Gartendenkmalpflege: Grundlagen der Erhaltung Historischer Gärten und Grünanlagen* (Stuttgart, 1985); Roy Strong, *The Renaissance Garden in England* (London, 1979).

Chapter 2: W. Hansmann, *Gartenkunst . . .* (1983); Georgina Masson, *Italian Gardens* (London, 1961; paperback 1966); Margherita Azzi Visentini ed., *Il Giardino Veneto* (Milan, 1988); K. Woodbridge, *Princely Gardens* (1986); William Howard Adams, *The French Garden, 1500–1800* (New York, 1979); Robert W. Berger, *In the Garden of the Sun King* (Washington, D.C., 1985); J. D. Hunt ed., *the Dutch Garden in the Seventeenth Century* (Washington, D.C., 1990); J. D. Hunt and Erik de Jong eds., 'The Anglo-Dutch Garden in the Age of William and Mary', a special double issue of *Journal of Garden History*, vol. 8, nos 2 & 3 (1988); David Jacques and Arend Jan van der Horst, *The Gardens of William and Mary* (London, 1988); J. D. Hunt, *Garden and Grove* (1986); D. Hennebo and A. Hoffmann, *Geschichte der Deutschen Gartenkunst*, vol. II (1965; 1981); D. Hennebo ed., *Gartendenkmalpflege* (1985); Ernest de Ganay, *André Le Nostre, 1613–1700* (Paris, 1962); Alfred Marie, *Naissance de Versailles: le château, les jardins* (Paris, 1968); Alfred and Jeanne Marie, *Versailles au temps de Louis XIV* (Paris, 1976); F. Hamilton Hazelhurst, *Gardens of Illusion: The Genius of André Le Nostre* (Nashville, 1980).

Chapter 3: W. Hansmann, *Gartenkunst . . .* (1983); D. Hennebo and A. Hoffmann, *Geschichte der Deutschen Gartenkunst*, vol. II (1965; 1981); D. Hennebo ed., *Gartendenkmalpflege* (1985); Ingrid Dennerlein, *Die Gartenkunst der Régence und des Rokoko in Frankreich* (Worms, 1981); Iris Lauterbach, *Der Französische Garten am Ende des Ancien Régime* (Worms, 1987); W. Howard Adams, *The French Garden . . .* (1979); G. Masson, *Italian Gardens* (1961; 1966); David Jacques, *Georgian Gardens: The Reign of Nature* (Lon-

don, 1983); Peter Martin, *The Pleasure Gardens of Virginia: From Jamestown to Jefferson* (Princeton, 1991).

Chapter 4: D. Jacques, *Georgian Gardens . . .* (1983); George Carter et al, *Humphry Repton: Landscape Gardener 1752–1818* (Norwich, 1982); Brent Elliott, *Victorian Gardens* [London, 1986; paperback 1990]; D. Hennebo and A. Hoffmann, *Geschichte der Deutschen Gartenkunst*, vol. III (1962–65; 1981); D. Hennebo ed., *Gartendenkmalpflege* (1985); Harri Günther, *Peter Joseph Lenné* (1985; reprint 1991); Carla Oldenburger-Ebbers, *De Tuiningids van Nederland* (Rotterdam, 1989).

Chapter 5: David Ottewill, *The Edwardian Garden* (New Haven and London, 1989); Clive Aslet, *The Last Country Houses* (New Haven and London, 1982) and *The American Country House* (New Haven and London, 1990); Jane Brown, *Gardens of a Golden Afternoon* (London, 1982; paperback 1985) and *The English Garden in Our Time: From Gertrude Jekyll to Geoffrey Jellicoe* (Woodbridge, 1986); Diane Kostial McGuire ed., *Beatrix Farrand's Plant Book for Dumbarton Oaks* (Washington, D.C., 1980); Diane Kostial McGuire and Lois Fern, *Beatrix Jones Farrand: Fifty Years of American Landscape Architecture* (Washington, D.C., 1982); K. Woodbridge, *Princely Gardens* (1986); Michel Racine, *Le Guide des jardins de France* (Paris, 1990); Ernest de Ganay, *Les Jardins de France et leur décor* (Paris, 1949).

Detailed Bibliography and Notes

Introduction

P. 6: In general, the term 'formal' remains problematic for the garden historian – a fact recognized by Reginald Blomfield one hundred years ago. In recent years, 'geometric', 'regular' and 'architectural' have sometimes been adopted as alternatives, corresponding closely to 'der architectonische Garten' or 'le jardin régulier' used in German and French. These substitutes express more precisely the geometry – as an extension of the architecture – that determines the structure of such gardens; they also avoid confusion, since 'formal' has other meanings and connotations – the 'external forms' or the 'ceremonious' associations of a garden. Yet for all its inadequacies, 'formal' remains the widely accepted term in English. For the purposes of this study it is sufficient as a generic formula, but the reader should remain alert to the intricacies behind the label: to describe the park at Villa Lante as 'informal' helps to distinguish it from the geometric garden, but simplifies its elusive union of straight paths and naturalistic elements. Such hybrid forms reappear throughout the ages – in layouts and individual features of planting – and constitute a central theme in this work.

For discussion of 'formal' in this context, see Woodbridge (1986), p. 9. For an insight into some of the complexities behind the terms 'art' and 'nature' see Hunt (1986), Chapter 8.
P. 7: All information on Wrest Park is from the unpublished conservation report by Land Use

Consultants, *Historical Survey of Wrest Park* (1983); see here p. 17.
Pp. 7–8: For discussion of Claude Monet's garden, see Claire Joyes, *Monet at Giverny* (London, 1975), in particular p. 37; and Ottewill (1989), pp. 58–60.
P. 9: Recent discussions on carpet bedding include: Elliott (1986; 1990), pp. 154–58; and Clemens Alexander Wimmer, 'Die Kunst der Teppichgärtnerei' in *Die Gartenkunst*, vol. 3, no. 1 (1991), pp. 1–16.
For the Blomfield-Robinson debate, see R. Blomfield, *The Formal Garden in England* (London, 1892; this edition 1936).

Chapter 1 *Gardens of the Renaissance*
P. 11: For a more detailed discussion of Villa d'Este, see D. R. Coffin, *The Villa d'Este at Tivoli* (Princeton, 1960) and Lazzaro (1990), pp. 95–99 and 215–42.
Pp. 12–13: For an extensive discussion of the Villa Medici at Castello, see Lazzaro (1990), pp. 167–89.
Pp. 13–14: Lazzaro (1990), p. 30 and chapter 2 in general.
P. 14: For a wider discussion of the garden as 'theatre' and of 'cabinets of curiosity', see Hunt (1986), chapters 5 and 6.
Pp. 15–16: The Hortus Palatinus, Johan Vredeman de Vries and Furttenbach are discussed in articles in Mosser and Teyssot eds. (1991): Ulbe Martin Mehrtens writes on De Vries's *Hortorum Formae*, pp. 103–5; and Reinhard Zimmermann on the Hortus Palatinus, pp. 157–59; Dorothee Nehring writes on Furttenbach, pp. 160–62. See also Florence Hopper, 'The Dutch Classical Garden and André Mollet' in *Journal of Garden History*, vol. 2, no. 1 (1982), pp. 25–40.
P. 16: For the Cisterna garden, see G. Masson 'Italian flower collectors' gardens' in Coffin ed. (1972), pp. 63–80. For Bartolomeus Menkins, see Lazzaro (1990), p. 41. For English knots, see Strong (1979), pp. 36 and 40–43.
P. 25: See Christopher Thacker, *The History of Gardens* (London, 1979) p. 123 for the Idstein garden. See Woodbridge (1986), chapter 6, especially p. 108 for the *compartiment en broderie*.
Pp. 26–29: See Lazzaro (1990), pp. 243–86; Coffin (1988), pp. 340–62; and D. R. Coffin, 'The "Lex Hortorum" and Access to Gardens of Latium During the Renaissance' in *Journal of Garden History*, vol. 2, no. 3 (1982), pp. 201–32.
Pp. 30–32: See Coffin (1988), chapter 2 for *villeggiatura* and chapter 9 for Caprarola; see Lazzaro (1990), pp. 100–108 for planting.
Pp. 32–33: See Woodbridge (1986), pp. 70–73 and 81–83.
Pp. 34–36: See Strong (1979), pp. 120–21, 125–29, and 211–14.
Pp. 37–38: For the botanic garden at Padua see Lazzaro (1990), pp. 41–42. For Giardino Buonaccorsi, see Masson (1961; 1966), pp. 216–20; for Cisterna, see Masson in Coffin ed. (1972) and Ada Segre's current study for PhD, University of York; see also Lucia Tongiorgi Tomasi, 'Projects for Botanical and Other Gardens: A 16th-Century Manual' in *Journal of Garden History*, vol. 3, no. 1 (1983), p. 13.

For Germany and the Low Countries, see Hansmann (1983) pp. 74–77, and W. Hansmann, 'Parterres: Entwicklung, Typen, Elemente' in Hennebo ed. (1985), pp. 141–173, and especially pp. 163–64.

Chapter 2 *Baroque Gardens*
P. 41: For Villa Montalto etc. see Coffin (1988), pp. 365–69, and Lazzaro (1990), pp. 272–75. For Villa Aldobrandini, see Masson (1966), pp. 188–93. For Villa Garzoni, see Alessandra Ponte, 'The Garden of Villa Garzoni at Collodi' in Mosser and Teyssot (1991), pp. 181–84; and for French-style parterres in Italy, see Villa Allegri Arvedi in Visentini ed. (1988), pp. 135–37.
P. 42: Sten Karling argues for the role of the Mollets in developing broderie forms before the Luxembourg. See here 'The Importance of André Mollet and His Family for the Development of the French Formal Garden' in E. B. MacDougall and F. H. Hazelhurst eds., *The French Formal Garden* (Washington, D. C., 1974), pp. 3–25. For the Luxembourg garden, see Woodbridge (1986) pp. 134–38, and Hansmann in Hennebo (1985), pp. 150–51 and 158. For Liancourt, Brécy etc. see Woodbridge (1986), pp. 139–41 and chapter 9 in general.
Pp. 42–43: For Dutch gardens, see Eric de Jong, 'For Profit and Ornament . . .' and J. D. Hunt, ''But who does not know what a Dutch garden is?'' The Dutch Garden in the English Imagination' in Hunt ed. (1990), pp. 13–48 and pp. 175–206, and other articles; also entries in *Journal of Garden History* (1988).
P. 44: For German gardens, see Hansmann (1983), chapter 8 and especially pp. 227–29 for Gaibach, and pp. 252–55 for Herrenhausen; see also D. Hennebo, 'The Grosser Garten at Herrenhausen near Hanover' in Mosser and Teyssot eds., pp. 192–94, and Helmut Reinhardt's article in ibid., pp. 293–98.
P. 45: For British sites, see Hunt and De Jong eds. (1988), *passim*; and Jacques and Van der Horst (1988), *passim*. See also Hunt (1986), chapter 10. Cleves (Kleve) is discussed by Wilhelm Diedenhofen, '''Belvedere,'' or the Principle of Seeing and Looking in the Gardens of Johan Maurits van Nassau-Siegen at Cleves', in Hunt ed. (1990). For Rueil, see Woodbridge, (1986), chapter 8, and his article in Mosser and Teyssot eds. (1991), pp. 169–71.
Pp. 47–48: For the 1647 plan and view of Villa Aldobrandini, see Cesare D'Onofrio, *La Villa Aldobrandini di Frascati* (Rome, 1963); Giovanni Fontana, Orazio Olivieri and Jacques Sarrazin were involved with hydraulics and sculpture from the 1600s to 1621. See also Hunt (1986), chapter 4, pp. 45–48.
Pp. 73–76: See Woodbridge (1986), chapter 10, Adams (1979), pp. 80–84, and Hansmann in Hennebo ed. (1985), pp. 142–43, 147, 150–54, 158–59.
Pp. 76–79: See Woodbridge (1986), chapter 11, Adams (1979), chapter 3 and pp. 84–94, and Hansmann (1983), pp. 97–125. For the iconographical background, see Berger (1985). For Locke's visit and public access, see Ann Friedman, 'What John Locke saw at Versailles' in *Journal of Garden History*, vol. 9, no. 4 (1989), pp. 177–98, and Coffin in ibid., vol. 2. no. 3 (1982), p. 209. According to Woodbridge (1986), p. 227, climbers on trellis replaced hornbeam hedges after 1674. For recent rep-

lanting of the bosquets after storm damage, see information issued by Versailles public relations office.
Pp. 80–82: See K. H. D. Haley, 'William III as builder of Het Loo' and Florence Hopper, 'Daniel Marot: A French Garden Designer in Holland' in Hunt ed. (1990), pp. 1–11 and 131–50; also entries in *Journal of Garden History* (1988). For details of planting, see H. R. Barkhof and C. S. Oldenburger-Ebbers, 'Plants for the Restoration of the Baroque Garden of the Palace of the Loo at Apeldoorn' in ibid., vol. 1, no. 4 (1981), pp. 293–304; also the guidebook and a special issue of *Groen* (June 1984), available from Het Loo.
Pp. 82–85: See Hansmann (1983), pp. 236–52 and 259–67; and Hansmann in Hennebo ed. (1985), especially figs. 34, 39 and 50. For further information on 'Jeu des Passes' and board games like 'goose' that were transformed into garden features, see Georg Himmelheber, *Spiele* (Munich and Berlin, 1972), pp. 163 and 180. The Duke of Norfolk's Worksop had a hornbeam 'goose' course. Weikersheim: 'French formality' relates only to Versailles' pervasive influence on such sculptural programmes; the two-part orangery, in contrast, is closer to the Dutch Het Loo or German models. See here Klaus Merten's guidebook. Recent information that challenges the attribution to Daniel Matthieu as supplied by Herr Alfons Elfgang.
Pp. 86–89: See National Trust, *Westbury Court Garden* (1990) and Land Use Consultants' *Historical Survey of Wrest Park* (1983).

Chapter 3 *Eighteenth-century Themes*
P. 91: For Caserta, see George L. Hersey, 'Ovid, Vico, and the Central Garden at Caserta' in *Journal of Garden History*, vol. 1, No. 1 (1981), pp. 3–34; for Veitshöchheim and Schwetzingen, see Helmut Reinhardt, 'The Garden of the Prince-Bishop at Vietshöchheim' in Mosser and Teyssot eds. (1991), pp. 188–91, and Hansmann (1983), pp. 276–83 and 286–89; for Chantilly, see Dennerlein (1981), pp. 98–101; for pall-mall see Hansmann (1983), p. 246.
Pp. 91–92: See Anthea Taigel and Tom Williamson, 'Some Early Geometric Gardens in Norfolk' in *Journal of Garden History*, vol. 11, nos. 1 & 2 (1991), especially pp. 15–16. See R. Todd Longstaffe Gowan, 'Proposal for a Georgian Town Garden in Gower Street: The Francis Douce Garden' in *Garden History* vol. 15, no. 2 (1987), pp. 136–44. For Wormsley, see Fiona Cowell, 'Richard Woods (?1716–93): A Preliminary Account' part III in *Garden History*, vol. 15, no. 2 (1987), pp. 115–35. For Thomas Wright, see Jacques (1983), pp. 70–71 and 82. For Hartwell, see Mark Laird, '''Our Equally Favorite Hobby Horse'': The Flower Gardens of Lady Elizabeth Lee at Hartwell and the 2nd Earl Harcourt at Nuneham Courtenay' in *Garden History*, vol. 18, no. 2 (1990).
Pp. 93–94: For Neufforge and Chantilly, see Lauterbach (1987), pp. 189–97 and 89–99. For Rambouillet, see Dennerlein (1981), 47–48; and for Waterland, see F. Hopper, 'The Dutch Régence Garden' in *Garden History*, vol. 9, no. 2 (1981), pp. 118–35.
P. 94: For St. Paul's Walden Bury, see English Heritage (HBMC) register of historic sites; for Canon, see Racine (1990), p. 237. For Nord-

kirchen and Nymphenburg, Vietshöchheim, Schwetzingen and Solitude, see Hansmann (1983), pp. 240–49 and pp. 276–89 respectively; see also Hansmann in Hennebo ed. (1985), figs. 39 and 50. For Italian sites, see Masson (1966), pp. 216, 242–46 and 273–74.
P. 95: For Bacon's Castle, see Nicholas Luccketti, 'Archaeological Excavations at Bacon's Castle, Surry County, Virginia' in William M. Kelso and Rachel Most eds., *Earth Patterns: Essays in Landscape Archaeology* (Charlottesville and London, 1990), pp. 23–42. For Middleton Place, Crowfield and Woodlands, see James D. Kornwolf, 'The Picturesque in the American Garden and Landscape before 1800' in Robert P. Maccubbin and Peter Martin eds., *British and American Gardens in the Eighteenth Century* (Williamsburg, 1983), pp. 97–98 and 100; see also Barbara Wells Sarudy, 'Eighteenth-Century Gardens of the Chesapeake' in *Journal of Garden History*, vol. 9, no. 3 (1989), pp. 125–40, and C. Allan Brown, 'Thomas Jefferson's Poplar Forest: The Mathematics of an Ideal Villa' in ibid., vol. 10, no. 2 (1990), esp. p. 121. See Coffin in ibid., vol. 2, no. 3 (1982), p. 211, for matters of public access.
P. 96: For St Paul's Walden Bury see English Heritage (HBMC) register. For connections to the Régence style, see Dennerlein (1981), pp. 40–41 (Sablé). Compare also Cassiobury as depicted by Kip and Knyff.
Pp. 121–23: For the first improvements (c.1715–19) and for other aspects of Chiswick, see the bibliography of previous studies in Hunt (1986), note 48 on p. 256, (and his exploration of Chiswick as museum, theatre etc. and the 'miniaturization' of classical and Italian forms); see also the guide, *Chiswick House and Gardens* (London, 1989). See J. D. Hunt, *William Kent . . .* (London, 1987); and Cinzia Maria Sicca, 'Lord Burlington at Chiswick' in *Garden History*, vol. 10, no. 1 (1982), p. 45 for theatre, opera and music in the garden. For contrasting grand spectacle in the Baroque gardens of August the Strong – patron of the arts and Burlington's contemporary – see Hansmann (1983) p. 259. Recent information on archaeology and conservation made available to me through Jan Woudstra. For hedgework at Schönbrunn, see Mosser and Teyssot eds. (1991), p. 197.
Pp. 123–24: See Hansmann (1983), pp. 272–76.
Pp. 125–27: See ibid., pp. 276–83; also Reinhardt in Mosser and Teyssot eds. (1991), pp. 188–91. The broderie has been largely replaced by lawn.
Pp. 128–31: See Hansmann (1983), pp. 286–89, (with notes referring to Jörg Gamer's study of the complex iconography) and Hennebo and Hoffmann (1965; 1981) pp. 361–69; also Hansmann in Hennebo ed. (1985), pp. 162–63 and 165–68, and Hubert Wolfgang Wertz, 'Wiederherstellung und Unterlagen von Parterreanlagen' in ibid., pp. 174–204.
Pp. 131–32: See Oldenburger–Ebbers (1989), p. 211, and her recent article, 'De Tuinarchitectuur van Johann Georg Michael (1738–1800)', of which she kindly sent me a copy.
P. 133: See Barbara Paca-Steele, 'The Mathematics of an Eighteenth-Century Wilderness Garden' in *Journal of Garden History*, vol. 6, no. 4 (1986), pp. 299–320; and Mark. P. Leone

and Paul A. Shackel, 'Plane and Solid Geometry in Colonial Gardens in Annapolis, Maryland' in Kelso and Most eds. (1990).

Pp. 134–35: See Martin (1991), chapter 6.

Pp. 136–37: See Hansmann (1983), pp. 267–71, and Hennebo and Hoffmann (1965; 81), pp. 269–77, also vol. III, pp. 55–59, 176–85, and figs. 117 and 118; also Hans-Christoph Dittscheid, 'The Park of Wilhelmshöhe: From the Baroque *Delineatio Montis* to the Heroic Landscape' in Mosser and Teyssot eds. (1991), pp. 317–19; and Teresa S. Badenoch, 'Wilhelmshöhe: A Unique Record of a Changing Landscape by J. H. Müntz (1786–1796)' in *Journal of Garden History*, vol. 6., no. 1 (1986), pp. 50–61.

Pp. 138–39: See Giuseppe Chigiotti, 'The Design and Realization of The Park of the Royal Palace at Caserta by Luigi and Carlo Vanvitelli' in *Journal of Garden History*, vol. 5, no. 2 (1985), pp. 184–202, and Hersey in ibid. (1981). See also Cesare De Seta, 'Gardens of the Palazzo Reale at Caserta' in Mosser and Teyssot eds. (1991), pp. 327–29.

Chapter 4 *Revivals and Eclecticism*
P. 141: See Jacques (1983), pp. 163–65 and p. 120, and Carter (1982), especially p. 59. For Mount Edgcumbe, see John Harvey, *Restoring Period Gardens* (Aylesbury, 1988), pp. 105–6. For Wilton, Trentham and Bowood, see Elliott (1990), pp. 74–77. For Lenné, see Günther (1991), pp. 67, 70 and 75. For the 1894 plan of Biltmore, see *The Oxford Companion to Gardens* (Oxford, paperback edition, 1991), p. 56.

Pp. 141–42: For M'Intosh and Nesfield, see Elliott (1990), pp. 56, 71–4 and fig. 28. For the original design by Marot, see Hunt ed. (1990), p. 148. For Levens Hall, see Elliott (1990), pp. 58–9.

P. 143: For Audley End, Wrest Park and Cliveden, see notes to pp. 164–70. For bedding and glasshouses, see Elliott (1990), pp. 17, 29, 50–51.

P. 144: For Andrew Murray, colour theory etc., see Elliott (1990), pp. 87, 123–28. For Germany, see Klaus von Krosigk, 'Wiesen-, Rasen- und Blumenflächen in Landschaftlichen Anlagen' in Hennebo ed. (1985), pp. 232–53. For Blickling and broderie, see Elliott (1990), pp. 161 and 138–46, and National Trust guidebook, *Blickling Hall* (1989), pp. 59–60.

P. 161: For carpet bedding, see references given for Introduction, p. 9. For foliage beds and pelargonium pyramids, see Elliott, pp. 130–31 and 152–54. See, for example, Mosser and Teyssot eds. (1991) for the emphasis on the public park or town planning, despite articles on Klein-Glienicke, cottage gardens and private gardens by Henri and Achille Duchêne; see also Mary Ann Wingfield, *Sport and the Artist*, vol. 1 (Woodbridge, 1988) chapters 6 and 13 for bowls, croquet etc. For Shrubland, see the series of articles in *The Cottage Gardener*, Sept. 29, 1853, pp. 495–97; Oct. 6, 1854, pp. 5–7; Sept. 23, 1856, pp. 452–54; and Sept. 30, 1856, pp. 469–71 especially.

Pp. 162–64; See here the guidebook, *Chiswick House and Gardens* (1989), pp. 33–34 and pp. 53–55 and Jacques (1983), p. 196; the unpublished report of Travers Morgan Planning (February 1985) and recent information from Jan Woudstra have been used in this account. See Charles M'Intosh, *The Book of the Garden*, vol. 1 (1853), pp. 619-20; Thomas Faulkner, *The History and Antiquities of Brentford, Ealing and Chiswick* (1845), pp. 428–29. See also David Stuart, *The Garden Triumphant: A Victorian Legacy* (London, 1988), pp. 116 and 129.

Pp. 164–65: See here the unpublished report by Land Use Consultants, *The Restoration of Flower Garden at Audley End* (March 1988).

Pp. 165–66: See Klaus von Krosigk, 'The Park at Klein-Glienicke, Berlin' in Mosser and Teyssot eds. (1991), pp. 421–23; and Krosigk in Hennebo ed. (1985), pp. 236–41.

Pp. 166–67: See Günther (1991), pp. 31–63.

P. 168: See unpublished *Historical Survey of Wrest Park* by Land Use Consultants (1983).

Pp. 169–70: See the National Trust guidebook, *Cliveden* (1990), and especially pp. 16–18; also Elliott (1990), pp. 136–37.

Pp. 170–72: See Elliott (1990), pp. 77–78; also the series in *The Cottage Gardener* as given above (for p. 161), especially Sept. 30. 1856, p. 470, and Oct. 20, 1857, p. 33.

Pp. 172–73: See Florence Hopper, 'Formality Enclosed by Water' in *Country Life* (August 26, 1976), pp. 540–42, and Oldenburger-Ebbers (1989), pp. 88–89 and 94–95.

Chapter 5 *The Past in the Present*
P. 175: See Blomfield (1892; 1936), pp. 1, 2 and 10; Elliott (1990), p. 227; Ottewill (1989), pp. 5–10; and Aslet (1982), p. 289.

P. 176: See Aslet (1982), p. 287–97 and Ottewill (1989), p. 2.

P. 201: For Duchêne's work, see Monique Mosser, 'Henri and Achille Duchêne and the Reinvention of Le Nôtre' in Mosser and Teyssot eds., (1991), pp. 446–50; and Woodbridge (1986), pp. 279–84; for Hautefort, see Racine (1990), p. 37. For I Tatti, see Lazzaro (1990), 284–86. See also Erika Neubauer, 'The Garden Architecture of Cecil Pinsent, 1884–1964' in *Journal of Garden History*, vol. 3, no. 1 (1983), pp. 35–47. For Villa Pisani, see Visentini ed. (1988), pp. 154–58. For Port Lympne, Tyringham and Ditchley Park see Ottewill (1989), pp. 190–93 and 196–200. For Vizcaya and Nemours see notes for pp. 214–19. Information on the Clarence Mackay estate from Alfred Branam. For Longwood, see Colvin Randall, *Longwood Gardens* (1987; second edition 1988), pp. 44–54.

Pp. 202–3: See Morley R. Brown and Patricia M. Samford, 'Recent Evidence of Eighteenth-Century Gardening in Williamsburg, Virginia' in Kelso and Most eds. (1990). Information on the recent appraisal for the Grosser Garten, Herrenhausen, from Dr. Erika Schmidt, 27 December 1990. See also William M. Kelso, 'Landscape Archaeology at Thomas Jefferson's Monticello' in Kelso and Most eds. (1990), pp. 20–21, and Monique Mosser, 'The Impossible Quest for the Past: Thoughts on the Restoration of Gardens' in Mosser and Teyssot eds., pp. 525–30.

Pp. 204–6: See Ottewill (1990), pp. 24–26; for Hestercombe, see Aslet (1982), p. 287, Ottewill, pp. 89–90 and Brown (1985), pp. 83–85 and 127.

Pp. 206–7: For Blickling Hall, see references to page 144.

Pp. 208–10: See Rose and Gustav Wörner, 'Parkpflegewerk Nordkirchen' in *Garten und Landschaft* (5, 1988), pp. 22–27. For Schlaun's West Gardens, which largely survived the 1830s landscaping unaltered and declined after 1918, see Hansmann (1983), pp. 247–49. For the possible inspiration that Colonna provided for the Colonnade, see Berger (1985), pp. 44–47.

Pp. 211–12: For Blenheim, see Ottewill (1989), pp. 200–201, and the guidebook, *Blenheim Park and Gardens* (1990); also Ann Friedman, 'The Evolution of the Parterre D'Eau' in *Journal of Garden History*, vol. 8, no. 1 (1988), pp. 1–30. For Courances, see Woodbridge (1986), pp. 280–83 and Racine (1990), pp. 145–49.

Pp. 213–14: See Woodbridge (1986), pp. 286–88; and his article, 'Doctor Cavallo and the Absolute' in *Garden History*, vol. 6, no. 2 (1978), pp. 46–68; also Monique Mosser in Mosser and Teyssot eds. (1991), p. 528.

Pp. 214–17: See Rebecca W. Davidson, 'Past as Present: Villa Vizcaya and the 'Italian Garden' in the United States' in *Journal of Garden History*, vol. 12, no. 1 (1992), pp. 1–28, and especially p. 22. See Aslet (1990), chapter 15. For the background history of Villa Gamberaia, see Judith A. Kinnard, 'The Villa Gamberaia in Settignano: The Street in the Garden' in *Journal of Garden History*, vol. 6, no. 1 (1986), pp. 1–18.

Pp. 217–18: See Mac Griswold and Eleanor Weller, *The Golden Age of American Gardens* (New York, 1991), pp. 139–41; further information supplied by Paul J. Lloyd of the Alfred I. du Pont Institute.

Pp. 219–22: See McGuire ed. (1980), especially pp. 59–66 and pp. 75–81; also McGuire and Fern eds. (1982), pp. 99–123.

Pp. 222–23: See Strong (1979), pp. 103–10; also the guidebook by The Marchioness of Salisbury, *The Gardens at Hatfield House* (1989). For Sutton Place, see George Plumptre, 'The Gardens of Geoffrey Jellicoe at Sutton Place, Surrey' in Mosser and Teyssot eds. (1991), pp. 516–18; for Eyrignac see Racine (1990), p. 37. For Galveston, see G. Jellicoe, *The Landscape of Civilisation, Created for The Moody Historical Gardens* (Northiam, 1989). On the question of past and present activities in the historic garden, see the forthcoming issue of *Die Gartenkunst* – papers delivered at the conference in Vienna, 3–5 October 1991: 'Der europäische Barockgarten und seine heutige Verwendung'; and also Gervase Jackson-Stops, *An English Arcadia: 1600–1990* (The National Trust, 1991) p. 15 (with information on the later history of 'mock battles' in landscape gardens). This exhibition catalogue also provides supporting documentation to many sites discussed here (Blickling, Cliveden, Powis Castle) and shows further evidence of formal/informal marriages in the British context.

Acknowledgments

The primary acknowledgment is to those who have given support in matters of documentation and illustration; the list below cannot do full justice to their contribution. The secondary acknowledgment – no less important – is to those whose research I have tried to introduce in these pages. Inevitably the scope and depth of their work has been reduced in distillation; but the bibliography acknowledges their original scholarship. Consulting these authorities is especially important in sites as complex as Versailles, Chiswick House or Schwetzingen; for in order to highlight the neglected area of historic planting, I have given only cursory attention to iconography, architecture and sculpture. Equally, the emphasis on formal traditions of planting at Chiswick House should not obscure the intimate and innovative aspects of the Burlington/Kent layout, to which other historians have given ample attention. Indeed, to speak of Chiswick as 'formal' is only a corrective to the equally inadequate term 'early landscape'; it remains for the specialists to refine their classifications – 'Rococo', 'transitional', 'late geometric' etc. Likewise,

I hope this work will prompt questions for the future – how gardens should best be conserved when original planting, décor and functions have vanished; and topics for further research – sport and gardens, the origins of the circular rosary, social and iconographical themes in the Victorian garden, the legacy of Dézallier d'Argenville.

I am especially grateful to a number of individuals who have given generous help over the year: Alfred S. Branam, Jr. for advice on the formal garden in North America; Douglas Chambers for reading through the manuscript; Rebecca W. Davidson for detailed help with Vizcaya; Carla Oldenburger-Ebbers for special assistance with some Dutch sites; Erika Schmidt for continual support in the German sphere, and Professors Jörg Gamer and Dieter Hennebo for illustrations; Ada Segre for access to her work on Cisterna and for help with access to Italian sites; and the team at Land Use Consultants for guidance on Audley End and Wrest Park. Others to whom I am equally indebted are as follows: Cathleen H. Baldwin, Krysia Bilikowski, Bruno Bellone, C. Allan Brown, Dominic

Cole, Walter Coultous, Fiona Cowell, Jennifer Dickson, Wouter Dooijes, Alfons Elfgang, Brent Elliott, Linda Dicaire Fardin, Richard Flenley, Jonathan Fraser, Geoffrey James, Madame Jean-Louis de Ganay, Giorgio Galletti, Eric Guillou, John Harvey, Eric T. Haskell, Florence Hopper, John Dixon Hunt, David Jacques, Elizabeth Kryder-Reid, Matthias Kuhn, Susan Taylor Leduc, Doris B. Littlefield, Paul J. Lloyd, The National Trust Archives, Mechtild Nienhaus-Wasem, Dean Norton, Therese O'Malley, John Phibbs, Michel Racine, Colvin Randall, Donna Salzer, Michael Symes, Lucia Tongiorgi Tomasi, Sally Wages, Robert Williams, Joachim Wolschke-Bulmahn, Jan Woudstra, Herman van der Mars (and staff at Het Loo), Monica Vittori. And the owners and administrators of sites who gave gracious permission for photography.

I would like to thank the librarians of Trinity College, University of Toronto for help with references. Above all I am grateful to Hugh Palmer for going 'the extra mile' – or thousand miles – in the search for the appropriate photograph.   MARK LAIRD

Acknowledgments for Illustrations

(t = top, b = bottom, l = left, r = right)
Photo **American Academy** in Rome 46 b; **Amsterdam**, Rijksprentenkabinet (photo Rijksmuseum) 45 tr; **Bedfordshire** Record Office, (Lord Lucas Collection, BRO L 33/128A) 88/89 t, (Lord Lucas Collection, BRO L 33/208) 168 r; **Berlin**, Kupferstichkabinett, Staatliche Museen Preussischer Kulturbesitz (photo Jörg P. Anders), 38/39; Kartenabteilung der Staatsbibliothek zu Berlin (PK) (photo Bildarchiv Preussischer Kulturbesitz) 167; Photo The **Biltmore** Company 142; Photo: From the **Bryant** Library Local History Collection, Roslyn, NY 202 tl; **Cadland** Trustees 140; **Caetani** Archive 37 tl; University of **California** at Berkeley. College of Environmental Design Documents Collection 176; **Chantilly**, Musée Condé (photo Giraudon) 43 t; **Cologne**, Museen der Stadt Köln (photo Rheinisches Bildarchiv) 44 t; Photo copyright **Country Life** 207; **Devonshire** Collection, Chatsworth. Reproduced by permission of the Chatsworth Settlement Trustees 88, 122 (photo Courtauld Institute, University of London), 143 l, 162 tl; **Dresden**, Sächsische Landesbibliothek (photo Deutsche Fotothek) 83; the **Dumbarton Oaks** Research Library and Collections, Washington DC (photo Dumbarton Oaks, Trustees for Harvard University) 47 br, 93 b, 220, 221; **English Heritage** Photo Library 164; **Florence**, Museo di Firenze com'era 13; Photo **Gabinetto Fotografico** Nazionale (Rome) 31; Photo courtesy of **Hagley** Museum and Library 203 tl; **Hanover**, photo Historisches Museum am Hohen Ufer Hannover 44 br, endpapers; **Heidelberg**, Kurpfälzisches Museum der Stadt 94 bl, 128; **Kassel**, Staatliche Kunstsammlungen 136 b, 137 t; The **Lamont Gallery**, Phillips Exeter Academy, Exeter, New Hampshire. Gift of Thomas W. Lamont. Class of 1888 95 bl; **London**, British Architectural Library Drawings Collection, RIBA 34 b, 169, 205; British Library (Map Library) 123; British Museum 33; Royal Horticultural Society, Lindley Library 170; Victoria and Albert Museum 92 tr; **Longwood** Gardens Photograph 202

b; Lord **Lucas** Collection 168 l; Photo Georgina **Masson** 12, 27, 90 bl, 95 tl, 95 tr; **Milan**, Archivio Civico di Milano 95 tl; The **Mount Vernon** Ladies' Association of the Union, Mount Vernon, Virginia 134; **Munich**, Bayerische Schlösser, Gärten und Seen 90 t, 125; Photo Alfred I du Pont Institute of the **Nemours** Foundation, Wilmington, Delaware 218; Photo The **New York** Public Library 203 tr; **Oxford**, Bodleian Library 92 br; **Paris**, Bibliothèque des Arts Décoratifs (photo Jean-Loup Charmet) 42; Bibliothèque Nationale 43 b, 162 br, 210 tr; Bibliothèque Nationale (Estampes) 7, 75, 94 tl, 212 bl; Musée des Arts Décoratifs (photo Musée des Arts Décoratifs/Laurent Sully Jaulmes) 209 t; Photo The Library Company of **Philadelphia** 203 br; **Potsdam-Sanssouci**, Stiftung Schlösser und Gärten (photo Stiftung Schlösser und Gärten) 124, 142 r; **Private Collection** 84, 92 tl, 172; Photo copyright **Réunion** des Musées Nationaux (Paris) 77, 78, 79 tl, 79 tr; Photo **Soprintendenza** alle Gallerie (Florence) 37 tr; **Versailles**, Musée de Versailles (photo copyright Réunion des Musées Nationaux) 77, 78, 79 tl, 79 tr; **Vienna**, Graphische Sammlung Albertina 15 t, 82 t; **Wageningen**, Library, Agricultural University (photo Agricultural University) 80 tl, 132 r.

All other photographs are by Hugh Palmer, with the exception of p. 108 r, which is by the author.

Illustrations taken from books: *The Architectural Review*, July 1917, 215; Robert Atkyns, *The Ancient and Present State of Glocestershire* (London 1768) 86; Jacques Boyceau de la Barauderie, *Traité du jardinage selon les raisons de la nature et de l'art* (Paris 1638) 42; E. Adveno Brooke, *The Gardens of England* (London 1858) 143 r, 171; S. and N. Buck, *Buck's Antiquities; or, Venerable Remains of above four hundred castles, monasteries, palaces, etc. etc. in England and Wales* (London 1774) 93 t; William Chambers, *Plans, Elevations, Sections and Perspective Views of the Gardens and Buildings at Kew in Surry* (London 1763) 90 br;

Delineatio Montis (Kassel 1706) 136 b; A. J. Dézallier d'Argenville, *La Théorie et la pratique du jardinage* ([Paris 1709] [1723 edition]) 162 br, 210 tr; G. B. Falda, *Le Fontane di Roma* (Rome 1675–91) 46 b; After G. B. Ferrari, *Flora overo cultura di fiori distinto in quattro libri* (Rome 1638) 37 b; Marcel Fouquier, *L'Art des jardins* (Paris 1911) 209 b; *The Garden Magazine*, August 1919, 203 tr; K. Götze, *Album für Teppichgärtnerei und Gruppenbepflanzung* (Erfurt c. 1900) 161 t, 161 b; *L'Illustration*, 1927, 9 tl; Supplement to *Journal for Horticulture and Cottage Gardener*, 29 July 1862, 170; J. Kip, *Britannia Illustrata* (London 1720) 87; Jean-Benjamin de Laborde, *Description générale et particulière de la France* (Paris 1781–1796) 7; G. Lauro, *Antiquae Urbis Splendor* (Rome 1612–28) 27; G. L. Le Rouge, *Détails des nouveaux jardins à la mode: jardins anglo-chinois* (Paris c. 1775–88) 93 b; D. Lucchese, *Delizie della Villa di Castellazzo* (Milan 1743) 90 bl, 95 tl; Charles M'Intosh, *Book of the Garden* (Edinburgh and London 1853) 162 tr; André Mollet, *Le Jardin de plaisir* (Stockholm 1651) title page; John Nichols, *The Progresses of Queen Elizabeth* (London 1823) 34 t; R. G. Mattheus Brouërius van Niedek, *Het Zegenpralent Kennemerlant* (Amsterdam 1729–32) 94 bl; *Nouveau guide dans le jardin de Schwetzingen* (Schwetzingen, Heidelberg 1830) (Crispin de Passe, *Hortus Floridus* (Arnhem 1614) frontispiece; *Les Plaisirs de l'Isle Enchantée ou les festes, et divertissements du Roy à Versailles ... de l'année 1664* (Paris 1676–78) 79 b; G. C. von Prenner, *Illustri fatti farnesiani coloriti nel real Palazzo di Caprarola* (Rome 1748) 31; J. Rigaud, *Recueil de cent vingt-une des plus belles vues de palais, châteaux et maisons royales du Paris et ses environs ...* (Paris 1730–85) 94 tl; L. Scherm, *Het Koninklijk Lusthof 'Het Loo'* (c. 1700) 80 tl; L Vanvitelli, *Dichiarazione dei Disegni del Real Palazzo di Caserta* (Naples 1756) 138/139 t.

Index

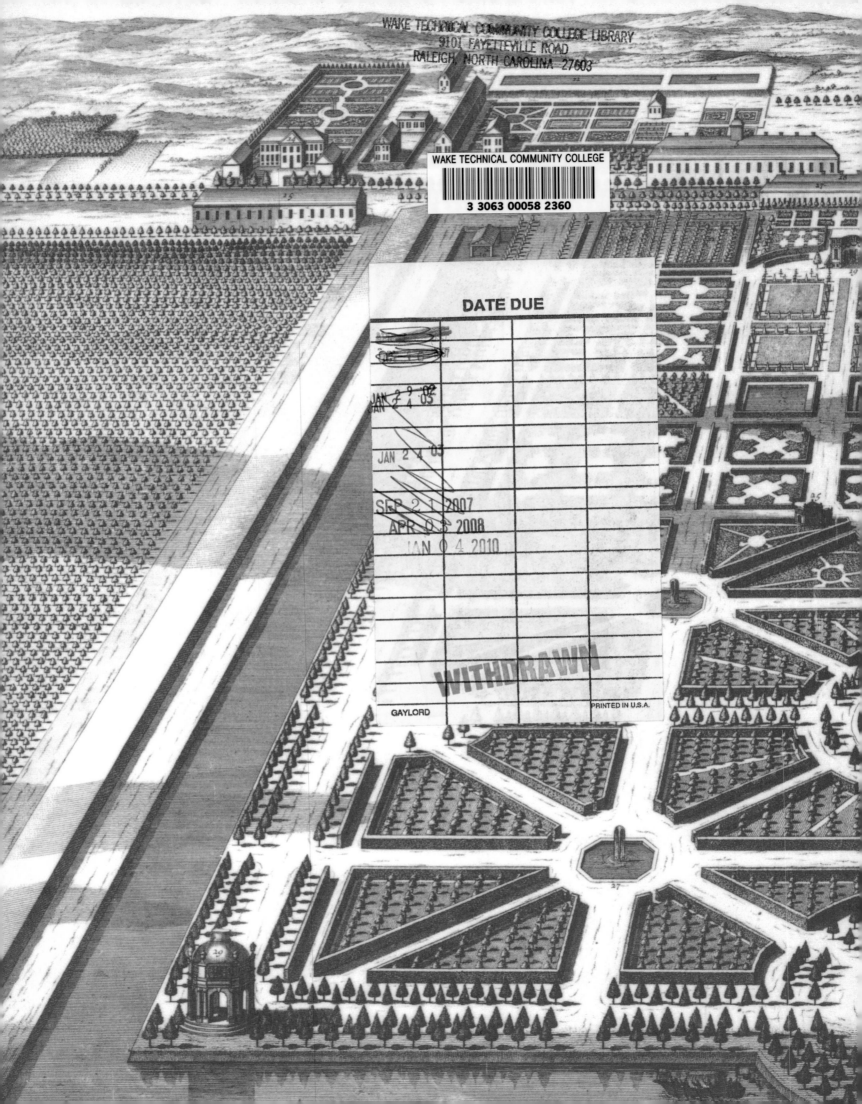